19.95

Build Your Own 486/486SX and Save a Bundle

2nd Edition

Aubrey Pilgrim

TAB BOOKS

Blue Ridge Summit, PA

SECOND EDITION
FIRST PRINTING

© 1993 by **TAB Books**.
TAB Books is a division of McGraw-Hill, Inc.

Library of Congress Cataloging-in-Publication Data

Pilgrim, Aubrey.
   Build your own 486/486SX and save a bundle / by Aubrey Pilgrim.—2nd ed.
      p.   cm.
   Includes index.
   ISBN 0-8306-4217-X   ISBN 0-8306-4216-1 (pbk.)
    1. Microcomputers—Design and construction—Amateur's manuals.
  I. Title.
  TK9969.P564 1992
  621.39'16—dc20   92-20328
                                     CIP

Acquisitions Editor: Ron Powers
Editor: Laura J. Bader
Managing Editor: Susan Wahlman
Director of Production: Katherine G. Brown
Book Design: Jaclyn J. Boone
Cover: Sandra Blair Design and Brent Blair Photography, Harrisburg, Pa.   EL1

Contents

Introduction

We are living in the best of all times. At no time in the past have people had so much freedom, had so many material things, and lived so well. And the future is going to be even better — especially after you have built your own 486 computer.

Assembling a 486 is very simple. You don't have to be an engineer to do it. You don't have to do any soldering or wiring, or use any electronic test instruments. The board-level components have already been installed and tested. All you have to do is insert the plug-in boards into the slots on the motherboard, connect some cables, install two screws to hold the motherboard in place, two more screws for the power supply, and five for the case. Once you have purchased all of the components, it should take you no more than an hour to assemble them. Anyone can do it. I will show you how easy it is.

Some of you might still be unconvinced. Some people are afraid of the computer and stand in awe of its mysterious and fantastic capabilities. You might be a bit reluctant to build your own, but you shouldn't worry.

A computer is primarily a bunch of transistors, resistors, capacitors, and other electronic components. I guarantee that it won't bite you. Computer voltages range from 5 to 12 volts dc (direct current). You can't even get an electric shock unless you ignore the warnings and remove the cover of the power supply. Then you have to put your hand in the power supply and touch the bare components while the power is on in order to get a shock. The power supply has an input of 110 volts ac (alternating current), which it transforms into low dc voltages.

The computer changes data into a form of low-voltage electricity that represents 0s and 1s. A voltage level of 3 volts might represent a 1, and 0 volts for a period of time might represent a 0. Computer programs use the electronic components to route and shape the small bits of electricity, causing them to perform all sorts of useful functions.

Billions of dollars worth of computer components and boards have been designed and manufactured. By using different boards a myriad of options are possible. You simply plug the option boards into the motherboard. There's no soldering, wiring, or technical expertise required.

A short history of electronics

Many of the good things that we enjoy today have come about in just the last few years. More than any other single factor, electronics has been one of the major contributors to our good life.

Electricity has been around for some time. In 1800, Alessandro Volta demonstrated the first battery. A battery is made up of two dissimilar materials, or *electrodes*. One element has an excess of electrons, the other has a deficiency. All elements have electrons flying around the nuclei of their atoms. Some have one or more excess electrons. If a proper medium is present, the excess electrons will flow from one electrode to the other. The electrons continue to flow until there is a balance between the two materials (electrodes). When this occurs, the battery is completely dead or discharged.

If a motor is placed in the circuit between the two poles, the flow of electrons through the motor will cause it to turn. Electric motors have contributed greatly to our present good life.

Relatively speaking, the first vacuum tubes were developed only a short time ago. The basic vacuum tube has a cathode and a plate with a grid between them. If a high positive voltage is placed on the plate and the cathode is heated by a filament, electrons are boiled off. They fly through the vacuum to the plate because of the high positive voltage. When this happens, current flows through the tube. A small negative voltage applied to the grid can block the flow of electrons and keep them from reaching the plate. In this case, no current flows through the tube. By varying the amount of voltage on the grid from positive to negative, the flow of current or voltage can be controlled so that it becomes a magnified image of the small input voltage. Using a small voltage on the grid of the tube to control a larger voltage is somewhat like using a faucet to control a stream of water.

Radio and television stations fling high-voltage signals into the atmosphere. Depending on the distance from the broadcast station and the station's broadcast power, the signal voltage might be only a few millionths of a volt when it reaches a radio or TV antenna. The signals are made up of alternating waves that vary from a positive level to a negative level. When these alternating signals are applied to the grid of a vacuum tube, the signals cause the current through the tube to be turned on and off, creating a mirror image or identical alternating copy of the input signal at the plate of the tube. The small input signal applied to the grid can cause the output copy of the signal voltage to be millions of times larger and stronger than the input. This replica of the small input signal is then strong enough to power a loudspeaker or to paint images on a television screen.

In the early 1940s, a group of scientists connected several thousand vacuum tubes together and created a primitive computer. It cost millions of dollars and filled a large room. However, it could do less computing than a modern $5 hand-held calculator. The vacuum tubes were crude and massive and used large amounts of power. In the late 1940s, at Bell Laboratories, three scientists (Barden, Brattain, and Shockley) invented the transistor. This invention changed the world as it had never been changed before.

Compared to a vacuum tube, the transistor is very small and requires only a small amount of voltage to operate. Yet it can do almost everything that the vacuum tube can do, as well as many things that the vacuum tube cannot do.

The electrons that cause a lamp to light or a computer to run are very tiny. We can't begin to see them, even with the most powerful microscope. Developers began reducing the size of transistors, and soon it was discovered that several transistors and other components could be placed on a single slab of silicon; this was the birth of integrated circuits (ICs). Integrated circuits were made smaller and smaller, and more and more transistors were added. These small ICs made it fairly easy to develop computers.

The central processing unit (CPU) is the brain of the computer. The more transistors it has, the more powerful the computer can be. In the early 1980s, Intel developed the 8088 CPU with 29,000 transistors on a single chip. The 80286 CPU came along a short time later with 125,000 transistors, followed by the 80386 CPU with 275,000 transistors. Today the 80486 CPU with 1,200,000 transistors on a silicon chip is about 0.4 inches wide and 0.65 inches long. By the time you read this, the 80586 P5CPU should be on the market with over 3 million transistors.

Figure I-1 shows a fairly modern vacuum tube. Above the tube, in the center, is a

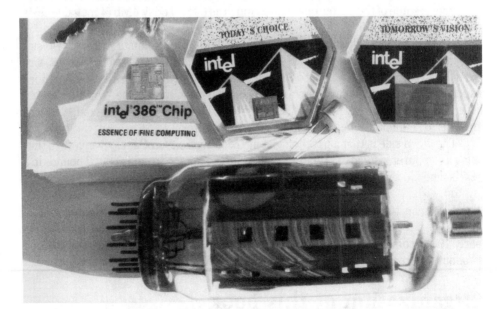

I-1   Evolution in electronics. A vacuum tube (bottom), a transistor (center), and (top, left to right) the original 386 chip with 275,000 transistors, the new 386 chip, and the 486 chip with 1,200,000 transistors.

single transistor. At the top left is a keychain with an original 386 chip with 275,000 transistors. Next to it is another keychain with the newer version of the 386. Note that it is about half the size of the original. At the far right is a keychain with a 486 chip. It has 1,200,000 transistors. This photo helps to put into perspective the tremendous advances that have been made in the last few years. It is now possible to integrate an entire computer on one or two chips. Intel has said that CPUs with over 100 million transistors will be a reality within the next 10 years.

The chips shown in Fig. I-1 were defective, so Intel embedded them in plastic and made them into keychains. Intel sells keychains similar to those pictured and several other Intel-unique products. Call (800) 544-4411 for a catalog.

The computer's impact

The computer has had a tremendous impact on our lives. It has revolutionized the way we do research and development. In the field of medicine alone, it has made new drugs possible that have helped reduce suffering and pain and have added years to our lives.

The computer has made it possible to land a man on the moon. New products are rolling off computerized manufacturing lines. All kinds of things from heart pacemakers to cameras to automobiles to mailing lists now depend on computers and high-tech electronics.

To say that computer technology is moving forward in leaps and bounds is an understatement. Electronics technology has made some extraordinary advances in just a few short years, but computer technology advancements have been even more dramatic. In the early 1980s, many of the desktop computers had only 16K (16 kilobytes) of memory; some of the better ones had as much as 64K. Today 4Mb (4 megabytes) is the minimum for a 486.

My first computer was a Morrow Designs with 64K of memory. It had two single-sided floppy drives that could hold only 140K on each diskette. In those days, single-sided diskettes cost from $5 to $10 each. Double-sided diskettes were even more expensive. Now you can buy them for $.20 apiece. I was able to use WordStar on my little Morrow to write my first book. Even with its limitations, this tiny computer was an order of magnitude better than using a typewriter.

The down side is that a psychologist at the University of Pennsylvania says that using a computer instead of a typewriter can cause a person to gain about 7 pounds in a year's time. So that is why I am getting fatter. I thought it was just because I was eating too well.

Less than 10 years after the early Apple, Morrow, Osborne, and other CP/M machines, we have the fabulous 486 desktop computer. It is about the same size as those early 1980s computers, but the difference between the early computers and the 486 is about as great as that of a biplane from World War I and the space shuttle.

Organization of this book

I go into some detail about the 486 system and list some of its hundreds of applications. I recommend some standard off-the-shelf software and explore such things as desktop publishing (DTP), local area networks (LANs), and other business and personal uses for the 486.

I describe the 486 and give reasons why a person should build their own. The 486SX CPU was announced after the first edition of this book was published. A description and some recommendations for this CPU are included in this edition. The instructions and photos in this book can be used to build any version of the 486. I also describe how to upgrade a PC, 286, or 386 to a more powerful 486. Descriptions of the parts and components needed to assemble a 486DX or 486SX are included and I tell you where you can get them.

The types and functions of floppy and hard disks are discussed. The importance of backups gets its own chapter, as do monitors, the function and operation of memory, keyboards and other methods of input to the computer, communications software and hardware (including modems, electronic mail (E-mail), and fax), and printers. I review a few of the accessories and adjuncts for the 486 and list some of the most useful software. A few tips on troubleshooting are included in case something goes wrong.

The glossary has hundreds of buzzwords and acronyms invented for the computer revolution. This extensive list should help you hold your own in any computer setting.

The subjects covered in each of the chapters will be of interest to the newcomer as well as the experienced user of computers — and especially to anyone who wants to build their own 486 and save a bundle.

1
The fantastic 486

You can build a fantastic 486, one of the fastest and most powerful desktop computers in existence today. You don't have to be an engineer or technician to assemble one. You don't have to do any soldering or wiring. In fact, you don't have to know anything about electronics in order to build a computer. If you know how to use a screwdriver and how to plug a few cables together, then you can do it. Once you buy all of the parts that are needed, it should take less than an hour to assemble.

The cost of a computer

I have been asked many times, "What does it cost to build a computer?" That is like asking, "How much does a car cost?" There are many different kinds of cars with hundreds of options and a wide variation in cost. The same situation applies to computers. The cost of a computer depends on where you buy the components, what types of components you buy, whether they are brand name or not, when you buy them, and who you buy them from. A big cost factor is how well you shop.

When someone asks me about cost, I answer with my own questions: "What do you want your computer to do?" and "How much do you want to spend?" Just as a Cadillac costs more than a Chevrolet, a 486 costs considerably more than a 286 or 386.

It is almost impossible to say exactly how much it costs to build, or even buy, a computer. Hundreds of options are available from thousands of different vendors. Prices in the computer business are also very volatile. They change constantly, usually downward, which is very good news for consumers.

To build or not to build

Should you build your own or buy a ready-made one? Some companies are offering 486SX systems for less than $1300. You can buy a 25-megahertz (MHz) 486DX system for $1500 that would have cost about $6000 a couple of years ago.

Brand-name systems such as IBM and Compaq still cost three or four times as much as the no-name clones. One of the reasons that IBM and Compaq cost so much more is that they usually have several distributors and middlemen between the manufacturer and final dealer. They also have large expensive showrooms and lots of salespeople, which adds considerably to the cost of the product.

Most of the clone dealers have very few distributors between the manufacturer and the end dealer, especially the large discount houses and mail-order firms. (At the time of this writing, IBM is rumored to be preparing to set up a direct mail-order division. The components that they would sell would not necessarily be manufactured by IBM.)

A couple of years ago, you could save from $1000 to $5000 by building your own computer. You won't be able to save that much today, but depending on what you put in it and how well you shop, you can still save from $200 to $1000. In answer to the question, I say by all means build your own. Because it can be assembled in less than an hour, I think it is well worth it. Most of us don't often get the opportunity to save money at the rate of over $200 an hour.

You might see ads for very low-cost systems that might cause you to believe that you can't save by building your own. You should read the ads very closely. Many of these low-cost systems do not include a hard drive, memory, or some other essential components.

Even if you save nothing at all, you are still better off building your own. You learn what is inside your computer. You acquire a knowledge and experience that is worth more than money. Also, you can't put a price on the sense of satisfaction that you derive from doing it yourself.

Build a minimum system

You might see ads for very low-priced bare-bones systems. A bare-bones system usually consists of a motherboard, a power supply, and a case, but you cannot do any computing with only these components. You still need a keyboard, a monitor and monitor adapter, a floppy drive, and a hard disk to have a minimum system. You easily can assemble a minimum 486 system for about $1200. You can spend $25,000 or more if you want a 50-Hz system with brand-name extras and goodies.

Build a 286 or 386 computer

If you are short of money, you can build a less expensive computer. You can use this book to build not only 486 systems, but also XT, 286, or 386 systems. They are all assembled the same way with the same basic components (except for the motherboards).

You can purchase your parts as you can afford them. Because all of the components are compatible, you can also buy them from different vendors or wherever you find the best prices. If you can get by for a while with something less than a 486 system, you can upgrade it later by replacing the motherboard. I discuss upgrades in more detail in chapter 4.

Some facts about the 486
The CPU

The central processing unit (CPU) is the brain of the computer. Just a very short time ago, the 386 seemed to be the ultimate desktop PC. The 386 CPU has 275,000 transistors integrated on a silicon chip. The original chip was about 0.375 inch by 0.4 inch. Using new technologies, they have been shrunk to about 0.225 inch by 0.275 inch. The 486 CPU has 1,200,000 transistors on a chip that is about 0.4 inch by 0.65 inch. It is the first chip ever designed with over 1 million transistors on it (Fig. 1-1). Figure 1-2 is a diagram of the 486 CPU.

Intel Corporation

1-1   The i486 chip with 1,200,000 transistors.

Processing speed

A 386 operating at 33 million cycles per second (33 MHz) provides performance 25 times greater than the original IBM PC. A 486 operating at 25 MHz provides performance 50 times greater than the original IBM PC. The 25-MHz 486 operates at a slower clock frequency than the 33-MHz 386, but its internal design allows it to process data with a fewer number of clock cycles. Its built-in cache also helps speed up processing considerably.

The original 486 chip operated at 20 MHz. Today they operate at 25 MHz, 33 MHz, and 50 MHz. Chips that operate at up to 100 MHz should soon be available. Of course, the higher the speed or frequency, the higher the cost.

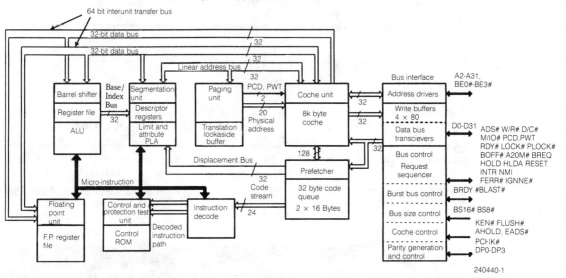

1-2 A block drawing of the functions of the i486. Intel Corporation

Backward compatibility

Despite all of its speed and power, the 486 is still compatible with the early 16K desktop PCs and can still run the same software. In addition, it can run all of the latest and most sophisticated software available. Actually, software that can take full advantage of the 486's capabilities has not yet been written. (We don't even have software that can fully utilize all of the 386's capabilities at this time.)

You also can use most of the billions of dollars worth of older boards and peripheral equipment that has been developed over the last 10 years. If you or your company has a large investment in PCs, XTs, 286s, or 386s, the 486 can use the plug-in boards, disk drives, printers, and most other equipment.

Built-in coprocessor

Another feature of the 486 is that it has integrated memory management with paging. The 486DX has floating point and cache memory units and a high-performance integer unit. It has a coprocessor, which is essential for running many software packages such as Lotus 1-2-3, dBASE, AutoCAD, and several others.

You might be tempted to buy a less expensive, but faster 386. You can buy a 33-MHz 386 motherboard for about $400. You can add a 387 coprocessor for the 386 for about $175, for a total of $575. A slower running 25-MHz 486 will cost about $650, but it can still process applications two to four times faster than a 386 running at 33 MHz with an external 387 coprocessor.

Unlike the 486DX, the 486SX does not have a coprocessor. Actually, the coprocessor is on the chip, but it might have a few defective transistors or be otherwise nonfunctional. More about the 486SX in the next chapter.

Built-in cache

The 486 CPU has 8K of on-chip cache memory in among its 1,200,000 transistors. It is designed so that it has a very high hit ratio. Because it does not have to traverse the circuits to an external cache memory, it is very fast. In addition to the built-in cache, most motherboards are designed so that a fast static random-access memory (SRAM) cache of up to 256K can be installed.

The 486 has an external 32-bit data bus to the on-board RAM, which can quickly refill the on-chip cache when a miss occurs. The 486 uses a new burst bus transfer mechanism that can read a double word from external memory each clock cycle and write it to the on-chip cache. In the burst mode, the 486 can throughput data at a rate of 80Mb per second. *Burst mode* means that the bus is taken over and a packet of data is sent as a single unit. The bus cannot be accessed by other requests until the burst operation is completed.

The 486 is capable of directly accessing 4Gb (4 gigabytes) or four billion (4,000,000,000) bytes of RAM. Using 1Mb chips, it takes 9 chips to make 1Mb. It would take 36,000 1Mb chips to make 4Gb. Even with the newer 4Mb chips, it would take 9000 chips. You probably would not be able to put that many chips into a desktop unit.

IBM and some of the Japanese companies are manufacturing 16Mb chips. It still takes 9 chips to make 16Mb. We should also have 64Mb RAM chips soon, considerably reducing the board space needed for memory.

RISC performance

The 486 offers all of the performance associated with the 32-bit reduced instruction set computing (RISC) used in many of the very large and powerful systems, such as those from Sun. RISC-type computers are usually very expensive and require special software. A single software program for these systems can cost from $25,000 to $50,000 or more. The 486 is 100% compatible with low-cost off-the-shelf disk operating system (DOS) software. But the 486 can also run Unix, Xenix, OS/2, and other engineering software. Most engineers need DOS compatibility because they use software for word processing, computer-aided design (CAD), business, graphics, and other functions, as well as engineering.

Multiprocessing and multitasking

The 486 supports multiprocessing and is able to communicate with other processors to make efficient use of shared resources. It also retains all of the multitasking features of the 386. To use these features you must have software that can take advantage of them.

Who needs a 486?

So who needs all the speed and processing power of a 486? The same question might have been asked in the early 1980s when it was decided to go from 16K memory to 64K. You can be sure the question was asked when it was decided to go from 64K to 640K memory. I had no trouble running dBASE II, SuperCalc, Lotus 1-2-3, or WordStar on my little 64K Morrow. When IBM first came out with a PC that could have a memory of 640K, it was very expensive. Many people didn't need the extra memory at the time, so they never bothered installing more than 128K or 256K at the most. Of course, you know the rest.

Very few programs today can run on anything less than 640K. Many of the new programs require up to 2 or 3Mb of hard disk space just to install them. Many of them can't run unless you have 4Mb or more of expanded or extended RAM.

Computer technology continues to grow and expand at a dizzying pace. At this very moment, engineers and programmers are developing and designing hardware and software that will require even more memory and capabilities than we have today. The even more powerful 586 will be out by the time you read this. Much of the technology that we have today will be obsolete tomorrow, but that doesn't mean that the software and hardware we have today won't still be useful tomorrow. Many people are still using 64K CP/M machines and running dBASE II and many other useful programs on them. After all, if it satisfies their needs, that is all that matters. But to many people and businesses, time is money. They cannot afford to wait for a computer. It can be a shameful waste of human labor and valuable resources to have to wait for a complex spreadsheet or database.

So who needs a 486? You do, if you or your business does programming or uses any kind of design software. You should have a 486 on your desk for such things as computer-aided design (CAD), computer-aided software engineering (CASE), or almost any kind of development and design. If you or your business does a lot of number crunching with spreadsheet programs such as Microsoft Excel, Borland's Quattro, Computer Associates SuperCalc5, or Lotus 1-2-3, then you need a 486. If you or your business uses programs such as dBASE IV, Paradox, askSAM, FoxBASE, R:BASE, or any of the other databases, then you need a 486. If you are a CPA, if you use accounting programs, if you do bookkeeping or taxes, then you could make good use of a 486. If you are in a manufacturing business that uses servers, networks, multitasking, or multiprocessing, then you need a 486. If you use graphics or do desktop publishing, you need a 486. If you are a lawyer, doctor, chiropractor, dentist, grocery store owner, or if you are involved in any one of a thousand other businesses where a fast and powerful computer is needed, then you need a 486.

Lots of photos and easy instructions

It is actually easier to assemble a 486 computer than it is to learn some of the so-called "user-friendly" software packages. I sometimes have great difficulty in learning some of the software that is supposed to be very easy to learn and use. Some of the problem might be my fault. I am like a lot of people; quite often I don't read the instructions all the way through or follow them completely. Sometimes, it might not be my fault entirely. Some of the manuals and instructions seem to be written for those people who already know the product. Often very important facts are glossed over or buried in the middle of a 500-page manual, or not even mentioned at all. Many of the manuals and instructions are almost worthless.

Because I have had so many bad experiences with manuals, I have tried very hard to avoid the mistakes made by others. I have tried to make this book as clear and easy to use as possible.

You can do it

Considering the power and sophistication of the 486, some of you might still have doubts about being able to build one. Would you have doubts about being able to build a lowly PC or XT? Please believe me, it is no more difficult to assemble a 486 than an XT, 286, or 386. Except for the motherboard, they are all assembled the same way.

You can build your own 486 and save a bundle doing it. The next chapter talks a bit about some of the components that you need to assemble a 486.

2

Components
and cost

Components needed

In this chapter I list and briefly discuss all of the major components needed to build a 486. In later chapters I go into much more detail about each of them. If you are new to computing, the chapters about the major components will help you make better purchase decisions. The next chapter has photographs and instructions for the assembly of a system, but I recommend that you read the chapters on the major components before buying the parts or starting your system.

All of the PCs use the same basic components. The main differences are the motherboard and the CPU. Because the components are all interchangeable, you can shop around for the best buys. Look at the ads in computer magazines such as *Computer Shopper, PC Sources, Computer Buying World, Computer Monthly,* and others for an idea of what is available. These ads also give you an idea of the cost of the various components and options. You can order the components through the mail, or if you live near a large city, go to a swap meet or to a local store.

Motherboards

The motherboard is the main board in the computer. It sits on the floor of the case. It has the all-important CPU, provisions for memory, slots for the plug-in boards, and a built-in clock, and it might have several other built-in functions such as parallel and serial ports, an integrated disk electronics (IDE) interface for hard disks, and other goodies.

The original standard-size AT or 286 motherboard was larger than the XT board. The original 386 and 486 motherboards were about the size of the standard AT board.

Most of the motherboards manufactured today are the baby size, or about the same size as the XT.

A couple of years ago, a 486 motherboard cost between $2500 and $5000. For my first 486, I bought a Micronics motherboard. (Micronics was one of the original gang of nine.) It was one of their first production models. It has 4Mb of memory and 256K of SRAM. I paid $4450 for it. Today a 486DX motherboard costs between $500 and $900. A motherboard for a 486SX costs between $350 and $650.

486DX versus 486SX

The 486SX CPU is the same as the 486DX except that it does not have a functional co-processor. The 486SX is usually slower and operates at 16 MHz, 20 MHz, or 25 MHz. If at all possible, try to buy a 486DX.

If you can't afford the price of a 486 motherboard, you might consider building a less powerful 386 computer. You can upgrade later by replacing the motherboard with a 486. The motherboard is the main difference in all PCs. The plug-in boards, disk drives, and other peripherals are basically the same in all of the computers. See chapter 5 for more information about motherboards and plug-in boards.

Table 2-1 lists the components that are common to all of the PCs and their approximate cost, followed by a comparison of the total costs of the common components plus motherboards for six popular computers. As you can see, there can be quite a large variation in the cost, depending on the particular components and whether they are brand names. There is also a large variation in cost from dealer to dealer. Some of the high-

Table 2-1. Common components

Item	Cost
Case	$ 35–105
Power supply	40–70
Monitor	65–900
Monitor adapter	40–200
Memory, 4Mb	140–180
Multifunction board	50–200
Floppy drive, 1.4Mb	55–75
Floppy drive, 1.2Mb	55–75
Hard disk drive, 80–300Mb	250–995
Disk controller	20–150
Keyboard	40–150
Total $790–3100	

	286	386SX	386DX	486SX	486DX	486EISA
Motherboard	$ 70–150	$100–350	$350–600	$350–650	$500–900	$900–1500
Total cost	$860–3250	$890–3450	$1140–3700	$1140–3750	$1290–4000	$1690–4600

volume dealers might charge less, so it pays to shop around a bit and compare prices. These figures are only rough approximations. The market is so volatile that the prices can change overnight. If you are buying through the mail you should call to check the advertised prices before ordering. Often the advertisements are made up one or two months before the magazine is published, so the prices might have changed considerably.

The variation in the cost of the motherboards depends to a large extent on the frequency of the CPU. The higher the operating frequency, or the faster the PC can operate, the higher the cost.

At the time of this writing, Intel was still the only manufacturer of 486 chips. But AMD, Chips and Technology, and several other companies are expected to have 486 CPU clones on the market soon. This competition will force the CPU prices down even more.

Options

I listed several options in the common components list that are not absolutely necessary for a bare-bones system. It is possible to build a minimum 486SX system for less than $1000, or a 486DX for less than $1200. If you are short of cash or if you don't need a lot of goodies at this time, you can buy the minimum components and add to your system later. For instance, you don't absolutely need two floppy drives. You can get by fine with only a 1.2Mb drive. You can also get by with just 2Mb of memory. You can save a little bit if you install a smaller hard drive, such as 50Mb for about $175. You will need a much larger one later, but this will get you started.

Case and power supply

There are several types of cases available. You can use whichever you prefer. The desktop type is still the most popular. Most desktop types are limited to three or four bays for mounting disk drives. If you want to install two hard disks, a 1.2Mb floppy, and a 1.44Mb floppy, you will need a case with at least four bays.

Depending on your needs, you might want to buy a tower case. The tower case sits on the floor, and the larger ones have space for up to eight drives. This provides room for two hard drives, two floppies, a tape backup, a CD-ROM, a write once read many (WORM) drive, and others. Tower cases are a bit more expensive than standard- or baby-size cases. There are three sizes of tower-type cases: a mini tower, a medium size, and a large size. The smaller sizes do not have as many bays for mounting drives. Most of the tower cases include a power supply and sell for $80 to $150 each. Many cases are sold with the power supply, but make sure that the power supply is at least 200 watts.

Memory

When a computer runs a program, the program is loaded into memory and is processed there. When the processing is completed, it is loaded back on the hard disk, printed out, or sent to wherever you want it to go. Many of the programs today require 2Mb of memory or more in order to run. There are many different types of memory. Chapter 6 goes into detail about the many types.

Floppy disk drives

You can get by with a single 360K floppy drive, but I recommend that you buy a 1.2Mb drive. It reads and writes to both 360K and 1.2Mb diskettes. You can store 3½ times more data on a 1.2Mb diskette than on a 360K diskette. The 360K drives cost about $50, the 1.2Mb about $55.

I also recommend that you buy a 1.44Mb 3½-inch drive. It can read and write to 720K diskettes as well as 1.44Mb diskettes. The 1.44Mb drives also cost about $55, about $5 more than the 720K drives. Both the 360K and the 720K drives are obsolete. I do not recommend them.

You might have to buy a floppy drive controller (FDC) board for your floppy drives. If you have a hard drive, it might have a hard/floppy drive controller (H/FDC) built in. If not, you can buy a floppy controller for about $20. You might not need a controller if your motherboard has a built-in IDE interface. See chapter 7 for more details on floppy drives.

Hard disk drives

It is possible to operate a computer without a hard disk, but it is difficult to do much productive work. If your time is worth anything at all, a hard disk can pay for itself in a very short time.

Several hard disk manufacturers offer hundreds of different models, sizes, and types of hard disks. IDE drives have all of the controller electronics on the drive itself, but still need an interface to the system. This might be built-in on the motherboard, or you might have to buy a low-cost interface that plugs into one of the slots. Other hard drives need a controller on a plug-in board. In many cases, the controller is made by some company other than the one that manufactures the hard drives. Because the controllers for IDE drives are made and matched by the same manufacturer, they operate a bit better. They might also cost a bit less than buying a drive and a separate controller. But it all depends on what you want and how much you want to spend. See chapter 8 for more details on hard drives.

Backup

It is very important that you keep copies or backups of all of your software programs and important data. You never know when your hard disk might crash or have a failure. There are thousands of ways that you can lose your very important data. You should always have a current backup. There are many methods of backup, some using hardware and some that require special software programs. See chapter 9 for more details.

Keyboards

The keyboard is a very important part of the computer. It is the main device for communicating with the computer. There are many manufacturers. Most of them have slight differences in the placement of the keys, the tactility, and special adjuncts such as trackballs, calculators, and keypads.

To run Windows and other graphical user interface (GUI) programs, it is essential to have a mouse, trackball, or other pointing device. Chapter 10 discusses keyboards and other input devices in some detail.

Modems, fax, and communications

You can use your computer to communicate with millions of other computers, with on-line services, and with a host of other services. You can download software from bulletin boards. You can send low-cost faxes to millions of other fax sites. You definitely need some communications hardware and software if you want to get the most from your computer. Communications are discussed in chapter 11.

Monitors

A large variety of monitors are available. You can buy a monochrome monitor for about $65. I like color even if I am just doing word processing, so I am willing to pay a little more for color. A good enhanced graphics adapter (EGA) color monitor can be purchased for about $200, a better video graphics adapter monitor (VGA) costs about $300, or you can spend $3000 or more for a large screen, very high-resolution monitor.

Monitor adapter

A plug-in adapter board is needed to drive the monitor (some motherboards have a built-in adapter). It might cost as little as $20 for a monochrome adapter. A standard VGA can be purchased for about $100. For very high-resolution color it might cost up to $600. See chapter 12 for more details about monitors and adapters.

Printers

You have lots of options when it comes to buying your printer. There are several manufacturers and hundreds of different types and models including dot matrix, laser, inkjet, daisywheel, and many others. Some types are better for particular applications than others, so your choice depends on what you want to do with your computer and how much you want to spend. Chapter 13 discusses the various types of printers.

Software

You will need software for your computer. Before you even turn it on, you will need operating software such as MS-DOS, DR DOS, or OS/2. Billions of dollars worth of off-the-shelf software have been developed. Some of the commercial programs are a bit expensive, but inexpensive public domain and shareware programs can do just about everything the commercial programs do. See chapter 16 for some software recommendations.

Sources

If you live near a large city, there are probably local stores that sell the parts you need. There are also computer swaps in most large cities. A computer swap is just a gathering of local vendors at a fairground, stadium, or some other area. The vendors set up booths and tables and present their wares. You usually find all that you need at these meets. The prices are usually very competitive and you might even be able to haggle for some real bargains.

Another good source for components is through mail order. At one time mail order could be a bit risky, but it is fairly safe today. See chapter 17 for more details on magazines, mail order, and other sources.

Troubleshooting

You shouldn't have any problems assembling your computer, but if you do, turn to chapter 18 for some help and suggestions.

What should you buy?

What you buy depends on what you are going to use your computer for. The 286 is a 16-bit system. The 386SX system processes data internally in 32-bit chunks, but the CPU communicates with memory over a 16-bit bus. The 386DX system processes data in 32-bit chunks and the CPU communicates with memory over a 32-bit bus. The 486SX and DX systems also process data in 32-bit chunks and communicate with memory over a 32-bit bus. All of the industry standard architecture (ISA) systems communicate with their plug-in boards and other input/output (I/O) peripherals over a 16-bit bus, the same as the lowly 286.

Some companies have developed what they call *local bus* ISA motherboards that have one or more slots with a 32-bit bus. One or more of the standard 16-bit slots have an additional special slot for the 32-bit bus. At this time there aren't many boards available for this system. Most of the boards that can use the 32-bit local bus are enhanced VGA cards. Microlink, (800) 829-3688, offers a motherboard with one local bus slot and one extended ISA (EISA) slot. The motherboard with a 33-MHz CPU lists for $595. The enhanced VGA card for the local bus costs $340. EISA systems are true 32-bit systems throughout. They communicate with memory and all I/O functions over a 32-bit bus.

Do you need an EISA motherboard for your 486? That depends on whether you will be using it for high-end applications such as CAD programs, large spreadsheets, or a network server. Because the EISA motherboard provides much more functionality than the ISA type, it is considerably more expensive.

In a few short years, EISA systems will be the most popular and most prevalent PCs. They will still be a bit more expensive than ISA systems, but because they offer so much more they are well worth it. If you have the money, go ahead and buy an EISA system even if you don't need the extras right away. It will make life a little simpler and less frustrating.

Buying a bare-bones unit versus components

Many companies offer "bare-bones" systems that include only a motherboard, a case, and a power supply. These systems do not include a keyboard, monitor, floppy and hard disk drives, and other essential components.

Even some of the complete systems might seem very attractive and difficult to beat. They might be fine for some people, but some of the components in these preassembled systems might not be what you want. For instance, you might want floppy drives that can read and write to all formats, a good high-resolution monitor and adapter, and a couple of good high-capacity hard drives.

If a price seems too good to be true, then the vendor has probably cut a few corners somewhere. There are some very good bargains out there, but you should be careful. Your best protection is to be fairly knowledgeable about the computer business. Computer magazines and books are good sources for this knowledge.

Component sources

If you are fairly new to computing, be sure to read the chapters on floppy disk drives, hard disk drives, monitors, keyboards, and the major components before you buy your parts.

There are billions of dollars worth of products available. Many of them are very similar in function and quality. What you buy depends on what you want your computer to do and how much you can afford to spend.

One of the better ways to find components and compare prices is to look through the many computer magazines such as *Computer Shopper* and *Computer Buying World*. You'll find the addresses of these and other computer magazines in chapter 17. Many of the ads in these magazines are from mail-order houses.

Another good source is to visit a computer show or swap meet. Of course, local vendors and computer stores will be most happy to help you. They might charge a bit more than a mail-order house, but if anything goes wrong, they are usually very quick to help you or make it right.

I hope you are convinced that you can build your own computer. Lots of photos and instructions in the next chapter show how easy it is to build your own computer and save a bundle.

3
Putting it all together

This chapter covers what you need to know to assemble your computer and how to do it. You will not have to do any soldering because all of the parts are connected together with cables and screws.

Configuration record

You will have to set switches and jumpers on some of your boards and components to configure them to your system. For instance, you need to know what device is set for COM1 and what is set for COM2. You will also have to use the setup system to tell your complementary metal oxide semiconductor (CMOS) system what type of hard drive you have. If you forget how your components are configured, you might have difficulty solving any problems that might develop later. I would advise that you write down the configurations on a tablet and keep it for reference.

You will need a floppy disk to boot up your computer once it is assembled. After that you will probably boot off of the hard disk. But don't lose your boot disk. It should have a copy of your autoexec.bat and config.sys, your device drivers, and the Mirror command. It should be updated whenever you make any changes.

Parts needed

The basic parts you will need for your computer include the motherboard, chassis, power supply, floppy drive, hard drive, floppy and hard drive controllers, cables for disk drives, monitor and adapter card, and keyboard. I recommend that you read the chapters on the basic parts before you buy them. You should also have a power strip with at least six outlets so that all of your equipment can be plugged into a single source.

Tools needed

You will need a Phillips head and a flat blade type screwdriver. It is helpful if they are magnetized. You can magnetize them yourself by rubbing them briskly on a strong permanent magnet. The magnets found on cabinet doors or the voice coil magnet of a loudspeaker will do fine.

Caution! Do not place a magnet of any kind near or on your floppy disks. It can erase them.

Though not absolutely essential, longnose pliers can come in handy. If you have to remove or replace any chips, it is helpful to have a small bent screwdriver for prying them out. The metal fillers on the back of the chassis are excellent tools for lifting chips (Fig. 3-1). A small flashlight is very handy for checking in dark places to make sure that everything is plugged in right.

3-1   The back panel cover for unused slots make a good tool for lifting out chips.

Software needed

You will need a copy of DOS to boot up the system. You can boot up with almost any version of DOS, but I strongly suggest that you use DOS 5.0 or DR DOS 6.0. You must have a boot disk that has been formatted with system files on it.

Benchtop assembly

If you have all of your components, you can start putting them together. Before I install a system in the chassis, I usually plug everything together and try it out on a workbench. If you don't have a workbench, just set it up on the kitchen table. Plug in all the cables, drives, and boards and make sure everything works. If something doesn't work properly, it is much easier to find the problem now than once everything is mounted in the chassis. Once you are satisfied that everything works, you can mount it in the chassis.

Caution! Before you open the plastic bags or handle any sensitive boards, you should ground yourself, especially if you are working on a floor that is carpeted. You can build up a static charge on your body of several thousand volts by just walking across a carpeted floor. This static voltage could possibly damage some of the fragile transistors and semi-conductors on the components. You can discharge yourself by touching almost any metal surface or any object that is plugged into a power outlet.

Instructions for assembly

Figure 3-2 shows the chassis, power supply, floppy disk drives, hard disk drives, cables, and disk drive controllers. Figure 3-3 shows a Micronics 486 motherboard. The eight plug-in connector slots are shown in the top right portion of the motherboard. Below the plug-in slots are the vertical slots for the single in-line memory modules (SIMMs). The four slots near the rear are filled with 4Mb of memory. To the right of the SIMMs is a white connector for the power connection from the power supply. Immediately above the power connector is the round connector for the keyboard cable.

3-2 Some of the basic components that are needed to assemble a computer.

3-3 My 486 motherboard.

Step 1. Connect the power supply to the motherboard

Plug the power supply cables into the white 12-pin connector on the motherboard. Figure 3-4 shows the power cables being connected.

Caution! It is possible to plug these connectors in backwards. If you do so it could cause severe damage to your motherboard and system. Note that the connectors from the

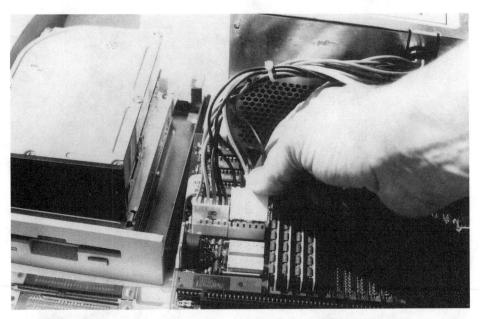

3-4 Plugging in the power supply to the motherboard. The two connectors are usually marked P8 and P9. P8 goes toward the rear. When properly connected, the four black wires are in the center.

power supply are usually in two parts, one marked P8 and one P9. P8 plugs in toward the back of the connection and P9 toward the front. Each connector will have two black ground wires. When connected properly, the four black wires will be in the center.

Step 2. Connect the floppy drives

Caution! Be very careful when installing the drive cables. Most of them can be plugged in backwards. This could cause severe damage to your drives or to the controllers.

You should have a wide 34-wire ribbon cable with a connector on each end and one near the center. The connector on one end has a split and several of the wires are twisted (Fig. 3-5). This connector plugs into the edge connector on the floppy that will be your drive A:, the drive that you boot from. You can hook up any drive as drive A:, but I recommend that you install a 5¼-inch 1.2Mb drive.

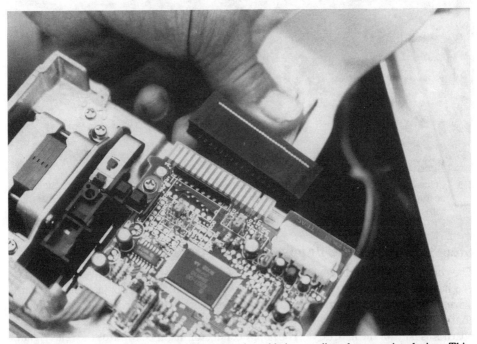

3-5 Connecting floppy disk drive A:. Note that the cable has a split and some twisted wires. This connector goes to drive A:. The edge connector on the drive should have etched numbers indicating pin 1 and pin 34. The edge connector also has a slot between pins 2 and 3.

Note that this connector can be plugged in backwards or upside down. A different color wire (blue, black, or red) on one side of the cable indicates pin 1. The floppy drive edge connector should have a 2 on one side and a 34 on the other. There should also be a slot cut into the edge connector between contacts 2 and 3. The colored wire side should be on the same side as the slot.

If you have a floppy drive B:, the center connector should be plugged onto the edge connector. You can use any drive for drive B:, but I recommend that you install a 3½-inch

1.44Mb drive. Again, the edge connector should have a slot cut between contacts 2 and 3, and the colored wire side should go to the side of the connector marked pin 1 or 2 (Fig. 3-6).

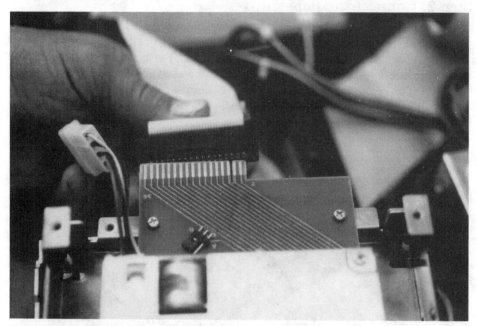

3-6 Connecting the B: drive to the connector in the middle of the cable. Note that the edge connector has a slot between pins 2 and 3. Note that the cable has a different color wire that indicates pin 1.

Step 3. Connect the floppy drives to the controller

The connector on the other end of the cable is connected to the floppy drive controller. If you have a hard disk controller, it is probably able to control two floppies and two hard drives. Check any documentation that you received with your controller. If it has a floppy controller, it will probably have two sets of 34 pins. The set of 34 pins in the center of the board is usually for the hard drive. The floppy connector might be towards the rear. Again, check your documentation. Pin numbers should be on the board indicating pin 1 (Fig. 3-7).

If you have a separate floppy controller, check for pin 1 and plug in the connector. Most of the newer floppy controllers have pins, but the older ones used an edge connector on the end of the board. Make sure that your controller cable has the proper type of connector for your controller. Figure 3-8 shows a floppy controller that has both types of connectors. It will control up to four floppies of any kind.

When connecting a cable to a board with pins, it is very easy to plug the connector in so that it contacts only one row of pins. Check to make sure that the connectors are installed properly.

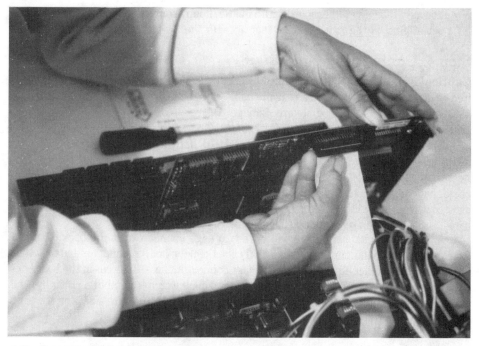

3-7 Connecting the floppy drive cable to a controller board that controls both hard disks and floppies. Check your documentation, but usually the floppy connector goes to the pins at the rear of the board. Make sure that the colored wire side goes to pin 1.

3-8 This is a controller for floppies only. It can control up to four floppies of any kind.

You might have a motherboard with a built-in floppy controller. In this case there will be a set of pins on the motherboard that accepts the 34-pin cable connector.

Step 4. Connect the hard drives

Caution! If you are installing a modified frequency modulation (MFM) or run length limited (RLL) hard drive, be aware that the cables for these drives can also be plugged in backwards. This could cause severe damage. Be very careful that you plug them in properly.

The flat 34-wire ribbon cable for MFM and RLL hard drives looks very much like the floppy cable. If you have only one hard drive, you might have a cable with just a single connector on each end, or you might have one with three connectors just like your floppy cable, but the connector might not have twisted wires like your floppy cable. If it has twisted wires, they will be in a different location on the hard drive cable than on the floppy cable, so the cables are not interchangeable.

An MFM or RLL hard drive will have two edge connectors at the back. One is a 34-contact edge connector that looks exactly like the floppy edge connector and the other is a smaller 20-contact edge connector. These connectors have slots cut in the board between contacts 2 and 3, so it is fairly easy to determine which is number 1. Plug the end connector of the cable into the edge connector so that the colored wire side is on the pin 1 side (Fig. 3-9).

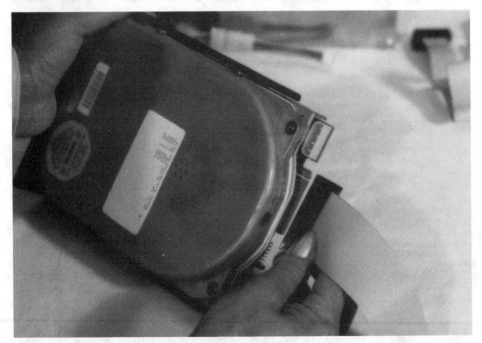

3-9   Connecting a hard disk. It will have a 34-wire cable that is similar to the floppy cable. The colored wire indicates pin 1. Note the slot on the edge connector between pins 2 and 3.

3-10 A closeup of the edge connectors of two hard drives. Note that they have a 34-pin and a 20-pin connector. The ballpoint pens point to the pins that have to be shorted out when connecting two drives. They also have removable resistor packs. The drive in the middle, or drive number two, should have the resistor pack removed. Check your documentation.

If you are installing a second hard drive, there are some pins between the two edge connectors that should be jumper configured (Fig. 3-10). In Fig. 3-10, the ballpoint pens point to the pins and black jumpers. If you have a straight-through cable, with no twisted wires on the end connector, the hard disk on the end connector should have a jumper on the set of pins nearest the 20-pin edge connector. Hard drive number two will have the second set of pins jumpered. If the cable has a twist in it, then the second set of pins on both hard drives are jumpered. Your drives might be different than these Seagate drives, so check your documentation.

A removable in-line terminating resistor pack is in the center of the boards in Fig. 3-10. The hard disk at the bottom shows the terminating resistor pack unplugged. The hard disk that is plugged into the center connector should have this resistor pack removed.

Figure 3-11 shows the 34-wire ribbon cable about to be connected to the hard disk

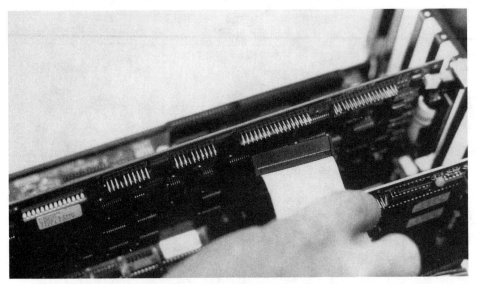

3-11 Connecting the hard disk cable to the controller. Note that the colored wire goes to pin 1.

controller. Again, be sure to install the connector so that the colored wire lines up with pin 1 on the board.

Install the 20-wire flat ribbon data cable connector on the hard disk (Fig. 3-12). Look

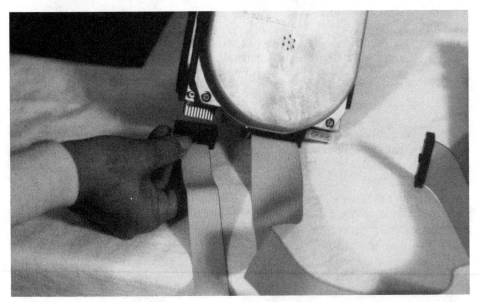

3-12 Connecting the 20-wire data cable to the hard drive. Note the colored wire and the slot between pins 2 and 3.

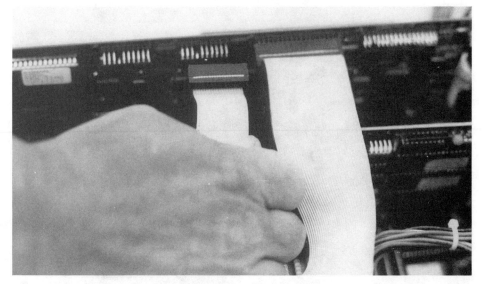

3-13 Connecting the data cable to the controller. The first hard drive connects to the set of pins nearest the 34-wire cable. Note that the colored wire goes to pin 1.

for pin numbers on the edge connector, or for the slot between contacts 2 and 3, and orient the connector so that the colored wire goes to that side.

Connect the 20-wire data cable to the hard disk controller (Fig. 3-13). There will probably be two sets of 20-pin connectors. Usually, the first hard disk is connected to the set of pins nearest the 34-pin hard disk connector. The 20-wire data cable from the second hard disk is connected to the other set of 20 pins. Again, check the documentation for your hard disks.

If you bought IDE hard drives and a motherboard with a built-in controller interface, there will be a set of pins on the motherboard for the 50-wire flat ribbon cable. This cable will also have a different colored wire on one side to indicate pin 1. This cable can be plugged in backwards, so make sure the colored wire side goes to pin 1 on the motherboard.

If your motherboard does not have a built-in IDE interface, you will have to buy a plug-in board for it. Most of the IDE interfaces also have an integrated floppy controller. Just make sure the cables are plugged in properly.

If you bought small computer system interface (SCSI) or enhanced small disk interface (ESDI) drives, you should have received some documentation with them. Make sure that any jumpers, switches, or shorting blocks on the controller boards are properly set. The cables for these drives will also have a different colored wire that indicates pin 1. Make sure that they are connected properly.

Your hard drives are probably already low-level formatted, especially if they are IDE, SCSI, or ESDI drives. However, they are probably not high-level formatted. Formatting is fairly simple and straightforward. If you are not familiar with the formatting of hard drives, read chapter 8.

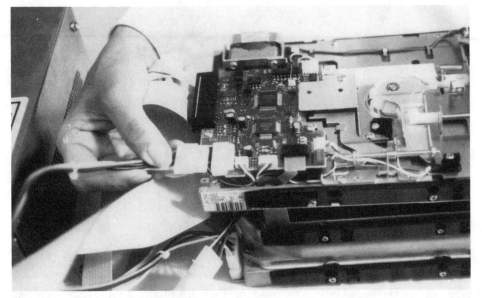

3-14   Connecting the power to the floppy drives. It can only be plugged in one way. The hard drives have the same connectors.

Step 5. Connect the power cables to the drives

The power supply should have four cables, each with four wires. They should be plugged into the matching connector on each drive. These connectors can only be plugged in one way (Fig. 3-14).

Step 6. Connect the keyboard, monitor, and power

Plug the keyboard into the socket on the back of the motherboard. Install the monitor adapter plug-in board and connect the monitor cable. Plug the monitor power cord into your power outlet. Check again to make sure that everything is plugged in properly. Connect the cord for the power supply to the outlet.

Figure 3-15 shows the system all connected and ready to go. Put your boot floppy disk in drive A: and turn on the power. You will probably get a message that your computer configuration needs to be set with instructions on how to set the time, date, and number and types of floppies and hard drives.

Step 7. Install the system in the chassis

If you have no problems, then install the system in the chassis. Figure 3-16 shows the floor of the chassis. Note the raised portions and the slots. Figure 3-17 shows the power supply

3-15 All connected on the benchtop and ready to try it out before installing in the case.

3-16 The case showing the raised channels with slots for the motherboard standoffs.

3-17   The power supply showing the raised tongues on the floor of the chassis. The power supply has matching slots to accept the tongues. Set the power supply over the raised tongues, slide it toward the rear and install two screws.

being installed. Note the raised tongues on the floor of the chassis. The power supply has two recessed cutouts on the bottom that slip onto the raised tongues. Two screws are then inserted through the back panel of the chassis to secure the power supply.

Figure 3-18 shows the back of the motherboard. The white objects are standoffs that fit in the slots on the floor of the chassis. Figure 3-19 shows the motherboard being installed. Line it up so that the standoffs drop into the openings of the slots, then slide the motherboard forward about one-half inch. The standoffs lock the motherboard so that it cannot be lifted. Screws should be installed, one in the center rear and one in the center front, to fasten the motherboard securely.

You will see several wires for the small speaker, the switches, and the light-emitting diodes (LEDs) on the front panel. Refer to the documentation that came with your motherboard as to where these wires should be connected. Most of the LEDs will have a black wire and a different colored wire. The colored wire should go to pin 1 on the motherboard, the black wire to ground.

Depending on the type of case you bought, your drives might have to have plastic slide rails installed (Fig. 3-20). Small clamps are then used to hold the drives in place.

Go back and check all of the cable connections again. Make sure that they are all plugged in properly and securely. Check all of the boards to make sure that they are seated properly.

3-18 The backside of the motherboard. The white objects are standoffs. The lower photo is a close-up of a standoff that has been removed.

You are now ready to install the cover. Slide it on and install a screw in each of the four corners on the back panel and one in the top center.

Congratulations! You have just saved about $1000.

3-19 Sliding the motherboard into the chassis. Position it so that the standoffs slide into the openings on the raised channels.

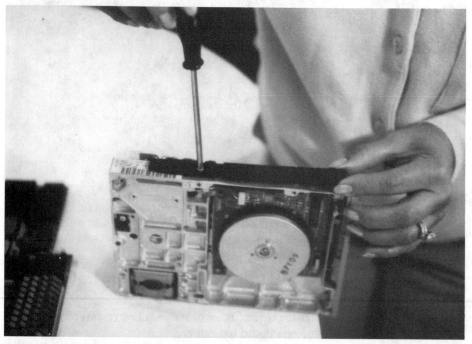

3-20 Installing the plastic slide rails on the floppy drive. Your system might be different. Some have metal slide rails.

Computer furniture

If you have your computer on the kitchen table, sooner or later your spouse will probably ask you to remove it. If you are setting up a home office, and you are not very rich or too proud, you might buy some used office furniture. Desks and filing cabinets might get dinged up and the paint might get scratched, but they seldom wear out. A used office furniture store can be found in most larger cities. Many of the larger stores, such as K-Mart, Sears, and Montgomery Ward, also carry computer furniture.

User groups

You should not have had any trouble putting your system together, but chances are you will have some software or hardware problems sooner or later and you will probably need some help. One of the best places to get help is from user groups. These are groups of people very much like you who have computers. Most of them have had problems like the ones that you will experience. They are usually happy to help you solve your problems.

Besides being a source of help, many of these groups provide their members with public domain software. Some have vendors come to their meetings to demonstrate products. Many of them use the combined buying power of the group to arrange for discount prices on software and hardware.

The Pasadena (California) user's group is one of the largest in the country, primarily due to their president, Steve Bass. He has had speakers and presenters from major companies come to the meetings. Often speakers and presenters give away some of their products, which are raffled off to the attending members.

Several of the members have volunteered to be in a skills bank. These members have an expertise in some phase of computing, such as using a particular program or in troubleshooting and diagnosis. One member put all of the volunteers' names and telephone numbers in a FoxBASE database and put it on the user group bulletin board and on floppy diskettes. The members can search the database to find an expert member who can help with a particular problem.

The meetings are enjoyable and fun. One member told an unusual computer story at one of the meetings. He said a friend bought a computer and set it up on the kitchen table. The table had one short leg and the computer started sliding off. He looked around for something to put under the table leg, but could not find anything the right size. He noticed that he needed something about the thickness of a checkbook, so he slid his checkbook under the table leg. It made the table perfect. He was probably the first person ever to use a checkbook to balance his computer.

Each month *Computer Shopper* publishes an extensive list of most of the user groups in the country. It also publishes a list of the bulletin boards. You can pick up a copy of *Computer Shopper* at most magazine racks, or better yet, subscribe (P.O. Box 51020, Boulder, CO 80321-1020). It is one of the largest magazines, both in circulation and in size, with about 800 pages of articles and ads every month. It is an excellent source for shopping and comparing of prices.

4
Upgrading
an old computer

If you have an old PC, XT, 286, or 386, you can easily upgrade it. Just pull out your old motherboard and install a new 486. You get all of the benefits of a new 486 system at a fairly reasonable cost. There are baby-size 486 boards that will fit in a PC or XT, or if you have an older standard-size 286 or 386, there are a few vendors who still offer standard-size 486 motherboards. If you want to, you can install a baby-size motherboard in a standard-size chassis. The mounting holes and the rear slots are the same so everything will line up.

486 ISA or EISA

You can install an ISA or EISA motherboard in any PC. The EISA board is a bit more expensive, but it is more versatile and powerful. All of the procedures described in this chapter apply to the 486SX, 486DX, or EISA upgrades.

Use your old components

Even if you are moving up from a PC or XT, you can use many of your old components such as the plug-in boards and disk drives. Unless your memory chips are a very fast 70 ns or better, you will not be able to use them. Besides, most of the new motherboards use SIMMs. For more about memory see chapter 6.

Keyboards

If you are upgrading from an old PC or XT, you might not be able to use your old keyboard. Although the PC, XT, 286, and 386 keyboards look exactly alike and have the same connector, the PC and XT keyboards will not work on the 286 or 386 because they have a different scanner frequency. Some of the keyboards have a small switch on the back that allows them to be switched from one type to the other. Some of the newer ones can detect which system they are connected to and switch automatically. The 286 and 386 keyboards will work on a 486 with no problems.

The price of keyboards has dropped dramatically. I have seen some fairly good ones at swap meets for $30 to $50. If possible, try the keyboard before you buy it. Some require only a very light touch. If you are heavy-handed like me, you might not be happy if it is too light. For more about keyboards see chapter 10.

Disk drives

There is no reason why you can't use an old 360K floppy disk drive on your new 486, but you might want to install a 1.2Mb and a 1.44Mb drive. These drives can read and write to 360K and 720K formats, as well as the high-density ones. The higher capacity makes them much better for backing up and archiving. For more about floppies see chapter 7.

If your old hard drive is less than 30Mb and is fairly slow, you should consider buying a new one, or at least a second one. Most controllers have the ability to control a second hard drive, although some controllers require that the second drive be the same size and type as the first one.

You definitely need a large hard drive. The new software packages require an enormous amount of disk space. Over 20Mb is required just to run OS/2 2.0. Most of the newer hard drives are much faster than earlier ones and have much greater capacities. For more about hard drives see chapter 8.

Monitors

An old monochrome or CGA monitor will work fine with the new 486. But depending on what you want to do with your new baby, you might not be too happy with it. To me, the monitor is one of the most important components of my system. I spend a lot of time looking at it. I like color, even if I am doing nothing but word processing, and I will spend a little extra for it. For more about monitors see chapter 8.

Deciding what to buy and where to buy it

One of the first things you have to do is decide what you want; or if you are like me, decide what you want at a price you can afford. I subscribe to about 50 computer magazines. (See chapter 17 for a listing of computer magazines.) These magazines have excellent articles and reviews of software and hardware, and of course they have lots of ads. The ads give me a good idea about the price I will have to pay for an item. There can be quite large variations in prices from dealer to dealer. Mail order might be one of the better ways to purchase your parts, especially if you don't live near a large city.

There are usually lots of computer stores in the larger cities. There are hundreds in the San Francisco Bay and Los Angeles areas. Computer swaps are going on almost every weekend. If I need something I go to one of the swap meets and compare the prices at the various booths. I often take a pad along, write the prices down, then go back and make the best deal I can. Sometimes you can haggle with the vendors for a better price, especially if it is near closing time.

Case size

The standard-size AT or 286 case is a bit larger than the XT case. The original XT case is 5 inches high, 19½ inches wide, and 16½ inches deep. The AT case is 6 inches high, 21½ inches wide, and 16½ inches deep. The XT motherboard is about 11 inches wide and about 13 inches long. The standard AT motherboard is about 14 inches by 14 inches. By combining several chips into single very large-scale integrated (VLSI) chips, the clone builders developed a "baby" 286 motherboard. It is about 1 inch longer than the XT motherboard, but it still fits in the XT case. The VLSI chips result in a savings on components, soldering, labor, and cost. They are also more reliable because there are fewer solder joints and components.

The 386 and 486 motherboards were originally designed to the standard AT size. In a very short time baby 386 and 486 motherboards were also developed. The baby size is the most prevalent and popular size today.

Figure 4-1 shows an XT motherboard on the left and the standard-size 486 motherboard on the right. Several companies manufacture baby 486 motherboards that are about the same size as the XT motherboard so you can remove an XT motherboard and install a baby 486.

At one time there were only two sizes of computers, the XT and the AT. But there are now dozens of different sizes and types. IBM developed a low-profile type and several

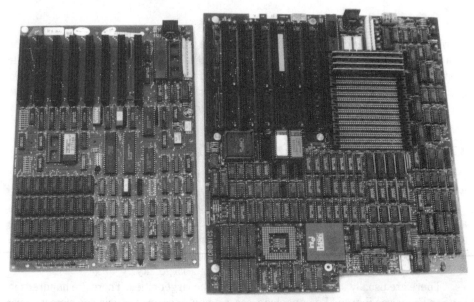

4-1   An XT motherboard on the left and a standard-size 486 motherboard on the right. A baby-size 486 motherboard is about the same size as the XT and can be installed in an XT case.

of the clone makers have developed similar types. The low-profile type has a single slot in the motherboard. A daughterboard is plugged into this slot. The daughterboard has two slots on one side and three on the other for plugging boards in horizontally. I don't like this type of motherboard. Most of them have several built-in options, but you are still limited to five plug-in boards. This type of system requires a special case with horizontal rear slot openings, so you cannot use an older case.

Some people like the tower-type case, which stands on the floor freeing up some of the desktop. Tower cases are even larger than the standard case and have space for more drives and other goodies. A tower case and power supply costs from $80 to $150, whereas a desktop case and power supply costs from $60 to $100. Tower cases come in three different sizes. Figure 4-2 shows a minitower for baby-size motherboards.

4-2   A mini tower case with the cover removed.

Instructions and photos

The basic instructions and photos in chapter 3 apply in most cases to the upgrading of any computer. Refer back to that chapter if you have any problems.

Upgrading a PC or XT to a 486

The original PC and XT use the 8088 CPU. This CPU has about 29,000 transistors and operates at 4.77 MHz. Computers perform their operations by moving blocks of data in precise blocks of time. The PC and XT can cycle 8-bit blocks of data at 4.77 MHz. That sounds fast, but it takes 8 bits to make a single byte. It also takes 8 bits to create a single character of the alphabet. It takes a whole lot more bytes if you are using graphics. It can be painfully slow if you have to run a CAD program or a large spreadsheet. The turbo XTs are souped up so that they can operate faster than their normal 4.77 MHz. Most have a "high gear" so that they can be shifted up to 8 MHz, or even 10 MHz or 12 MHz. A 486 can process data 50 to 100 times faster than a PC or XT.

If you have an original "true blue" IBM PC, it has only five slots. The case, or chassis, has five openings in the back panel. The XT has eight slots with eight openings in the back panel. Almost all motherboards now have eight slots. If you have an old PC case with the five openings in the rear panel, it will not accommodate an eight-slot motherboard. Your best bet is to scrap the old case with the five slot openings and buy a new case. It will only cost about $30 for a desktop case, or about $75 for one with a 200-watt power supply. If you are in love with the IBM logo and want to keep the old case, there are a few companies that make special motherboards for the old five-slot PC. But buying one of these special five-slot motherboards will cost much more than what a new case and an eight-slot motherboard would cost. It would be much better to buy a new case, rip the IBM logo off the old case, and tape it to the new one.

If you are upgrading an original PC, you should also buy a new power supply. The PC has a puny 63-watt power supply. The XT and later models have 135- to 150-watt power supplies. Depending on what you install in your 486, you might be able to get by with a 150-watt power supply, but you will be better off with a minimum 200-watt supply.

Upgrading a 286 to a 486

You can easily upgrade a 286 to a 486. The 286, or IBM AT (for advanced technology), uses the 80286 CPU. It has 125,000 transistors and is a 16-bit system. The original IBM AT operated at a very conservative speed of 6 MHz, but many of the 286 clones now run at 12 MHz, 16 MHz, and even up to 25 MHz.

The 286 CPU handles data in 16-bit chunks; twice that of the 8088. A 286 operating at 10 MHz is more than four times faster than an XT operating at 4.77 MHz. Because it handles twice as much data per cycle, the 286 is still more than twice as fast as an XT, even if the XT is operating at the same 10 MHz. Even the fastest 16-bit 286 is a slowpoke compared to the 32-bit 486. You should have no trouble replacing a 286 motherboard with a 486SX or 486DX.

Upgrading a 386 to a 486

The 386 system uses the Intel 80386 CPU. This CPU has 275,000 transistors and can handle data in 32-bit chunks, the same as the 486. But the 486 has 1,200,000 transistors and can handle data much faster than a 386.

The standard-size 386 and 486 motherboards are the same size as the original standard-size AT motherboards. There are many baby-size 486 motherboards that will fit in the standard-size or baby-size case. It is very easy to pull out a 386 motherboard and install a 486. You should have no problems using your 386 peripherals and plug-in boards. You might even be able to use the memory chips from your 386.

The Cyrix 486 CPU

The Cyrix Company has a 486 CPU that is pin-compatible with the 386DX chip. Just remove the 386 CPU and plug in the Cyrix CPU. This chip also comes with a coprocessor that plugs into to 387 socket. It gives you the coprocessing ability of the true 486DX systems.

The Cyrix 486 CPU operates internally at 40MHz, but it can be used in any 386DX system. This CPU can also be used in the PS/2 386 systems. This upgrade provides almost all of the power and functionality of a true 486DX 33MHz system. The Cyrix 486 CPU costs less than half as much as the Intel 486DX 33MHz chip. It is the easiest and least-expensive way I know of to upgrade to 486 power.

Upgrading a 386SX to a 486

The 386SX can also be easily upgraded to a 486. Simply pull out the motherboard and install the same size 486 motherboard. The 386SX CPU uses 32 bits internally, but only 16-bit lines externally. The 16-bit external operation causes it to be a bit slower than the 32-bit 386DX. A 386SX motherboard costs from $100 to $350. You should have no problem removing and replacing a 386SX motherboard with a 486 motherboard.

Upgrading a 486 system
CPU upgradables

Some systems can be upgraded by simply replacing the CPU. Some vendors have developed proprietary motherboards that can accept several different versions of the 386DX, 486SX, or 486DX CPUs. They did this by installing different CPU sockets on the motherboard. Intel and some of the motherboard manufacturers are promoting these systems as "upgradables." You can start off with a 386DX CPU then later replace it with any of the 486 CPUs.

Most of the companies have developed these upgradable motherboards for use with their own systems. At the present time it is rather difficult for an end user to find one, especially one that has the 386 option. There might be several available later. Check the computer magazines for ads.

Northgate, Dell, and several others are promoting systems that will let you upgrade later. You should be aware that it will cost you much more if you buy one of these systems than if you do your own upgrade. An article in a recent issue of *PC Sources* listed Dell's prices for upgrades as follows: from 486SX/20 to 486SX/25, $499; from 486SX/20 to 486DX/33, $1099; and from 486SX/25 to 486DX/33, $699.

If you must start out with a 486SX, you can make these upgrades yourself and save from $300 to $600. You should be able to buy a 486SX/20 CPU for about $250. If you later decide that you need the 486DX, the CPU will cost you about $400.

This might be a good deal if Intel or other dealers would let you trade in your old 486SX, but there is no trade-in, so you lose the $250 that it cost you. Essentially you end up spending about $650 for a $400 486DX CPU.

The ZIF socket

Most of the vendors who sell the upgradable systems use a zero insertion force (ZIF) socket. It can be very difficult to remove a 168-pin CPU from its socket. The ZIF socket has a small lever that opens the internal contacts so that the CPU can be inserted or removed very easily. Once inserted, the lever is pressed down and the contacts make a tight connection around each pin. If you plan to make a lot of CPU changes, you might look for a motherboard with a ZIF socket. If you don't have a ZIF socket, you can use a small bent screwdriver to pry up chips from their sockets. You can also use the metal fillers for the unused slots on the back panel of the case.

The 487 coprocessor

If you insist on buying a 486SX and you later find that you need a coprocessor, you can buy an Intel 487SX. This is essentially a full-functioning 486DX with a built-in coprocessor. When plugged into the empty socket alongside the 486SX, it disables the 486SX. It would be nice if you could remove the 486SX CPU and sell it to someone else, but even though the SX becomes nonfunctional, it must remain plugged in. You cannot plug the 487SX into the CPU socket because it has 169 pins, one more than the 168 pins on a standard 486.

Upgrading to a faster CPU

The early 486 operated at 20 MHz, but they now operate at 25 MHz, 33 MHz, and 50 MHz. You can remove a slower CPU and replace it with a faster one. You might also need to replace your quartz oscillator which determines the system frequency. The quartz oscillator is usually in a small metal container. If you install a faster CPU, you might also have to install faster memory and reset some jumpers and switches on your motherboard.

The 486DX2

The 486DX2 series of CPUs doubles and internal processing frequency. They still operate externally at 25 MHz or 33 MHz, but they can process data internally at 50 MHz or 66 MHz. The DX2 provides a 50% to 150% increase in the overall processing speed depending on the application being processed.

It is very easy to upgrade with one of these chips. Just remove the old CPU and plug in the DX2. There is no need to set any switches or install faster memory. Again, neither Intel nor their dealers offer a trade-in for your old CPU. You might be able to take it to a swap meet and sell it, or you might find a small dealer who will buy it. Don't expect to get full price for it.

The overdrive chip

The overdrive CPU is basically a 486DX2 designed to replace the 487SX. It plugs into the 169-pin coprocessor socket on the 486SX board and disables the 486SX. Like the 486DX2, the overdrive doubles the internal processing speed of the system. A 20-MHz system with an overdrive chip will process data internally at 40 MHz; a 25-MHz system will operate internally at 50 MHz. The 486 overdrive provides all of the math coprocessor and other functions of a true 486DX. The suggested list price of the 20-MHz overdrive chip is $549, and $699 for the 25-MHz chip.

The Cyrix CPU

Cyrix has developed a hybrid chip that is part 386 and part 486. It uses the same pinout and is the same size as the 386SX, but it uses a 486 instruction set. It is very easy to use this chip to make a 386 faster and more powerful.

Upgrading to EISA

It is very easy to pull out any of the previously mentioned motherboards and replace them with an EISA motherboard. There are both standard-size and baby-size EISA boards.

Upgrading an AT&T 6300 or Zenith 151

These computers have a different type of case. You should be able to use most of your present components, but to add a new motherboard you will have to buy a new case and power supply.

What to do with your old parts

You might be able to take your old motherboard and other parts to a swap meet and sell them. Most swap meets have a consignment table where parts like this are sold. You might advertise in the local paper and sell them. You might even be able to sell them to a local dealer.

Installing the motherboard

Now that you have a new motherboard, it is easily installed in a few simple steps. The following procedures can be used for installing any motherboard.

Step 1. Remove the cover

The first thing to do is remove the cover from your computer. Unplug the power and remove the screws at each corner of the rear panel and the one at the top center. Slide the cover off.

Step 2. Remove the plug-ins

Make a rough diagram showing where the cables and the boards are connected. You might even take pieces of tape or a marking pen and mark each board and cable with a number. You can use fingernail polish to paint a stripe on the cable connectors and components before they are disconnected. When you replace the cables, just line up the painted stripes. Notice that the ribbon cables have one wire that is a different color. This indicates pin 1. Pay close attention as to how the connectors are oriented. On most boards that have vertical connections, pin 1 will be towards the top. If the connection is horizontal, pin 1 is usually toward the front of the computer. But this might not always be so. Check the boards for a small number or some indication as to which is pin 1. Note the colored wires on the ribbon cables and record their position on your diagram. If possible, leave the cables from the disk drives connected to the plug-in boards.

Note that the connectors from the power supply are connected so that the four black wires are in the center. When reconnecting the cables, it is possible to replace the cable connectors upside down, backwards, or in the wrong connector. Make sure that your diagram is complete before disconnecting anything.

Remove all of the plug-in boards, the keyboard cable and other wires, and cables that are connected to the motherboard. If at all possible, leave the cables connected to the disk controllers. Just pull the boards out and lay them across the power supply. It should not be necessary to remove the disk drives or the power supply.

Step 3. Remove the motherboard

Depending on the type of computer you have, you might have nine standoffs holding the motherboard off the chassis. If so, there should be nine small nuts on the bottom of the chassis. The standoffs might be made of plastic. If they are plastic they will be held in place by flared portions of the body of the standoff. Use pliers to press the flares together so that the standoff can be removed.

Step 4. Install memory chips

If you got a motherboard without memory it might be possible to use the chips from your old 386 motherboard. But you probably will not be able to use chips from an older machine. It depends on how fast your new board operates and what kind of chips it uses. Most of the 486 motherboards use the SIMM-type chips.

For the older 4.77-MHz PCs and XTs, 200 ns was plenty fast enough. You will probably need at least 70 ns for your 486. Some systems use wait states so that you can use slower memory chips. The size and speed of the chips are usually marked on the top along

4-3   The back panel cover for unused slots makes a good tool for lifting out chips.

with the vendor's name and other information. You might see something like 100–70, indicating 1000K or 1Mb at 70 ns.

If you are going to use your old memory chips, you will need a small screwdriver or some other tool to pry them out of their sockets. The blank fillers on the back panel where there are no boards installed are a very good tool for lifting chips out of their sockets (Fig. 4-3).

You should have received some kind of diagram or information with your motherboard that tells you what kind of memory to install and where. Be very careful when inserting chips or SIMMs so that they are oriented in the proper direction and the proper location. Ordinarily, most of the chips on the boards will be oriented in the same direction. Be careful not to bend the legs, and make sure that all of the legs are inserted.

Step 5. Install the new motherboard

Plug all of the components together outside of the case and try them out. If they don't work, it is fairly easy to troubleshoot. If there are no problems, install them in the case, try them again, and install the cover.

Use the same procedure to install the motherboard that was detailed in chapter 3. Most of the new boards use a standoff system that is different than that used in the old PCs and XTs. Most of the new cases have raised channels on the floor of the chassis. The channels have holes with elongated slots. Plastic standoffs with rounded tops and a thin groove fit in the holes. The standoffs are pressed into the holes in the motherboard. The board is placed so that the standoffs fit into the holes in the raised channels. The board is moved to the right so that the grooves slide into and are locked in the narrow elongated slots. One screw at the back center of the board and one at the front center locks the board in place.

Step 6. Replace the boards and cables

You are now ready to start replacing your components. Reconnect the power to the board from the power supply. Make sure that it is oriented so that the four black wires are in the center. Replace your plug-in boards and any cables that were disconnected. Make sure that they are connected properly with the colored wire going to pin 1. If you made a diagram before you removed them, you shouldn't have any problems.

Amaze your friends

I have been told that Paul Newman, the movie actor who loves racing, has a beat-up old Volkswagen. He pulled out the VW engine and replaced it with a powerful V8. In this beat-up old VW, he pulls up alongside someone in a powerful car, then pulls away and leaves them in his dust. The looks of amazement and disbelief must have been worth all the money and effort he put into that old VW.

You can do about the same thing with an old PC or XT. On the outside it might still look like a lowly PC or XT, but underneath the hood is a veritable powerhouse. If your friends or coworkers don't know that you have upgraded to a 486, you can astonish and amaze them with the speed and power of your new machine.

5
Motherboards

The motherboard, along with its CPU, is the unique component that identifies each type of PC. It is mounted on the floor of the case, or chassis. It has eight slots for plug-in boards.

Some motherboard options
Size

The two sizes of motherboards are the standard-size AT and the baby size. When IBM developed the first ATs and 286s, they had several more chips than the XTs and they used a board that was about 1 inch longer and about 3 inches wider.

It wasn't long before Chips and Technology developed a series of VLSI chips. By integrating several of these chips into a single package, they were able to develop an AT motherboard that was the same size as the XT. Almost everyone called it a baby-size AT.

When the 386 and 486 are introduced, several manufacturers used the standard size AT motherboard, but many of them opted for the baby size. The majority of all boards sold now are the baby size. Using even more and denser VLSI chips, several companies have developed half-size boards for the 286, 386, and 486 systems. They are about half the size of the standard AT board and two-thirds the size of a baby-size board. One company that offers these half-size boards is QDI Computer.

There never seem to be enough slots. Several companies have developed standard-size motherboards with 12 slots (see Fig. 5-1). One company that offers these motherboards is Pioneer Computer.

ISA and EISA

There are two primary types of motherboards. The most popular one is the ISA board, which used to be known as the IBM standard. It has a 16-bit bus. The EISA board has a

5-1   A motherboard with 12 slots.

32-bit bus. It was developed to compete with IBM's microchannel architecture (MCA). I discuss MCA, ISA, and EISA in greater detail later in this chapter.

An EISA motherboard is more expensive than an ISA type, but it offers much more functionality, speed, and power. By 1995 EISA boards will be the most popular motherboards sold. At the present time, EISA motherboards cost from $1000 to $1600, about $400 to $700 more than ISA types.

Price comparisons

The *Reseller News* is a large weekly computer magazine with a large advertising section in the back of each issue. The magazine is free to qualified subscribers. See chapter 17 for the address and details on how to qualify. Table 5-1 lists some advertised prices for various 486 motherboards.

Notice that there are wide variations in the prices. It might be that some of the motherboards have other utilities and goodies besides the cache. Check current computer magazines for the latest prices.

There are a large number of motherboard vendors and each one tries to differentiate its product from the others with various options and prices. The competition among the many vendors helps to keep the prices down.

Note also that there are only a few EISA boards listed. There will be many more in a very short time, and as more manufacturers enter the EISA market, the competition will force the prices down. Within the next 5 years, EISA-type systems will be the most prevalent system in the PC industry. In a very short time, EISA motherboards will cost no more than a 386DX costs today.

Table 5-1. Price comparison of various motherboards

ISA 33 MHz		ISA 50 MHz		EISA 33 MHz		EISA 50 MHz	
Cache	Cost	Cache	Cost	Cache	Cost	Cache	Cost
256K	$ 609	256K	$1859	256K	$1150	256K	$ 879
256	570	256	950	256	1010	256	1650
256	659	256	975	256	1145	256	1599
256	595	256	845	128	1452	256	1460
256	605	256	995	64	1215	128	1932
256	715	64	1435	64	1480		1645
256	580	64	819	64	1040		1599
256	639	64	799		850		1395
128	569	64	990		1130		
128	590		849		995		
128	599		819		1035		
64	870		915		1350		
64	1025		945		1030		
64	585		1257				
64	900		1335				
64	579		799				
64	528						
64	545						
64	525						
64	599						
64	630						
	730						
	509						
	579						
	895						
	735						
	615						
	635						
	663						
	628						
	607						
	715						

EISA/ISA combo

Some manufacturers have developed EISA/ISA combination motherboards. These motherboards have from two to six EISA slots with the remaining slots for the ISA bus. Figure 5-2 shows a combination EISA/ISA motherboard. It has six EISA slots and two ISA slots. These motherboards cost from $800 to $1200, or about $200 to $400 more than the ISA ones.

The combination EISA/ISA motherboards are a good idea because about $10 billion worth of good low-cost 16-bit ISA products are still available. In many cases you don't need the full 32-bit power of EISA. It will be some time before EISA products replace these plug-in boards.

5-2 An EISA/ISA combination motherboard.

Local bus

The 386DX, 486SX, and 486DX systems process data 32 bits at a time and communicate with memory over a 32-bit bus. All of the ISA systems communicate with their plug-in boards and other I/O peripherals over a 16-bit bus, the same as the 286 systems.

Some companies have developed what they call local bus ISA motherboards that have one or more slots with a 32-bit bus. One or more of the motherboard's standard 16-bit slots have an additional special slot for the 32-bit bus (see Fig. 5-3). At this time, there aren't many boards available for this system. Most of the boards that can use the 32-bit local bus are enhanced VGA cards.

Microlink, (800) 829-3688, offers a motherboard with one local bus slot and one EISA slot. The motherboard with a 33-MHz CPU lists for $595. The enhanced VGA card for the local bus costs $340.

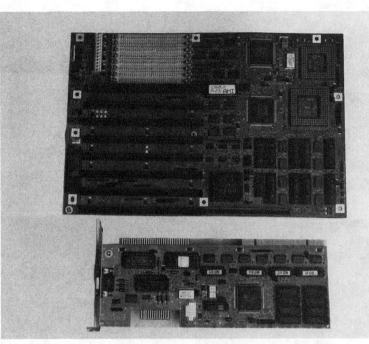

5-3   A motherboard with a local bus slot and adapter card.

CPU

I have seen lots of ads for 486 motherboards for as little as $150, but in small print it says, "w/o CPU." The CPU costs from $350 to more than $500. You have to pay close attention to the ads. Some are rather misleading.

One reason some vendors don't list a price for the 486 motherboard with a CPU is that you can choose several different CPUs. Intel manufactures over 30 different CPUs. You might choose the 20-MHz or 25-MHz 486SX for about $250 more than the cost of the motherboard without a CPU. There are 25-MHz and 33-MHz 486DX CPUs available, adding about $400 to the cost of the motherboard. The 50-MHz 486DX adds about $600 to the basic motherboard price.

The 486DX2

The 486DX2 is similar to the 386SX in one respect: The 386SX handles data in 16-bit chunks externally, but processes it 32 bits at a time internally. The 486DX2/50 handles data at a speed or frequency of 25 MHz externally, but it processes data internally at a speed of 50 MHz. The 486DX2/66 handles data at 33 MHz externally, but processes it at a rate of 66 MHz internally. The 50-MHz and 66-MHz 486DX2 adds $600 to $1000 to the cost of the motherboard.

One reason the CPU can't handle the data at the faster rate both externally and internally is that the higher the speed, the more heat that develops. The actual CPU chip is only about 0.4 inches by 0.6 inches and is paper thin. But the assembled unit is about 2 inches by 2 inches and is over 0.25 inch thick. A large part of the CPU assembly is a heat sink designed to absorb and carry away the excess heat that is generated.

Some vendors have devised methods to cool the CPU so that it can be operated at a higher frequency. Some use fans and large elaborate heat sinks. One vendor uses a thermoelectric cooling system to achieve the higher frequencies. Intel takes a dim view of the practice of "pushing" the frequency above their specifications. They do not guarantee a CPU that is operated outside their guidelines and specifications.

The 486SX

The 486SX is the same as the 486DX except that it operates at a slower frequency and its built-in math coprocessor is nonfunctional.

The manufacturing process

The 486 CPUs are etched onto a thin slab of silicon. Several CPUs can be etched onto a single slab. The chips go through several stages of processing. At the end of the processing, the individual CPUs are cut, separated, tested, and selected.

Coprocessors

A considerable number of the 1,200,000 transistors on the 486 are devoted to its built-in coprocessor. This makes the 486 very fast for applications that can utilize a coprocessor, such as spreadsheets and CAD programs. But many software applications do not require a coprocessor. The coprocessor is useless unless the software application is designed to use it. Except for the 486, almost all motherboards and computers are usually sold without a math coprocessor. An empty socket is provided on the motherboard so that a coprocessor can be added later.

The 486DX CPU chip has 168 pins. Intel has insisted that manufacturers of 486SX motherboards provide a 169-pin socket for a coprocessor. Intel has developed a 487SX coprocessor for the 486SX. It is actually a 486DX with an extra pin. When plugged in, it disables the 486SX and takes over all of the CPU and math coprocessor functions. The 487SX operates at the same frequencies as the 486SX: 16 MHz, 20 MHz, or 25 MHz. Figure 5-4 shows a 486SX with a 487SX coprocessor.

5-4   A 486SX with a 487SX coprocessor.

The overdrive

I mentioned the overdrive chip in the previous chapter. The 486 overdrive CPU does the same thing that the 486DX2 does. It is plugged into the coprocessor socket of a 486SX to double the internal processing speed.

Testing and selection

When a batch of chips are processed, some chips may have defective transistors or circuits. The chips that are not completely dead are tested for several specifications and parameters. Some of them operate at a higher voltage, higher frequency, or higher temperature than the others. They are also tested to meet several other important specifications and criteria. The CPU chips are separated and selected according to the tests that they pass. A single batch might have a few chips that can operate at 50 MHz, a few at 33 MHz, and some at 25 MHz, while some operate reliably only at 20 MHz. Most people want the faster chips, so a chip that is limited to 20 MHz is sold as a 486SX.

The coprocessor section represents a fairly large portion of the 486 chip, and it might have some defective transistors in this area. If the chip is otherwise okay, it can be used as a 486SX, otherwise it would be scrapped. Essentially, these "floor sweepings" increase the yield of salable chips for each batch that they manufacture. A spokesperson for Intel denies that this is the way 486SX chips are produced. Intel says that the 486SX is so popular, they have a manufacturing line devoted to it.

The fading 486SX

Despite what Intel's spokesperson says, I don't believe that the 486SX is all that popular. I don't think it will survive. When the 486SX first came out a large number of vendors developed 486SX systems. They were a very hot item. I recently attended a swap meet in Los Angeles with about 300 vendors present. I found only two vendors who were offering the 486SX motherboard. I talked to several of the vendors and they said that most people who build their own 486s want a 486DX with a coprocessor.

The overdrive chip won't help much. Why would a person pay $300 to $400 for a 486SX, then pay another $400 to $600 for an overdrive chip? They can save $300 to $400 if they buy the 486DX in the first place.

If you look through the computer magazines you will see very few ads for 486SX systems. If you can afford the extra $150, I recommend that you bypass the 486SX and buy the 486DX. Get the fastest one that you can, even if you have to eat hamburger now and then instead of steak.

Memory

Your motherboard should have sockets, or provisions, for the installation of at least 8Mb of RAM. Most motherboards have provisions for 16Mb and up to 128Mb of memory. The majority of the motherboards use SIMM-type sockets. This allows for the most memory to be installed in the least amount of space. You might find a few 486 boards that use single in-line package (SIP) sockets. But the SIP-type memory is not as popular as the SIMM type. Very few, if any, 486 boards use the older dual in-line package (DIP) memory chips. They require too much board space. You can install about 32Mb of SIMM memory in the space that 1Mb of DIP memory requires.

Your motherboard will probably be sold without memory. Make sure that you order the type and speed of memory that is required for your board. You can probably get by with 80 ns for a 20-MHz 486SX. For 25 MHz you will want 60 ns to 70 ns, and at least 60 ns for 33-MHz and faster systems.

It is very easy to install SIMMs. Just follow the documentation that you receive with your motherboard and make sure that you orient them properly when you plug them in. If you are not filling all of the sockets, check your documentation. You might have to install memory in multiples of two; that is 2Mb, 4Mb, or 8Mb. The sockets are usually numbered. If you are only installing 2Mb or 4Mb, the SIMMs have to be plugged into in the proper sockets.

There are probably some switches or jumpers on the motherboard that have to be set to tell the system how much memory is installed. Again, your motherboard documentation should tell you how to do this.

Many of today's motherboards are designed for 1Mb SIMMs. By the time you read this there should be lots of boards designed for 4Mb SIMMs. Look for the 4Mb systems. There should be 16Mb SIMMs available in the very near future.

Cache

When processing data, quite often the same data is used over and over again. Having to traverse the bus to retrieve the data can slow the system down considerably. This is especially so if the data is on a hard disk. Even fetching data from RAM can slow the system.

The 486 has a built-in 8K cache which contributes to its speed. But 8K is not nearly large enough for some programs, so many motherboards have sockets for adding a very fast cache. This cache is usually made from SRAM. SRAM is discussed in more detail in chapter 6.

Write through and write back

After the data is processed it is returned to RAM. The older write through systems send the data back to RAM. System operations are delayed while the data is being written to RAM. The delay might be only microseconds, but if you are processing a lot of data, it can add up. The newer write back systems keep the data in the cache until there is a break in operations, then they write the data to RAM.

Disk cache

Programs that are to be processed are usually loaded from a hard disk. Portions of the program might have to be retrieved from the hard disk over and over. Some software programs, such as Windows, can set aside a section of RAM that acts as a disk cache. A disk cache can also be set up by some hard disk controllers. This can speed up processing of some programs considerably.

Built-in goodies

The motherboard has eight slots and hundreds of different boards can be plugged into these slots. These boards can be used to configure your computer to do almost anything you want. There are boards to control scanners, fax and modem boards, network interface boards, CD-ROM interface boards, graphics boards, tape drive controller boards, and many, many others. Depending on how you want to configure your computer, the eight slots can be filled in a hurry.

Certain functions are common to all computers. They all need such things as hard and floppy drive controllers, a monitor adapter, and serial and parallel ports. Most of these functions can be integrated on VLSI chips and mounted on the motherboard. This can save several of your precious slots for other uses.

IDE interface

Some motherboards have a built-in interface for IDE hard drives. This interface is usually a set of 50 pins that accepts the hard disk cable connector. It is possible to plug this connector in backwards, so look for the different colored wire on one edge of the ribbon cable; it goes to pin 1 on the motherboard.

There is usually a floppy drive controller — a set of 34 pins — along with the IDE interface. This cable connector can also be plugged in backwards, so look for the colored wire and some sort of marking on the motherboard. The pins should be oriented the same as the IDE pins.

Check your documentation. You will probably have to set some switches or jumpers. If you want to use a hard disk other than an IDE type, you should be able to set the switches or jumpers so that a hard disk controller can be plugged in one of your slots.

Parallel and serial ports

If the motherboard has built-in ports, the parallel printer port (LPT1) should be a set of 25 pins. You might have a short ribbon cable for this port with a connector that plugs into the pins. Look for the colored wire and pin 1 on the motherboard. The other end of the cable should have a 25-pin, D-type connector. There should be a cutout on the back panel to mount this connector.

COM ports

The two serial ports, COM1 and COM2, will probably be two sets of 10 pins each. You should also have short ribbon cables for these ports. Look for the colored wire on the cable and pin 1 on the motherboard. The pins will probably be oriented the same as the LPT1 pins. Note which set of pins is COM1 and which is COM2. The cables will have 25-pin, D-type connectors that are mounted in cutouts on the back panel. Using a marking pen or adhesive labels, label the connectors COM1 and COM2.

Most systems only have two COM ports, but you might have two additional IRQ (interrupt request) addresses available. Ordinarily you only use one COM port at a time. You can have two other serial devices connected so that they use the COM3 and COM4 IRQ addresses. This allows you to have a modem, an SCSI device, a serial printer or plotter, and a mouse. Check your motherboard documentation. You will probably have to set some switches or jumpers to indicate that you intend to use the on-board ports.

You don't have to use the built-in goodies. If one of the built-in ports becomes defective, or for some reason you don't want to use it, you can always plug a board with ports into one of the slots.

Monitor adapter

Some motherboards have a built-in monitor adapter. Again, there will be a set of pins and a short cable. Look for the colored wire and pin 1 on the motherboard. Plug the cable in and mount the connector on the back panel. Check your motherboard documentation. There should be some switches or jumpers to set. If you want to use an adapter board instead of the built-in adapter, the switches should be set accordingly.

Network interface

Several companies manufacture plug-in interface boards for the different network systems. These boards cost from $100 to $800 each and they require the use of one of the eight slots.

Several companies have developed VLSI chips for network interfaces. These chips can easily be integrated onto motherboards. These chips will add from $30 to $40 to the cost of the motherboard, but more importantly, they will save a slot. If there is a possibility that your computer might be used in a network, look for one of these motherboards.

The most popular type of network is the Ethernet system. IBM's Token-Ring is another system that is popular. The VLSI chip set developed by Chips and Technology offers an interface for either system. It has been dubbed "Eithernet."

BIOS

Several companies manufacture basic input/output system (BIOS) ROM chips. There are slight differences among them as to the utilities and extra functions that they offer. For instance, the AMI BIOS has several very useful diagnostic routines.

Shadow RAM

Most of the BIOS chips support shadow RAM. This allows the BIOS to be copied from the relatively slow read-only memory (ROM) into the much faster RAM. BIOS functions can be executed much faster and this increases the overall speed of the system.

As you can see there are many different options to consider. What you intend to use your computer for should be a determining factor in what you choose.

MCA

The 8-bit IBM XT motherboard has eight slot connectors for plug-in boards. Each of the slot connectors have 31 contacts on each side for a total of 62. The plug-in boards have 62 matching contacts. The slot connectors are all connected together pin to pin. You can plug a board into any one of the eight slots because they are all wired the same. This is the bus. It is more than sufficient for the power, grounds, refresh cycles, RAM, ROM, and all of the other I/O functions for an 8-bit system.

There are 20 lines on this bus that are used to move data back and forth between the CPU and the RAM. These 20 lines allow the machine to address 1Mb of memory or 2^{20}. In the early days, 1Mb of memory was more than sufficient. Actually, only 640K was available to the user. The other 384K was reserved for the BIOS and for monitor video.

When IBM introduced the 16-bit AT, it was designed so that it could address 16Mb of memory, so a total of 24 lines (2^{24}) were needed. Several other new bus functions were also added to the AT bus. They needed the 62 pins already in use on the bus, plus several more for the new functions. A larger connector was needed, but a new connector would make all of the hardware that was available at that time obsolete. Someone at IBM came up with a brilliant design. They simply added a second 36-pin connector in front of the standard 62 pins. The new connector readily accepted 8-bit or 16-bit boards.

Later when the 386 and 486 were developed, they continued to use the standard AT bus. Many of the early 386 and 486 ISA machines had a special 32-bit connector for plug-in memory boards. Today almost all motherboards have sockets for 32-bit memory chips. Other than the 32-bit bus for the memory, all of the other I/O functions use the standard 16-bit AT bus.

In 1987, IBM introduced its new PS/2 line with Micro Channel Architecture (MCA). This new system added many new functions to the computer, but it also used a new bus system that was completely incompatible with the older hardware. Users were in the same boat as Apple users; they had only one vendor and the prices were very high.

To ensure that it remained the only vendor, IBM took out patents on almost every aspect of its PS/2 design. IBM let it be known that its stable of high-powered attorneys were ready to pounce on anyone who violated any of the patents. IBM published all of the schematics and documentation for its original PCs, so it was easy for the clone makers to design compatible machines. This time IBM has been very careful not to publish any data, so it is difficult for a cloner to know whether it is violating any of IBM's MCA patents. But IBM said, don't worry. Just send in your designs and we will tell you whether you are in violation. Not many have done this.

IBM magnanimously offered a license to anyone who wanted to clone its PS/2, but it wanted a rather high fee and a percentage of the price of each unit sold. In addition, IBM wanted back royalties from anyone who had sold IBM compatibles in the past, amounting to millions of dollars. Many of the smaller vendors couldn't possibly pay it.

It was readily admitted that MCA offered some real advantages over the original IBM standard. One of the excellent features of the MCA system is the programmed option select (POS). The MCA plug-in boards have a unique identification (ID). When a board is plugged in, the bus recognizes it by its ID and automatically configures the board for use with the system interrupts, ports, and other system configurations. Also, if there are switches on the board, it tells you how they should be set. I recently spent almost a whole day trying to install a board that had three DIP switches and three different jumpers. The switches and jumpers had to be set so that the board would not conflict with the rest of the system. The three DIP switches mean that there are eight different possible configurations (2^3), then include the three different jumpers for another eight possible configurations, or 64 possible combinations. By the time you turn the computer off, set the switches, then turn it back on and wait for it to reboot, it can be awfully time-consuming and frustrating. I had a manual, but like most of them, it was practically worthless. A PS/2 with MCA POS could have saved me a lot of time and frustration.

MCA offers several other very good features such as bus arbitration. This system evaluates bus requests and allocates time on a priority basis, relieving the CPU of some of its burdens. The MCA bus is also much faster than the old AT bus. MCA has several other excellent benefits, but IBM is still the single source. A few clones and a few third-party MCA boards are available, but they must pay a license fee to IBM, so they are rather expensive. IBM is the sole owner of the design. MCA users are completely at the mercy of IBM, and many people do not believe that the advantages of MCA are great enough to abandon the large supply of inexpensive IBM-compatible hardware that is readily available.

ISA

ISA is what used to be known as the IBM standard. For the vast majority of applications, ISA systems are more than adequate. Figure 5-5 shows a standard-size ISA motherboard from Micronics. It has sockets for 16Mb of SIMM memory, but only 4MB of RAM is installed. This is 32-bit memory with a bus that connects to the CPU. Figure 5-6 shows a baby-size ISA motherboard from A.I.R. This was an early design that used a plug-in board for its 16Mb of SIMM memory. Figure 5-7 shows a different type of baby-size ISA motherboard from Monolithic with 16Mb of SIMM memory.

One of the greatest advantages of the ISA system is the extraordinary versatility and flexibility that it offers. There are at least $10 billion worth of IBM-compatible, or ISA, computer components in existence. One of the reasons why there are so many ISA components available is the open system architecture.

5-5 My standard-size 486 board.

5-6 A baby-size 486 board with memory on a plug-in board.

Advanced Integration Research

Monolithic Corp.

5-7 A baby-size 486 with 16Mb of on-board memory.

Most ISA components are interchangeable. You can take any board or peripheral from a genuine IBM XT or AT and plug it into any of the clones and it will work. You can also plug any component found in a clone into a genuine IBM or into another clone and it will work. Because there are so many clone products and vendors, they are readily available almost anywhere and they are relatively inexpensive.

The EISA revolution

Many of the clone manufacturers were rather unhappy with IBM and its MCA PS/2 systems. IBM had introduced a system that was no longer compatible with most clone manufacturers. IBM was counting on the large users to abandon the clones and jump on the PS/2 bandwagon. Many of them did and it was clear that the cloners were being hurt.

A group of manufacturers got together and developed the extended industry standard architecture (EISA). This group included Advanced Logic Research (ALR), AST Research, Compaq Computer, Epson America, Everex Systems, Hewlett-Packard, Olivetti, Micronics, NEC, Tandy, Wyse Technology, and Zenith. The EISA system is a 32-bit system for memory and for the I/O bus. The EISA standard includes the bus speed, arbitration, bus mastering, POS, and other functions found on MCA systems. But unlike MCA systems, the EISA bus is downward compatible. The new EISA standard is designed so that the older-style XT and AT boards can still be used. It doesn't matter whether your boards are 8, 16, or 32 bit; the EISA bus accepts them.

In some areas, the EISA system outperforms the MCA system. But one of the biggest advantages of EISA over MCA is that it is downward compatible and allows you to use the earlier hardware.

The EISA connector

I noted earlier that IBM designed a 16-bit AT bus by simply adding an extra 36-pin connector to the 8-bit, 62-pin connector. This idea was excellent because all of the earlier 8-bit boards could still be used.

The AT bus, or ISA, has 49 contacts per side, or 98 total. Each contact is 0.06 inches wide with 0.04 inches of space between them. The total connector contact area of the board is 5.3 inches long.

The IBM MCA system needs 116 contacts. IBM designed the MCA board by miniaturizing the contacts. Each of the MCA board contacts is 0.03 inches wide with 0.02 inches between them, half the width on an ISA board. The total connector contact area of a board is 2.8 inches long, making any older ISA boards unusable in an MCA system.

The EISA system also needs more contacts, so 100 more were added for a total of 198 contacts, 82 more contacts than the MCA system has. More functions can be added to the EISA system than the MCA system. The extra contacts were added on the EISA plug-in boards below the ISA contacts. The lower EISA contacts are connected with etched lines that interleave the 98 ISA contacts.

Unlike the MCA system, the EISA connector is designed so that it is compatible with all of the previous 8-bit and 16-bit boards, as well as the new 32-bit EISA board. The socket is twice as deep as the original ISA slot or connector socket. This new socket has two sets of contacts, one set at the bottom of the socket and one at the top. At certain locations across the bottom of the socket, narrow tabs act as keys. These tabs prevent the insertion of an 8-bit or 16-bit board to the full depth of the socket. The contacts of the 8-bit and 16-bit boards mate with only the upper contacts.

The EISA board connectors have two sets of contacts, one set directly below the other. The 0.05-inch space between each ISA contact is used to connect to the lower EISA contacts. The boards have notches cut in them to coincide with the keys on the bottom of the EISA socket, allowing EISA boards to be inserted to the full depth.

Figure 5-2 shows an EISA motherboard from Micronics. Figure 5-8 shows the evolution of connectors. An 8-bit board is shown on top, then a 16-bit board, an MCA board, and an EISA board on the bottom. (The EISA board shown is a communications controller, primarily for use on local area networks, or LANs.)

ISA boards cannot be inserted deep enough to contact the EISA contacts, so they touch only the top ISA contacts. However, an EISA board can be inserted into an ISA connector. Because it cannot be inserted to its full depth, the EISA contacts touch the ISA contacts.

Which motherboard should you buy?

You can never have a computer that is too fast or too powerful. Even if you don't need it at the moment, buy the biggest, most powerful, and fastest motherboard with the most built-in goodies that you can afford.

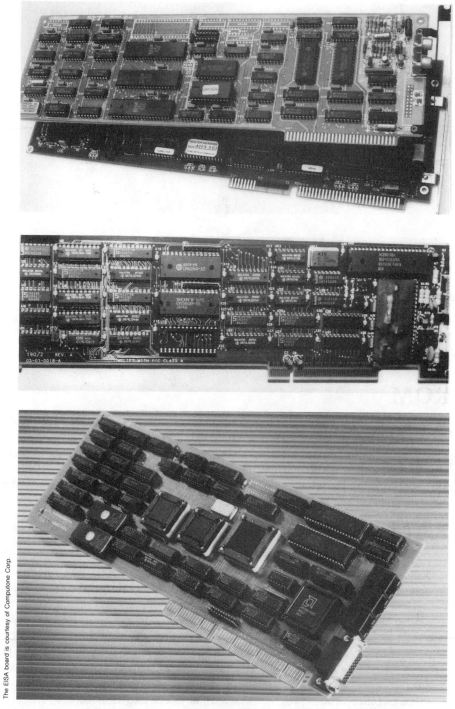

The EISA board is courtesy of Computone Corp.

5-8 The evolution of connectors. The board on top is 8 bit, the next one is a 16 bit, the next one is IBM's MCA, and the bottom is the EISA connector.

6
Memory

Memory is one of the most crucial elements of the computer. Computing as we know it would not be possible without memory. The PC uses two primary types of memory: ROM and RAM.

ROM

Read-only memory (ROM) is memory that cannot be altered or changed. The principle use of ROM in PCs is for the BIOS. The BIOS contains routines that set up the computer when it is first turned on. It facilitates the transfer of data among peripherals. The ROM programs are usually burned into electrically programmable ROM chips. The ROM BIOS for an early XT could be programmed onto a 128K chip. The 486 ROM BIOS needs 512K.

RAM

If you open a file from a hard disk, the files and data are read from the disk and placed in random-access memory (RAM). Actually it is dynamic RAM (DRAM). When you load in a program, be it word processing, spreadsheet, database, or whatever, you are working in the system RAM. If you are writing or programming you are working in RAM.

Being able to randomly access the memory allows you to read and write to it. It is somewhat like an electronic blackboard. Here you can manipulate the data, do calculations, enter more data, edit, search databases, or do any of the thousands of things that software programs allow you to do. You can access and change the data in RAM very quickly.

Besides the application programs that must be loaded into the 640K of RAM, certain DOS programs must be in RAM at all times. These are programs such as command.com and the internal commands. There are over 20 internal commands such as COPY, CD, CLS, DATE, DEL, MD, PATH, TIME, TYPE, and others. These commands are always in RAM and are available immediately. The config.sys file and any drivers that you might have for your system are also loaded into RAM.

Terminate-and-stay-resident (TSR) files are normally loaded into the 640K of RAM. They are memory-resident programs like SideKick Plus and others that can pop up anytime you press a key. Portions of RAM can also be used for very fast RAM, disk buffers, and print spooling.

All of these things contribute to the utility and functionality of the computer and make it easier to use. Unfortunately, they take big bites out of your precious 640K of RAM. Less than 400K might be left for running applications after loading all these memory-resident programs.

Many application programs do not run if you have less than 600K of free RAM. Some programs are now so large that they need up to 4Mb in order to run properly. These programs are designed to run in extended or expanded memory.

DR DOS 6.0 from Digital Research and MS-DOS 5.0 from Microsoft can now load much of the operating system and TSR files in upper memory. Several other memory management programs have been developed to help alleviate this problem. One excellent program is DESQview from Quarterdeck Office Systems, (213) 392-9701.

An important difference between ROM and RAM is that RAM is volatile. That is, it disappears if the machine is rebooted or if you exit one program and another one is loaded into memory. If power to the computer is interrupted, even for a brief instant, any data in RAM is gone forever. You should get in the habit of frequently saving your files to disk, especially if you live in an area that has a lot of power failures. One of the excellent features of WordStar is that it can be set up so that it automatically saves open files to disk at frequent intervals. If your data is crucial, you might consider using an uninterruptible power supply.

CMOS

The complementary metal oxide semiconductor (CMOS) uses very little power to keep it alive. Several of the computer features that are configurable, such as the time, date, type of disk drives, and other features that can be changed by the user are stored in CMOS.

A lithium or rechargeable battery keeps the data alive when the computer is turned off. If your computer is not used for a long period of time, you might have to reset the time. If you have to reset the time quite often, you might need a new battery. The early IBM AT used batteries that only lasted a couple of years. Most motherboards today have lithium batteries that last about 10 years.

A brief explanation of memory

Computers operate on binary systems of 0s and 1s, or off and on. A transistor can be turned off or on to represent 0 and 1. Two transistors can represent four different combinations: both off; both on; one on, one off; and one off, one on. A bank of 4 transistors can represent 16 different combinations. With 8 transistors, there are 256 different combinations. It takes eight transistors to make one byte. With them you can represent each letter of the alphabet, each number, and each symbol of the extended American Standard Code for Information Interchange (ASCII). With 8 lines, plus a ground, the 8 transistors can be turned on or off to represent any of the 256 characters of the ASCII code.

Need for more memory

Depending on what you intend to use your computer for, you might need to buy more memory. For some applications, you might need to buy several megabytes more. In the old days you could get by with just 64K of memory. Your new 486 needs at least 4Mb; 8Mb are even better. Many of the new software programs, such as spreadsheets, databases, and accounting programs, require a lot of memory. Lotus 1-2-3 release 3 requires about 2Mb of RAM in order to run.

If you bought your new 486 motherboard through the mail, you might have received it with OK memory. The price of memory fluctuates quite a lot. Because of the fluctuating prices, some vendors do not advertise a firm price for memory. Besides, if they included the price of the memory, it might frighten you away. They usually invite you to call them for the latest price.

Things to consider before you buy memory

There are several different types, sizes, speeds, and other factors to consider when buying memory. You should buy the type that is best for your computer.

DRAM

DRAM is the most common type of memory used today. Each memory cell has a small etched transistor that is kept in its memory state, either on or off, by a very small capacitor. Capacitors are similar to small rechargeable batteries. Units can be charged with a voltage to represent 1 or left uncharged to represent 0. Those that are charged begin losing their charge immediately. They must be constantly "refreshed" with a new charge. A computer might spend 7% or more of its time refreshing the DRAM chips. Also, each time a cell is accessed, it must be refreshed before it can be accessed again. If it has a speed of 70 ns, it takes 70 ns plus the time it takes to recycle, which might be 105 ns or more before that cell can again be accessed.

The speed of the DRAM chips in your system should be 70 ns or less. You might be able to install slower chips, but your system will have wait states. Wait states deprive your system of one of its greatest benefits, speed. If the DRAM is too slow, the CPU and the rest of the system have to sit and wait while the RAM is accessed and refreshed.

Refreshment and wait states   During the time that a chip is being refreshed, it cannot be accessed by your programs. After it has been accessed, it must be refreshed before it can be accessed again. If the CPU is operating at a very high frequency, it might have to sit and wait one cycle, or one wait state, for the refresh cycle. The wait state might be only a millionth of a second or less. That might not seem like much time, but if the computer is doing several million operations per second, it can add up.

It takes a finite amount of time to charge the DRAM. Some DRAM can be charged much faster than others. For instance, the DRAM chips needed for an XT at 4.77 MHz might take as long as 200 ns to be refreshed. A 486 running at 25 MHz needs chips that can be refreshed in 70 ns or less. Of course, faster chips cost more.

Interleaved memory   Some systems have been developed so that the memory is divided in half. One-half of the memory is refreshed on one cycle, then the other half. If the CPU needs to access an address that is in the half already refreshed, it is available immediately. This method can reduce the amount of waiting by one-half or more.

SRAM

Static RAM (SRAM) is made up of actual transistors. They are turned on to represent 1 or left off to represent 0 and stay in that condition until receiving a change signal. They do not need to be refreshed, but they revert back to 0 when the computer is turned off or the power is interrupted. They are very fast and can operate at speeds of 25 ns or less.

A DRAM chip needs only one transistor and a small capacitor. Each SRAM chip requires four to six transistors and other components. Besides being more expensive, SRAM chips are physically larger and require more space than DRAM chips. Because of the physical and electronic differences, SRAM and DRAM chips are not interchangeable. The motherboard must be designed for SRAM.

Many laptops use SRAM because it can be kept alive with a small amount of current from a battery. Because DRAM needs to be constantly refreshed, it takes a lot of circuitry and power to keep it alive.

The cost of SRAM is coming down. I bought a Toshiba laptop in 1989 and added 2Mb of SRAM on a cartridge. It cost $900, or about the same as the original price of the entire laptop. That same 2Mb SRAM cartridge today sells for less than $200.

The speed and static characteristics of SRAM make it an excellent tool for cache systems. The 486 chip has an on-board built-in 8K cache system. It is very fast, but 8K is fairly small. Many of the 486 motherboard designers have included sockets for up to 256K of SRAM cache.

Cache memory   Another scheme is to install a small amount of very fast DRAM or SRAM in a cache near the CPU. The cache might be from 64K to 128K or more. When running an application program, the CPU often loops in and out of certain areas and uses the same memory over and over. If this often-used memory is stored in the cache, it can be accessed by the CPU very quickly.

You can't arbitrarily add cache to any system. The motherboard usually has to be designed for it. If you are going to need a very fast system, you should look for a motherboard that has a cache on it. Most of the cache motherboards are designed for the 386DX and 486. There are only a few 386SX cache motherboards.

A cache system can speed up operations quite a lot. The computer is slowed down considerably if it has to search the entire memory each time it has to fetch some data. The data that is used most frequently can be stored in the fast cache memory, increasing the speed by several magnitudes.

Cache memory should not be confused with disk caching. Often a program might need to access a hard disk while running. If a small disk cache is set up in RAM, the program will run much faster.

Flash memory   Intel has developed flash memory that is similar to erasable programmable read-only memory (EPROM). It is on small plug-in cards about the size of a credit card. It is available on some small palm-size computers, such as the PSIONs. It is still rather expensive, but several foreign companies have begun development along the same lines. A JEIDA standard has been proposed that would make the cards interchangeable among the various laptops.

Motherboard memory

The XT motherboard can accept 640K of memory. The 286 and 386SX can accept up to 16Mb, but many of them have provisions for less. Extra memory can be added to these motherboards with a plug-in memory board.

Bus systems

The XT communicates with its plug-in boards and memory chips eight data bits at a time. Etched copper lines that physically connect each plug-in socket and the motherboard memory chips are called the bus. The 286 and 386SX are 16-bit systems and the motherboards use a 16-bit bus.

The 386DX and 486 have 32-bit memory systems and a 32-bit bus to communicate with memory. Some of these motherboards have SIMM connectors that will accept up to 128Mb of DRAM. Even though the 386 and 486 are 32-bit systems, except for communicating with memory over a 32-bit bus, they use a 16-bit bus to communicate with the plug-in boards. A plug-in memory board on a 32-bit system will slow it down because of the 16-bit bus.

Dual in-line package (DIP)

The early DRAM chips had two rows of eight pins. They were bulky and used up a lot of motherboard space. The 16 pins also imposed limits on them. Later 1Mb DIPs were developed that had 18 pins. You won't find DIPs on motherboards very often now. They are used mostly for VGAs and special uses.

Single in-line memory module (SIMM)

Your computer motherboard probably has sockets for SIMMs. A SIMM is an assembly of minature DRAM chips. There are usually nine chips on a small board that is plugged slantwise into a special connector. They require a very small amount of board space.

Single in-line package (SIP)

Some motherboards have SIP memory. It is similar to a SIMM except that it has pins. At the present time, 4Mb DRAM chips are the largest generally available. You should be able to buy 16Mb chips very soon. Several companies are working on 64Mb DRAM chips, but it will be some time before they get to market.

If you plan to add extra memory, be sure that you get the kind and type that's right for your machine. Make sure that it is fast enough for your system. Check your documentation. It should tell you what speed and type of chips to buy.

Electrostatic voltage

If you have memory chips or SIMMs to install on your motherboard, one of the first things that you should do is discharge any electrostatic charge that might have been built up on you. If you have ever walked across a carpet and been shocked when you touched the door-knob, then you know that you can build up static electricity. It is quite possible to build up 3000 to 5000 volts of static electricity in your body. If you touch a fragile piece of electronics that normally operates at 5 to 12 volts, you can severely damage it. You can discharge this static electricity from your body by touching any metal that goes to ground. The metal case of the power supply in your computer is a good ground if it is still plugged into the wall socket. The power does not have to be on for it to connect to ground. You can also touch an unpainted metal part of a lamp or other appliance that is plugged into a socket. You should always discharge yourself before you touch any plug-in board or other equipment where there are exposed semiconductors.

How much memory do you need?

The amount of memory you need depends on what you intend to use your computer for. When you run a program, data is read from the disk into RAM and is operated on there. For word processing or small applications, you can get by with 640K. You should have at least 4Mb if you expect to use Windows, large databases, or spreadsheets.

Having a lot of memory is like having a car with a large engine. You might not need that extra power very often, but it sure feels great being able to call on it when you do need it.

The 640K DOS barrier

At one time it was believed that 1Mb of RAM was more than sufficient for any eventuality, and DOS was designed for that limit. How little they knew. The 8088 CPUs found in all PCs and XTs can access 1Mb of RAM, but only 640K is available for applications. The other 384K is reserved for internal use of the BIOS, the display, and other functions.

The PCs and XTs use an 8-bit bus that has 20 lines for memory access. These 20 lines limit them to 2^{20} or 1,048,576 bytes. The 16-bit 286 systems have 24 bus lines for memory access. They can address 2^{24} or 16,777,216 bytes (16Mb). The 386 and 486 32-bit systems can address 2^{32} or 4,294,967, 296 bytes (4Gb). The 486 can address 4Gb of RAM, but DOS will not let you access more than 640K. (Incidentally, 4Gb of DRAM, in 1Mb SIMM packages, would require 4096 modules. You would need a fairly large board to install that much memory.) There are several software programs that let you break the 640K barrier, but first a few basics about the different types of memory.

Types of memory
Conventional memory

This is the 1Mb of memory that includes the 640K. The 384K of memory above 640K is reserved for video, ROM BIOS, and other functions (see Fig. 6-1).

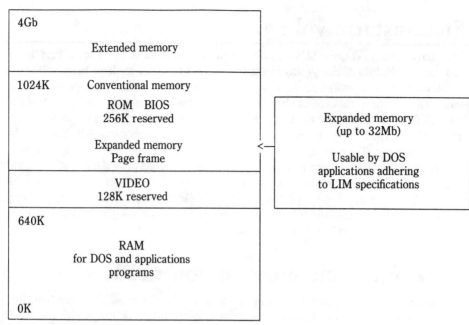

6-1   Memory arrangement.

Extended memory

Extended memory is memory that can be installed above 1Mb. If it weren't for the 640K limitation of DOS it would be a seamless continuation of memory. Windows 3.1 and several other software applications will let 286 and larger computers use this memory (see Fig. 6-1).

Expanded memory

Some large spreadsheets require an enormous amount of memory. A few years ago in a rare instance of cooperation among corporations, Lotus, Intel, Microsoft, and some other large corporations got together and devised a system and standard specification called the Lotus-Intel-Microsoft expanded memory specification (LIM EMS) It allows a computer, even a PC or XT, to address up to 32Mb of expanded memory (see Fig. 6-1).

The memory is divided into pages of 16K each. Expanded memory finds a 64K window that is not being used above the 640K of the 1Mb conventional memory. Pages of 16K expanded memory can be switched in and out of this window.

LIM EMS also includes functions to allow multitasking so that several programs can be run simultaneously. The system can treat extra memory on the 286, 386, and 486 as extended memory with the proper software and drivers.

Memory modes

The three different memory modes are real, standard or protected, and enhanced 386.

Real mode

The real mode is the mode that most of us have been using until now. When any application is being processed, the program is loaded into RAM. The CPU uses the RAM to process any data that is input. Computations, changes, or calculations are done in memory and are sent back to the disk, screen, printer, or other device. For most single-user applications, this processing is done in the standard 640K or less of RAM.

Operating in the real mode doesn't cause much of a problem if you are running fairly small programs that can fit in the available RAM. But if you are trying to update a spreadsheet that has 2Mb in it, you are in trouble.

Breaking the 640K barrier with LIM EMS

The Lotus-Intel-Microsoft Expanded Memory Specification (LIM EMS) system was designed to solve the 640K-barrier problem. Expanded memory can be accessed, a small amount at a time, through memory above 640K. Expanded memory is like adding an extra room onto a building. When the building is full, you can store extra material in the added room. But to use the extra material, you have to go through a door and move a small amount in or out. The LIM EMS system allows up to 32Mb of expanded memory to be added to a system, but it can only be accessed through a small window above 640K. Only 64K of data can be moved in or out of the window at a time. The LIM EMS system works on the XT as well as the larger AT-type machines.

Standard or protected mode

The XT can only address 1Mb. This 1Mb is 640K of lower memory and 384K of upper memory reserved for the ROM BIOS and video. The ROM BIOS and video usually does not require all of the reserved 384K, and portions of it can be used to access expanded memory.

The 286, the 386, and even the 486 is also limited to 640K in the real mode. However, with the proper software the 286 can address 16Mb and the 386 can address 4Gb. With Windows 3.1 and the proper application software, you can use extended memory on a 286, 386SX, 386, or 486.

In the protected mode, with the proper software applications, you can also load two or more programs into memory and process both of them at the same time. If you tried this in the real mode, the data from both programs would be mixed together. The data from both programs is just 0s and 1s. If you mix them together it would be like mixing a gallon of hot water with a gallon of cold water. The CPUs of the 286, 386, and 486 have a built-in system that can put a "wall" around 1Mb of RAM and let it work just as if it were a separate 8086 computer. Essentially, you can have several 8086 computers working on different applications all at the same time.

The 386 enhanced mode

With the proper software applications, the 386SX, the 386DX, and 486 can use all of the extended memory available. It will also set aside a portion of your hard disk and use it as virtual memory. This allows programs of 32Mb or more to be processed all at once. The 286 cannot operate in this mode, but it can do just about everything the 386SX can do.

OS/2 2.0

Operating system/2 (OS/2) was originally designed for high-end advanced applications. The development was a joint effort by Microsoft and IBM. Microsoft put the development of OS/2 on the back burner and devoted most of its energies and resources to developing and promoting Windows. After several missed deadlines by Microsoft, IBM took over all responsibility for OS/2.

The OS/2 system allows you to break the 640K barrier, do multitasking, use the protected mode and virtual memory, provides networking facilities, and can run all DOS software. The presentation manager portion of OS/2 is much like Windows, so OS/2 provides high-level DOS functions plus Windows functions. OS/2 2.0 is an excellent system for your 486.

Windows 3.1

Windows runs on top of DOS. Windows 3.1 also lets you go beyond the 640K barrier. It lets you do multitasking and lets you take advantage of the 486's virtual and protected modes. It works with a mouse and performs even better than a Macintosh. Windows is also very inexpensive. Every 486 should have Windows 3.1. If you have an older copy of Windows, you can easily upgrade to Windows 3.1. You can get more details by calling (800) 426-9400.

Microsoft is developing Windows New Technology (Windows NT), which should compete head-to-head with OS/2 2.0. This high-end system should be on the market by the time you read this.

DESQview

DESQview is an excellent program that lets you take advantage of the 486's virtual 8086 and 32-bit protected modes. It lets you run multiple DOS programs simultaneously, switch between them, run programs in the background, and transfer data between them. DESQview is very inexpensive and no 486 system should be without it. For more details, call (213) 392-9701.

7
Floppy drives and disks

You can run a computer with just a floppy drive. For several years only floppy drives were available. My first computer had two single-sided 140K drives. It was slow and required a lot of disk swapping. Floppy systems have come a long way since those early days. The 140K systems were soon replaced with 320K double-sided systems, then 360K, 1.2Mb, 1.44Mb, 2.88Mb, and now even 21Mb.

Floppy disks and floppy drives are a very important part of your computer. The majority of all software programs come on floppy disks. The program is then copied from the floppy disks to a hard disk. Floppy disks are also needed to archive programs and backup your hard disk.

There are about 40 million 360K drives still in use, so most programs are still distributed on 360K disks. The old 360K format has served us well, but it is now obsolete. The 5¼-inch 1.2Mb drive reads and writes to the 360K format as well as to the high-density format. The 3½-inch 1.44Mb drive reads and writes to the 720K format as well as to the high-density format. The 720K drive is also obsolete.

Although both the 360K and 720K drives are obsolete, many vendors are still advertising and selling them for about the same price as that of the high-density drives. I recommend that you buy 1.2Mb or 1.44Mb drives. Or better yet, buy both of them. You will then be covered for all formats.

Many computers provide only three or four bays to mount drives. You might not have space to mount two floppies, two hard drives, a tape backup, and a CD-ROM. CMS Enhancements noted this problem and created an all-media floppy drive by combining a 1.2Mb and a 1.44Mb floppy drive in a single unit. This allows both drives to be installed in a single drive bay. They can even share some of the drive electronics.

How floppy disk drives operate

The floppy drive spins a disk much like a record player. The floppy disk is made of a plastic material called polyethylene terephthalate coated with a magnetic material made of iron oxide. It is similar to the tape used in cassette tapes. The drive uses a head that records (writes) and plays back (reads) the disk much like the record/playback head in a cassette recorder. When the head writes on the iron oxide surface, a pulse of electricity causes the head to magnetize a spot on the track beneath the head. When the tracks are read, the head detects whether each portion of the track is magnetized or not. If the spot is magnetized, it creates a small voltage signal to represent a 1; if it is not magnetized, it represents a 0.

Types of disks

The 5¼-inch 360K and 3½-inch 720K disks are called double-sided double-density (DS/DD). The 5¼-inch 1.2Mb and 3½-inch 1.44Mb disks are called high-density (HD). The 3½-inch double-density disks are usually marked DD; the high-density are usually marked HD. The 5¼-inch 360K and the 1.2Mb disks usually have no markings. They look exactly alike, except that the 360K disks usually have a reinforcing ring or collar around the large center hole. The high-density 1.2Mb disks do not have the ring.

One of the major differences between the 720K and 1.44Mb disks is that the 1.44Mb disks have two small square holes at the rear of the plastic shell, while the 720K disks have only one. Compare the disks in Fig. 7-1. The two disks on the top are 1.44Mb, the two on the bottom are 720K disks.

7-1   Some 3½-inch floppy diskettes. Note the metal hubs that help to ensure head-to-track accuracy. The diskette at the top right is 1.44Mb, the one on the bottom right is 720K. Note the extra square hole in the 1.44Mb diskette. The square hole on the right corner of the diskettes has a slide that can cover the hole to write-enable it or uncover the hole to write-protect it. This system is just the opposite of the 5¼-inch write-protect method.

The hole on the right rear of the shell has a small slide that can be moved to cover the hole. A microswitch on the drive checks the hole when the disk is inserted. If the hole is covered, then the disk can be written on. If it is open, then the disk is write-protected.

The 3½-inch write-protect system is just the opposite of the system used by the 5¼-inch disks. The 5¼-inch disks have a square notch that must be covered with opaque tape to prevent writing or unintentional erasing of the disk. (You must use opaque tape.) The 5¼-inch system uses a light that shines through the square notch. If the detector in the system sees light through the notch, then the disk can be written on. Some people have used clear tape to cover the notch, with disastrous results.

On most of the 1.44Mb 3½-inch drives, a microswitch checks for the hole on the right rear of the disk. If you insert a disk and the drive finds a hole in the right rear it allows you to format, read, and write the disk as a 1.44Mb disk. If you cover the hole with tape, the disk formats as a 720K disk.

Disk format structure
Tracks

A disk must be formatted before it can be used. This consists of laying out individual concentric tracks on each side of the disk. If it is a 360K disk, each side is marked or configured with 40 tracks, numbered from 0 to 39. Figure 7-2 is a representation of the tracks and sectors of a 360K disk.

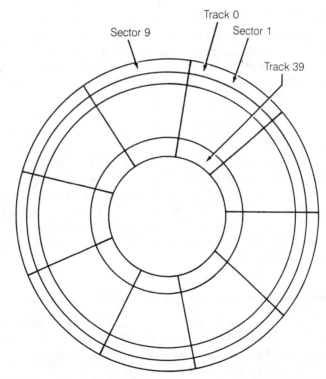

7-2 The relationship between tracks and sectors on a floppy diskette.

If the disk is a 1.2Mb, 720K, or 1.44Mb, each side is configured with 80 tracks, numbered from 0 to 79. The tracks have the same number on the top and bottom of the disk. The top is side 0 and the bottom is side 1. When the head is over track 1 on the top, it is also over track 1 on the bottom. The heads move as a single unit to the various tracks by using a head positioner. When data is written to a track, as much as possible is written on the top track, then the head is electronically switched and it continues to write to the same track on the bottom side. It is much faster and easier to electronically switch between the heads than to move them to another track.

Sectors

Each of the tracks are divided into sectors. Each track of the 360K and 720K disks is divided into 9 sectors, each of the 1.2Mb tracks is divided into 15 sectors, each of the 1.44Mb tracks are divided into 18 sectors, and each of the 2.88Mb tracks are divided into 36 sectors. Each sector contains 512 bytes. Multiplying the number of sectors times the number of bytes per sector times the number of tracks times two sides gives the amount of data that can be stored on a disk. For instance, a 1.2Mb disk has 15 sectors times 512 bytes times 80 tracks times 2 sides ($15 \times 512 \times 80 \times 2$) equals 1,228,800 bytes. The system uses 14,898 bytes to mark the tracks and sectors during formatting, so there is actually 1,213,952 bytes available on a 1.2Mb floppy.

Clusters or allocation units

DOS allocates one or more sectors on a disk and calls it a cluster or allocation unit. On the 360K and 720K disks, a cluster or allocation unit is two sectors. On the 1.2Mb and 1.44Mb disks, each allocation unit is one sector. Only single files or parts of single files can be written into an allocation unit. If two different files were written into a single allocation unit, the data would become mixed and corrupted.

File allocation table

During formatting, a file allocation table (FAT) is created on the first track of the disk. This FAT acts like a table of contents for a book. Whenever a file is recorded on a disk, the file is broken up into allocation units. The head looks in the FAT to find empty units, then records the file in any empty units it can find. Part of the file might be recorded in sector 5 of track 10 and part in sector 8 of track 15. It records the location of all the various parts of the file in the FAT. With this method, parts of a file can be erased, changed, or added to without changing the entire disk.

Tracks per inch

The 40 tracks of a 360K disk are laid down at a rate of 48 tracks per inch (TPI) so each of the 40 tracks is $\frac{1}{48}$ inch wide. The 80 tracks of a 1.2Mb disk are laid down at a rate of 96 TPI, so each track is $\frac{1}{96}$ inch wide. The 80 tracks of a 3½-inch disk are laid down at a density of 135 TPI or $\frac{1}{135}$ inch per track.

Read accuracy

The 5¼-inch disks have a 1⅛-inch center hole. The drives have a conical spindle that comes up through the hole when the drive latch is closed. This centers the disk so that the heads are able to find each track. The plastic material that the disk is made from is subject to environmental changes and wear and tear. The conical spindle might not center each disk exactly so head-to-track accuracy is difficult with more than 80 tracks. Most of the 360K disks use a reinforcing hub ring, but it probably doesn't help much. The 1.2Mb floppies do not use a hub ring. Except for the hub ring, the 360K and 1.2Mb disks look exactly the same.

The tracks of the 3½-inch floppies are narrower and greater in density per inch than the tracks of the 5¼-inch disks. But because of the metal hub, the head tracking accuracy is much better than that of the 5¼-inch systems.

Hard disks have very accurate head tracking systems. Some have densities of up to 3000 TPI, allowing much more data to be stored on a hard disk.

Rotation speed

Floppy disks have a very smooth lubricated surface. They rotate at a fairly slow 300 rpm. Magnetic lines of force deteriorate very fast with distance, so the closer the heads, the better they can read and write. The heads directly contact the floppy disks.

Hard disks rotate at 3600 to 6400 rpm. The heads and surface of the disk would be severely damaged if they came in contact at this speed, so the heads "fly" a few millionths of an inch above the surface.

Differences in disks

There are about 70 million PCs in use. Over half of them have 360K drives. Most software companies still distribute software on 360K disks because almost everybody can read that format. Many of them are now using high-density disks. Even then, some of the software programs, such as Windows, DOS 5.0, OS/2 2.0, and many others, have grown so much that the data has to be compressed on the high-density disks.

360K and 1.2Mb

The 360K and 1.2Mb disks look exactly alike except for the hub ring on the 360K disks. But there is a large difference in their magnetic materials which determines the oersted (Oe) of each one. Oersted is a measure of the resistance of a material to being magnetized. The lower the Oe, the easier the material is to magnetize. The 360K disks have an Oe of 300; 1.2Mb disks have an Oe of 600. The 360K disks are fairly easy to write to and require a fairly low head current. The 1.2Mb disks are more difficult to magnetize and require a much higher head current. This current is switched to match whatever type of disk you are using.

It is possible to format a 360K disk as a 1.2Mb disk but it will have several bad sectors, especially near the center where the sectors are shorter. These sectors are marked and locked out. The system might report that you have over 1Mb of space on a 360K disk. I do not recommend that you use such a disk for any data that is important. The data might eventually deteriorate and become unusable.

720K and 1.44Mb

The 3½-inch disks have several good features. A 720K disk can store twice as much data as a 360K disk, and a 1.44Mb disk can store four times as much in a smaller space. These disks have a hard plastic protective shell, so they are not easily damaged. They also have a spring-loaded shutter that automatically covers and protects the head opening when the disk is not in use.

Another feature is the write-protect system. A plastic slide can be moved to open or close a small square hole in the shell. When the slide covers the opening, the disk is write-enabled. When the slide is moved to open the square hole, it is write-protected. This system of write protection is exactly opposite of that used in the 5¼-inch system.

If the square notch on the 5¼-inch system is left uncovered, light shines through, allowing the disk to be written to or erased. If the notch is covered with opaque tape, the disk can only be read. Do not use clear tape. The system depends on a light shining through the notch. If clear tape is used, the disk can be written on or erased.

It is possible to insert a 5¼-inch floppy upside down, backwards, or sideways. The 3½-inch disks are designed so that they can only be inserted properly. They have arrows at the top left indicating how they should be inserted into the drive.

Converting 720K to 1.44Mb

The Oe of the 720K and 1.44Mb disks is about the same at around 600 to 700. Some companies have devised tools for punching an extra hole in the right rear corner of 720K disks, thus converting them to 1.44Mb disks. These tools can cost up to $40.

You can do it without a tool. Just take two disks and open the write protect slide. Place one disk on top of the other so that the metal hubs are contacting. Put a pencil through the small square hole and trace the outline to the other disk. Then use a pocket knife or drill and put a dimple in the area. The disk cover is made of two layers of soft plastic. The dimple only has to penetrate the bottom layer. The area of the dimple is not too important. Try to format the disk as a 1.44Mb. If it doesn't work, enlarge the dimple.

Most manufacturers advise against this practice. There might be some danger of losing data. If it is vital data, you should use quality high-density disks, especially now that the prices are so low.

Table 7-1. Capacities of various disk types

Disk type	Tracks per side	Sectors per track	Unformatted capacity	System use	Capacity available	Maximum dirs
360K	40	9	368,640	6,144	362,496	112
1.2Mb	80	15	1,228,800	14,898	1,213,952	224
3½"	80	9	737,280	12,800	724,480	224
3½"	80	18	1,474,560	16,896	1,457,664	224
3½"	80	36	2,949,120	33,792	2,915,328	224

Formatting

Assuming that the 1.2Mb drive is the A: drive, to format a 360K disk with the 1.2Mb drive, type FORMAT A/4. To format to 1.2Mb, you need high-density disks. If the system is configured and the controller allows it, you only have to type FORMAT A:. If you insert a 360K disk, it will try to format it to 1.2Mb and will probably find several bad sectors.

To format a 720K disk on a 1.44Mb drive, type FORMAT B:/T:80/N:9. To format a 1.44Mb disk, just type FORMAT B:, or you might have to type FORMAT B:/T:80/N:18.

Format .bat files

Here are some batch files that save me a lot of time in formating disks. Here is how I made my batch files:

```
COPY CON FM36.BAT
C: FORMAT A:/4
^Z

COPY CON FM12.BAT
C: FORMAT A:/T:80/N:15
^Z

COPY CON FM72.BAT
C: FORMAT B:/T:80/N:9
^Z

COPY CON FM14.BAT
C: FORMAT B:/T:80/N:18
^Z
```

The ^Z is made by pressing F6. With these batch files I only have to type fm36 for a 360K disk, fm12 for a 1.2Mb disk, fm72 for a 720K disk, or fm14 for a 1.44Mb disk.

The above statements and .bat files apply to DR DOS 6.0 and versions of MS-DOS through version 4.01. MS-DOS version 5.0 will also format a 360K disk in a high-density drive unless you tell it differently, but the command has been changed. A switch has been added that can be invoked with the FORMAT command. It eliminates the need to type in parameters for the various formats. To format a 360K disk, type FORMAT A:/f:360; for a 1.2Mb disk type FORMAT A:/f:1.2; for a 720K disk type FORMAT B:/f:720; and for a 1.44Mb disk type FORMAT B:/f:1.44. All of these commands could be considerably shortened if made into .bat files similar to those above.

If you try to reformat a disk that has been previously formatted, MS-DOS 5.0 will try to format it the same way. For instance, if you make a mistake and format a 360K disk as a 1.2Mb disk, MS-DOS 5.0 will insist on formatting the disk as a 1.2Mb disk if you don't use the /f:360 switch.

Cost of disks

All floppy disks are now priced quite reasonably. The 360K DS/DD disks are selling for as low as $.19 each and 720K disks are going for as little as $.33 each. The 1.2Mb HD disks are selling at discount houses for as little as $.33 apiece. The 1.44Mb HD disks are selling for as little as $.55 each.

These are real bargains. You can buy 10 of the 1.44Mb disks or 14.4Mb of storage for $5.50. This is about $.38 per megabyte. You can buy 10 of the 1.2Mb HD disks for only $3.30. You can store 12Mb of data on them at a cost of less than $.28 per megabyte. If you use a good compression software such as Norton or Fastback Plus, you can store over 28Mb on ten 1.44Mb disks, or about 24Mb on ten 1.2Mb disks.

Discount disk sources

Here are just a few of the companies that sell disks at a discount. There are several others. Check the computer magazines for ads.

- MEI/Micro Center   (800) 634-3478
- The Disk Barn   (800) 727-3475
- Americal Group   (800) 288-8025
- MidWest Micro   (800) 423-8215

Floppy controllers

A floppy disk must have a controller. In the early days the controller was a separate board full of chips, but now it is built into a single VLSI chip that is integrated with a hard disk controller or IDE interface. It might also be integrated with a multifunction board or built-in on the motherboard.

Higher-density systems

Floppy technology continues to advance. Several new high-capacity drives and disks are now available.

Extended density drives

Several companies are now offering 3½-inch extended density (ED) 2.8Mb floppy drives. The 2.8Mb disks have a barium ferrite media and use perpendicular recording to achieve the extended density. In standard recording, the particles are magnetized so that they lie horizontally in the media. In perpendicular recording, the particles are stood vertically for greater density.

The ED drives are downward compatible and can read and write to 720K and 1.44Mb disks. At the present time, ED drives are still rather expensive at about $350 for the drive and about $10 each for the disks.

The ED drives require a controller that operates at 1 MHz. The other floppy controllers operate at 500 kHz. Eventually this controller will be integrated with the other floppy controllers. Figure 7-3 shows an ED floppy controller.

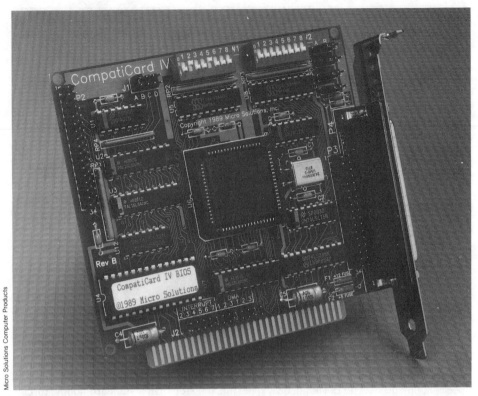

Micro Solutions Computer Products

7-3 A floppy controller for the 2.8Mb extended density drive.

Very high-density drives

Brier Technology, (408) 435-8463, and Insite, (408) 946-8080, have developed very high-density (VHD) 3½-inch drives that can store over 20Mb on a disk. There is no standard among the competing systems, and they use different methods to achieve the very high density.

One of the problems that had to be overcome in VHD drives was that of tracking. The drives have little trouble reading and writing to the 135 TPI of the standard 3½-inch disk, but 20Mb requires many more tracks that are much closer together. Brier Technology's Flextra uses special disks that have magnetic servo tracks embedded beneath the data tracks. The Insite disks have optical servo tracks that are etched into the surface with a laser beam. The heads lock onto the servo tracks for accurate reading and writing to the data tracks. The Insite drive has a head with two different gaps allowing it to read and write to the 20Mb format as well as the 720K and 1.44Mb formats. The Brier drive is being distributed by the Q'COR Company. Several companies, including Iomega, are now distributing the Insite Floptical. The VHD drives cost about $450 and special disks for these systems cost about $20 each. Figure 7-4 shows a Brier external QuadFlextra drive along with its 3½-inch floppy disk.

7-4 The Brier Technology Flextra 20Mb 3½-inch floppy. It uses a special floppy diskette.

Bernoulli drives

Iomega has a high-capacity Bernoulli floppy disk system that can record up to 90Mb on special floppy disks. The Bernoulli disk spins much faster than a standard floppy, forcing the flexible disk to bend around the heads without actually touching them. This is in accordance with the principle discovered by the Swiss scientist, Jakob Bernoulli (1654–1705). The average seek time for the Bernoulli systems is 32 ms. The better hard drives have seek times of about 15 ms. The Bernoulli box has always been a bit expensive at about $750 for the drive and about $70 for each disk. But VHD systems are now giving them some competition and prices should start coming down.

Data compression

Data compression can double your disk capacity. Programs such as Stacker from Stac Electronics, (800) 522-7822, and SuperStor from AddStor, (800) 732-3133, can double the size of a disk. DR DOS 6.0 comes with SuperStor as one of its utilities. Stac Electronics has both software and hardware compression systems.

At one time, data compression wasn't completely trusted. Compression has matured and it is now trustworthy and reliable. Bulletin boards have been using it for years with very few problems. Many of the backup programs use compression so that fewer disks are needed. Compression programs are now fast and transparent to the user.

Stacker can double the size of any disk — 360K, 1.2Mb, 1.44Mb, or any floppy disk. Stacker works great on VHD 20Mb floppies and on Bernoulli disks. I have used a Stacker system for over two years with no problems.

What to buy

Many vendors are still advertising and selling 360K and 720K drives. I don't know why anyone should buy one. They are obsolete. I recommend the 1.2Mb and 1.44Mb drives, or the extended density 2.88Mb drives.

If you live near a large city, there should be lots of stores nearby, as well as computer shows and swap meets. If you don't live near a good source, the next best source would be a mail-order house.

CD-ROM

CD-ROM is very much like an audio CD except that CD-ROM is for digital data. One CD-ROM can store the same amount of data as about 1500 floppies. Several advances have been made in the technology in the last few years. The prices of the drives and the disks have come way down. There is also a much greater variety of data and information available. Look through the computer magazines for ads.

8
Choosing and installing a hard disk

For those of you completely new to computing, a hard drive is an assembly of platters or rigid disks with magnetic plating. Depending on its capacity, a hard drive might have several disks on a common spindle. A read/write head is on the top and bottom of each disk. The head "flies" just a few millionths of an inch from the disk on a cushion of purified air. Figure 8-1 shows a hard disk with its cover removed.

A hard disk is a precise piece of machinery. The tracks might be only a few millionths of an inch apart. The head actuator must move the heads quickly and accurately over a specified track.

In the early 1980s, a 20Mb hard disk cost over $2500. You can buy a 20Mb hard disk today for about $100, or a 200Mb drive for about $500. For such a precise piece of machinery, that price is absolutely amazing.

The need for a hard drive

It is possible to run your 486 with only floppy disk drives, but that is like buying a 400-horsepower Cadillac and using a couple of horses to tow it around. I can't imagine anyone running a 486 without a good hard drive.

Factors to consider

You need to decide what type and size of disk to buy. Of course that depends on what you need to do with your computer and how much you want to spend. Some of the factors that should influence your decision are discussed in the following paragraphs.

Capacity

Buy the biggest you can afford. You might have heard of Mr. C. Northcote Parkinson. After observing business organizations for some time, he formulated several laws. One

Seagate Technology

8-1　A hard disk with the cover removed.

law says, "Work expands to fill up available employee time." A parallel law that paraphrases Mr. Parkinson's immutable law says, "Data expands to fill up available hard disk space." It is almost as if those little bytes on the hard disk reproduce themselves.

So don't even think of buying anything less than 100Mb, or better yet, 200Mb. New software programs have become more and more friendly and offer more and more options. Most of the basic application programs such as spreadsheets, databases, CAD programs, word processors, and many others require 2Mb to 3Mb of disk storage space. OS/2 2.0 requires over 25Mb of disk space.

Over the years I have accumulated hundreds of programs on 5¼-inch disks. I might never have a use for many of them, but I copy them onto my hard disk. If I ever do need them, they are right at my fingertips, just a keystroke away. This is very convenient, but it uses a lot of valuable space on my hard disk. Someday I hope to find time to reorganize my hard disk and delete a lot of the junk that I have accumulated. But deciding what to keep and what to erase is a real chore. The way disk prices keep coming down, I think it would be easier to buy a bigger hard disk than to reorganize.

Speed or access time

Speed or access time is the time it takes a hard disk to locate and retrieve a sector of data, including the time it takes to move the head to the track, settle into place, and read the data. For a high-end, very fast disk, this might be as little as 9 ms. Some of the older drives and systems required as much as 100 ms. An 85-ms hard drive might be fine for a slow XT; a 28-ms drive might not be fast enough for a 386. For disk-intensive uses on a 486, a 15-ms IDE, SCSI, or ESDI system is advisable. Of course, the faster the hard disk, the more expensive it is.

Types of actuators — stepper or voice coil

The head actuator is the method used to move the heads to the desired track. Most of the less-expensive hard drives use a stepper motor that moves the heads in discrete increments across the disk until they are over the track to be read or written. You can hear a definite click as they move from track to track.

The voice coil type of actuator is quieter, a bit faster, more reliable, and, of course, more expensive. Voice coil drives can be recognized because their spec sheets show that they have an odd number of heads. Actually, they have an even number of heads — one on the top and bottom of each disk — but one head and disk surface is used only as a servo control for the heads. By using calibrated voltages and the servo tracks, a voice coil system can smoothly, quietly, and quickly move the heads to the desired track. The high-end SCSI, IDE, and ESDI drives use the voice coil technology.

Types of drives

The two most popular types of drives are the SCSI and IDE drives. The ESDI is a good high-end drive, but it is usually more expensive than an equivalent IDE or SCSI drive. The older MFM and RLL drives are obsolete and are not recommended for high-end applications.

SCSI

Most drive manufacturers do not manufacture controllers. In many cases, you buy a drive from one manufacturer and buy a controller from another manufacturer. Small computer system interface, or SCSI, drives have most of the disk controlling functions integrated onto the drive. This makes a lot of sense because the control electronics can be optimally matched to the drive. The electronics still require an interface card to transmit the data in eight-bit parallel to the disk, much like a parallel printer port. Because it can handle eight bits of data at a time, it can have very fast transfer rates. MFM, RLL, and ESDI drives are serial systems that transfer data one bit at a time.

SCSI systems allow recording of up to 54 sectors per track, compared to 17 sectors with MFM systems, so more than twice as much data can be stored on a disk. They can also be more than twice as fast as an MFM system.

Many companies are making smaller capacity low-end SCSI drives. Seagate has several such models. The low-end models format each track to 26 sectors, the same as the RLL models. I recently bought a low-end SCSI system, a Seagate ST138N, 30MB, 28-ms drive (Seagate uses an N after the model number to denote SCSI). It is a stepper motor system, which makes it a bit slow, but it is reliable and rugged.

SCSI systems need a host adapter, or interface card, to drive them. A Seagate ST02 host adapter with a built-in floppy controller costs about $40. The ST02 interface has a very brief installation guide. Several jumpers on the board configure it to your system's interrupts, BIOS address, and the type of floppy drives you have.

The SCSI interface has its own drivers, so it does not require you to enter the type number into your CMOS setup. The setup lists several drive types that describe the hard disk characteristics. If your drive does not fit the listed types, the setup will usually allow you to type in the characteristics. More about the CMOS setup later.

The main reason I bought the SCSI drive was for backup. This type of backup is very fast. For my purposes, it is much better than using floppy disks for backup. I can quickly and easily copy files from my main IDE disk to the SCSI disk. I don't have to worry about swapping floppy disks in and out. I don't have to worry about labeling and storing floppy disks. And I can quickly find any file that I want and copy it back to the original disk.

Figure 8-2 shows the 50-wire flat ribbon cable being installed on the drive. Figure 8-3 shows the 3½-inch ST138N SCSI hard disk. Figure 8-4 shows the ST02 host adapter. There are many different types of SCSI controllers with many different functions and prices. In contrast to the $40 adapter, Fig. 8-5 shows a high-end EISA SCSI controller from Interphase, (214) 919-9000, which costs about $1500. It is very fast and can handle up to 14 different devices.

IDE- or AT-type drives

Several companies have developed IDE drives. They are sometimes called AT drives because they were first developed for use on the 286 AT. The drives are similar to the SCSI drives in that all of their controller electronics are integrated on the drive. They need only a very inexpensive interface to connect with the bus. This interface can be plugged into any of the eight slots. Figure 8-6 shows an IDE interface that can control two hard disks and two floppies.

Because the interface is so simple, some vendors have designed motherboards with the interface built-in by providing a set of pins on the motherboard. A single cable is plugged into these pins to control two IDE drives. This saves the cost of a controller and

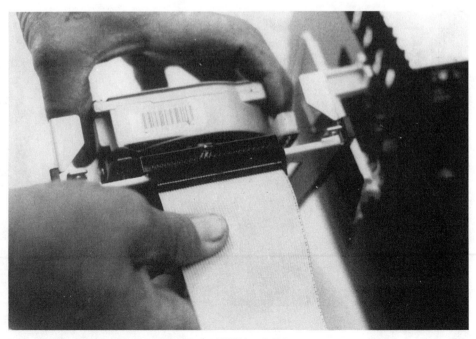

8-2 Connecting the 50-wire cable to the SCSI hard disk.

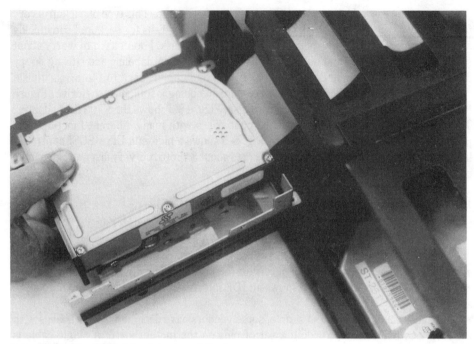

8-3 Sliding the SCSI drive into one of the bays.

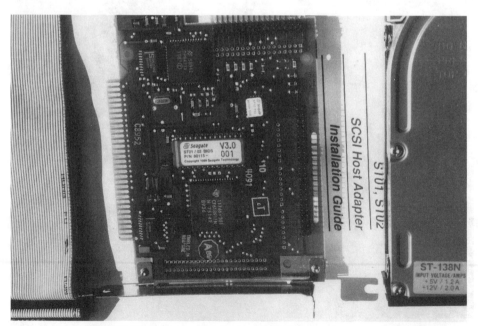

8-4 The Seagate SCSI host adapter. This is the ST02 that can also control two floppies.

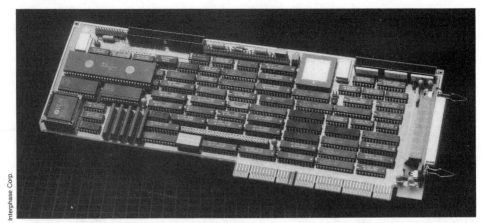

Interphase Corp.

8-5 An E/4810 Barracuda high-end dual SCSI host bus adapter for EISA systems.

8-6 An interface board for IDE systems.

also saves one of your slots. Many motherboards also have a built-in controller for floppy drives. A set of pins that are similar to the hard drive connector pins is provided. When plugging the connector into the pins for the floppy and hard drives, be very careful that you locate pin 1 on the board and plug the cable in so that the colored wire goes to the pin 1 side.

IDE drives cost about the same as SCSI drives. A recent *Computer Shopper* had several ads that listed 200Mb IDE and SCSI drives for less than $500. One major difference is that the IDE interface might cost nothing if it is built-in, or about $10 if you have to buy a plug-in board. An interface for a high-end SCSI costs $150 to $1500, but there are many more functions and options available with the SCSI, such as a fast disk cache.

ESDI

The enhanced small device interface, or ESDI (pronounced ezdy), is another modification of the MFM system. Most ESDI drives are large capacity, usually over 100Mb. ESDI drives can be formatted to 34 sectors or more per track so they can store more than twice as much data as the 17 sectors of a standard MFM drive. They have a very fast access speed, usually 15 ms to 18 ms and a data transfer rate of 10Mb to 15Mb or more per second.

ESDI drives don't offer as many options as SCSI drives. They are often more expensive than SCSI or IDE drives. Many vendors seem to be phasing them out. The May 1992 issue of *Computer Shopper* had a list of 1500 hard drives. Out of the 1500, less than 100 were ESDI drives. They are good drives, but if you buy one, you might be left with an orphan. Orphan products are those that are no longer being manufactured or have no technical support.

MFM

Modified frequency modulation (MFM) was an early standard method for disk recording. In the early 1980s, Seagate Technology developed the ST506/412 interface for MFM, and it became the standard. This method formats several concentric tracks on a disk like those laid down on a floppy diskette. MFM systems divide the tracks into 17 sectors per track, with 512 bytes in each sector. They usually have a transfer rate of 5Mb per second. The MFM method can be used with drives from 5Mb up to several hundred megabytes.

MFM drives are physically large, clunky, and slow. They are rather inexpensive and are fine for an XT or 286, but they are obsolete and I do not recommend them for a 486 system.

RLL

The run length limited (RLL) system is a modification of the MFM system. An RLL drive, when used with an RLL controller, formats a disk to 26 sectors per track. This allows the storage of 50% more data than on an MFM drive; for instance, a 20Mb can store 30Mb, a 40Mb can store 60Mb. RLL systems have a transfer rate of 7.5Mb; 50% faster than MFM systems. Not all drives are capable of running RLL. Seagate uses an R after the model number to denote RLL drives.

Except for being just a bit faster and being able to store 50% more data, RLL drives cost about the same as MFM types. As with MFM drives, RLL drives are practically obsolete. I do not recommend them for a 486 system.

Cost per megabyte

If two drives from different manufacturers have the same specifications, you might consider the cost per megabyte. For instance, a 210Mb drive might cost about $500, or 500/210 = $2.38 per megabyte. A 340Mb drive might cost about $900, or $2.65 per megabyte. A 668Mb drive might cost about $1250, or $1.87 per megabyte. Just a couple of years ago, the least expensive hard drive cost about $4.50 per megabyte. Within a couple of years you should be able to buy a 600Mb drive for about $1 per megabyte.

Physical size

The original full-height drives were about 3½-inches high and almost 6 inches wide. The disk platters were 5¼-inches in diameter. It wasn't long before the technology advanced to where you could get full-height capacity in a half-height, 5¼-inch form. But 5¼-inch platters have to be fairly thick in order to be rigid enough. As the technology advanced still further, you could get full-height capacity in a half-height, 3½-inch form. These smaller disks were made thinner and were still rigid enough. More platters were added in the same amount of space. The smaller diameter design has less mass and needs less wattage to spin the disks. Because they are smaller, it takes less time for the actuators to move the heads to a particular track, therefore, the access time is much less.

The technology continues to advance. Several companies are now manufacturing 2½-inch, 1.8-inch, and 1.3-inch drives.

Interfaces and controllers

If you buy an IDE drive, the interface might be built-in or you might have to buy an inexpensive plug-in interface board. If you buy a SCSI drive, you will need to buy a plug-in interface. For a high-end system, the interface can cost from $150 to $1500.

If you buy an MFM, RLL, or ESDI hard disk you will need a controller card that plugs into one of the slots in your computer. In the past, very few of the hard disk companies made controllers for their disks, but many of them are now making controllers for their high-end ESDI drives and interfaces for their SCSI drives. The controllers and drives are then tested and tuned for optimum operation and sold as a pair.

Most of the hard disk controllers (HDCs) have floppy disk controllers (FDCs) integrated onto the same board. This saves space and is very convenient. These HDC/FDC boards will control 360K, 1.2Mb, 720K, and 1.44Mb disk drives, as well as two hard disks. By the time you read this, there should be HDC/FDC controllers available that also include the 2.88Mb floppy disks.

Note that the advertised price of most disk drives does not include the controller or the necessary cables. An HDC/FDC controller costs as little as $40. The cables cost from $5 to $10.

Hard cards

Several companies have developed hard disks on plug-in cards. These cards have the disk on one end of the card and the controller on the other. They make it very easy to add a second hard disk to your system. You simply remove the cover of your computer and plug the card in.

The original hard cards were 20Mb, but many now have over 100Mb. Plus Development developed the first hard cards and they have remained in the forefront. Figure 8-7 shows one of their hard cards. Hard cards are an excellent tool for data storage or backups.

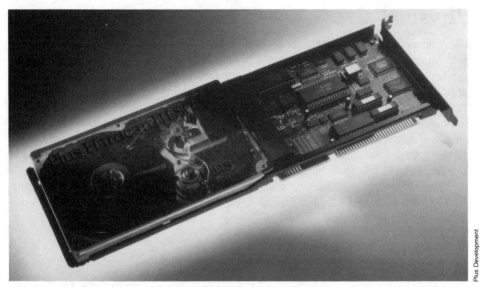

Plus Development

8-7   The Plus Development Hard Card II 80. It is only 1 inch wide and fits in a single slot, and is very easy to install.

Mean time before failure (MTBF)

Disk drives are mechanical devices. If used long enough, every disk drive will fail. Manufacturers test their drives and assign them an average lifetime that ranges from 40,000 to 150,000 hours. Of course, the larger the figure, the longer the drive should last (and the more it will cost). These are average figures, much like the figures quoted for a human lifespan. The average man should live to be about 73 years old. But some babies die very young, and some men live to be over 100. Likewise, some hard disks die very young, and some become obsolete before they wear out.

I have difficulty in accepting some of the manufacturers' MTBF figures. For instance, to put 150,000 hours on a drive, it would have to be used 8 hours a day, every day, for over 51 years. If the drive was operated 24 hours a day, 365 days a year, it would take over 17 years to put 150,000 hours on it. Because hard drives have only been around about 10 years, I am pretty sure that no one has ever done a 150,000-hour test on a drive.

Adding a second hard drive

You never know when a hard disk might fail. You should always have them backed up. A hard drive can be backed up to another hard drive in just seconds. The probability that both drives will fail at the same time is quite small.

I mentioned the fact that the need for storage is seldom satisfied. Even if you have a disk with 1Gb of storage, you will soon be trying to store 2Gb of data on it. A second hard drive can help this problem.

Some controllers cannot handle two different sizes and types of hard drives. If you can afford it, you should buy two drives of the same type. If you can't afford it at this time, buy a well-known brand. Several drive manufacturers have gone out of business, and if you buy an off-brand drive, you might not be able to get a second one later to match your first one. If you decide to add a second hard drive later, you should get some sort of documentation with your drive that tells you what switches or jumpers to set on the drive.

Data compression

I discussed data compression in chapter 7. It can give you all of the benefits of a second hard drive with much less trouble and expense.

Word processors versus ASCII

If you really need a bit more space and you have a lot of text files, you might consider storing them in the ASCII format. This chapter on hard disks requires over 52K in the Word-Star 7.0 format. When I store it as an ASCII file, it requires only 42K.

Formatting

Formatting organizes the disk so that data can be stored and accessed easily and quickly. If the recording of data was not organized, it would be very difficult to find an item on a large hard disk. I have about 3000 files on my two hard disks. Those files are on tracks and sectors that are numbered. A FAT is set up to record the location of each track and sector on the disk. The FAT is similar to an index in a book. When a request is sent to the heads to read or write to a file, they go to the FAT, look for the location of the file, and go directly to it. The heads can find any file, or parts of any file, quickly and easily.

I often forget what is in each of the 3000 files on my hard disks or where I might have stored something. I use the Magellan program from Lotus to instantly tell me where my data is stored. It is great.

Formatting is not something that is done every day, and it can be rather difficult in some cases. Very little literature on the subject is available. Unless you are fairly knowledgeable, try to have your vendor format your hard disk for you.

One reason the disks do not come preformatted from the manufacturer is that there are so many options. There are also many different controller cards. The controller cards are usually designed so that they will operate with several different types of hard disks, so most have DIP switches that must be set to configure your particular hard disk. Usually some documentation comes with the hard disk controller. Like most other manuals and documentation, the instructions are sometimes difficult to understand, especially if you are a beginner.

Low-level format

A floppy diskette is formatted in a single procedure, but a hard disk requires two levels of format — a low level and then a high level. You should have received some sort of documentation with your hard disk and controller. Most hard disks now have the low-level format already performed at the factory, especially the SCSI and IDE drives.

The low-level data recorded on a hard disk with a low-level format might deteriorate with time. Several programs can check MFM and RLL drives and reformat them if necessary. Two are Spin-Rite, (714) 830-2200, and Disk Technician, (619) 274-5000. These programs do not work with SCSI, IDE, and some other nonstandard disks. You should never try to low-level format IDE and SCSI drives unless you have specially designed software for that purpose. One company that provides diagnostic software that works with IDE drives is Micro-2000 at (818) 547-0125. Their Micro-Scope diagnostic software can low-level format IDE drives. It can also perform several other diagnostic tests on hard drives and all floppy drives. It can read, write, and edit data on any track of a floppy or hard drive. It can also check the IRQ assignment of devices in the event of a conflict.

If the hard disk has been low-level formatted, you can type FDISK, and it will allow you to partition the disk. If the hard disk does not allow you to do FDISK, or if you are using a controller other than an MFM, then you must do a low-level format. If the hard disk has not been formatted, use whatever software or instructions you received with the disk.

Using the debug command   CAUTION! Do not try to low-level format SCSI or IDE drives!

With many MFM and RLL controllers, you can use the DOS DEBUG command to invoke the low-level format. Type DEBUG and when the hyphen comes up, type G = C800:5. It looks like this:

```
A > DEBUG
 - G = C800:5
```

The following message is then displayed:

This is a FORMAT routine. It will DESTROY any existing data on your disk! Press <RET> if you wish to continue or <ESC> to abort.

Bad sector data   If you press Return, you will be asked several questions. One question is if you want to input any bad sector data. It is almost impossible to manufacture a perfect hard disk. The disk usually comes with a list of bad sectors that the manufacturer discovered during his testing. If they are very bad, your controller might detect them, but if they are marginal it might not. When you input the list of bad sectors, DOS marks them so that they are not used. As much as 100K or more space might be in bad sectors; a small percentage compared to the disk's capacity.

Utility programs for low-level format   Some controllers will not let you use the DEBUG command to do a low-level format. Utility programs that let you do a low-level format include

- Check-It   (800) 531-0450
- Disk Technician   (619) 274-5000

- SpinRite   (714) 830-2200
- DOSUTILS   (800) 752-1333
- QAPlus   (408) 438-8247

High-level format

If the low-level format has been done, you can do the high-level format. Boot up from your floppy disk drive with a copy of DOS and type DIR C:. If you get the message, "Invalid drive specification," put in a copy of DOS that has the FDISK command on it in drive A:.

When you type FDISK, the following message will be displayed if you are using MS-DOS 5.0:

```
MS-DOS Version 5.00
      Fixed Disk Setup Program
      Copyright Microsoft Corp. 1983, 1991
      FDISK Options
      Current Fixed Disk Drive: 1
      Choose one of the following:
      1. Create DOS partition or Logical DOS Drive
      2. Set active partition
      3. Delete Partition or Logical DOS Drive
      4. Display partition information
      5. Change current fixed disk drive
      Enter choice: [1]
      Press ESC to exit FDISK
```

If you choose 1 and the disk has not been prepared, a screen like this comes up:

```
Create DOS Partition or Logical DOS Drive
Current Fixed Drive: 1
Choose one of the following:
1. Create Primary DOS partition
2. Create Extended DOS partition
3. Create logical DOS drive(s) in the Extended DOS partition
Enter choice: [1]
Press ESC to return to FDISK Options
```

If you want to boot from your hard drive (and I can't think of any reason why you would not want to), then you must create a primary DOS partition and make it active.

DOS 3.3 and earlier versions could only handle hard disks up to 32Mb. If you bought a 40Mb hard disk, you could only use 32Mb of it unless you used special software such as DiskManager. DOS 4.0 and later versions allow very large partitions, up to 2Gb.

I do not recommend making a partition of more than 50Mb. If there are several partitions on a disk and one of them fails, you might be able to recover the data in the other partitions.

After the FDISK options have been completed, return to drive A: and high-level format drive C:. Because you want to boot off this drive, you must also transfer the system and hidden files to the disk as it is being formatted by using a /S to transfer the files. Type FORMAT C:/S. DOS will display a message that says

WARNING! ALL DATA ON NON-REMOVABLE DISK DRIVE C: WILL BE LOST!

Proceed with Format (Y/N)

If you press Y the disk light should come on, and you might hear the drive stepping through each track. After a few minutes, it will display

Format complete
System transferred
Volume label (11 characters, ENTER for none)?

You can give each partition a unique name, or volume label, if you wish to.

You can test your drive by doing a warm boot by pressing Ctrl-Alt-Del. The computer should reboot. Now that drive C: is completed, if you have other partitions or a second disk, format each of them.

Some hard disk basics

Here are some basic details that explain how a hard disk operates.

Tracks and sectors

Basically a hard disk is similar to a floppy disk. It is a spinning disk that has a coating that can be magnetized. Hard disks also have tracks that are similar to those on a floppy disk. A 360K floppy disk has only 40 TPI; hard disks might have from 300 to 3000 TPI. Each of the 40 tracks of the 360K floppy are divided into 9 sectors per track. Older hard disks have 17 sectors per track, while some newer ones have up to 54 sectors per track.

Speed of rotation and density

Another major difference between the floppy and hard disk is the speed of rotation. A floppy disk spins at about 300 rpm. A hard disk spins from 3600 to 6400 rpm. As the disk spins beneath the head, a pulse of voltage through the head causes the area of the track that is beneath the head to become magnetized. This pulse of voltage is turned on for a certain amount of time, then turned off for a certain amount of time, representing the writing or recording of 1s and 0s. Hard disks spin much faster than floppies so the duration of the magnetizing pulses are much shorter and at a higher frequency. This allows much more data to be recorded in the same amount of space.

Everything that a computer does depends on precise timing. Crystals and oscillators are set up so that certain circuits perform a task at a specific time. These oscillating circuits are usually called clock circuits. The clock frequency for the standard MFM method of reading and writing to a hard disk is 10 MHz per second. To write on the disk during one second, the voltage might turn on for a fraction of a second, then turn off for the next period of time, then back on for a certain length of time. The head sits over a track that is moving at a constant speed. Blocks of data are written or read during the precise timing of the system clock. Because the voltage must be positive or zero in order to write 1s and 0s, the maximum data transfer rate is only 5Mb per second for MFM, just half of the clock frequency. RLL systems transfer data at a rate of 7.5Mb per second. SCSI and ESDI systems have a transfer rate of 10 to 15Mb or more per second.

You have probably seen representations of magnetic lines of force around a magnet. The magnetized spot on a disk track has similar lines of force. To read the data on the disk, the head is positioned over the track and the lines of force from each magnetized area cause a pulse of voltage to be induced in the head. During a precise block of time, an induced pulse of voltage represents a 1, the lack of a pulse represents a 0.

The amount of magnetism that is induced on a diskette when it is written to is very small. It must be small so that it will not affect other recorded bits or tracks near it. Magnetic lines of force decrease as you move away from a magnet by the square of the distance. For this reason it is desirable to have the heads as close to the disk as possible.

On a floppy disk drive, the heads actually contact the diskette. This causes some wear, but not a lot, because the rotation is fairly slow and the plastic disks are coated with a special lubricant that makes them fairly slippery. However, the heads in a hard disk system never touch the disk. The fragile heads and the disk would be severely damaged if they made contact at a speed of 3600 rpm. The heads "fly" over the spinning disk, just microinches above it. The air must be pure because the smallest speck of dust or dirt can cause the head to crash. Most hard disks are factory sealed for this reason. You should never open one.

The surface of the hard disk platters must be very smooth. Because the heads are only a few microinches from the surface, any unevenness can cause a head crash. The hard disk platters are usually made from aluminum, which is nonmagnetic, and are lapped to a mirror finish. They are then coated or plated with a magnetic material. Some companies are now using tempered glass as a substrate for their platters.

The platters must also be very rigid so that the close distance between the head and the platter surface is maintained. You should avoid any sudden movement of the computer or any jarring while the disk is spinning because it could cause the head to crash onto the disk and damage it. Most of the newer hard disk systems automatically move the heads away from the read/write surface to a parking area when the power is turned off.

Another difference in the hard disk and the floppy is that the floppy comes on only when it is needed. Because of its mass, the hard disk takes quite a while to get up to speed and to stabilize. It comes on whenever the computer is turned on and spins as long as the computer is on. This means that it is drawing power from the power supply all the time. This could cause some problems if your system is fully loaded with boards and has a small power supply.

Clusters

A sector is only 512 bytes, but most files are much larger than that. Many systems lump two or more sectors together and call it a cluster. If an empty cluster is on track 5, the system will record as much of the file as it can there, then move to the next empty cluster, which could be on track 20. The location of each part of the file is recorded in the FAT so that the computer has no trouble finding it.

Cylinders

If you could strip away all of the tracks except track 1, top and bottom, on all of the platters, you would have something that looks somewhat like a cylinder. Cylinder refers to each of those tracks with the same number on a stack of platters or on a double-sided diskette.

Multiple platters

A hard disk can have from 2 to more than 10 platters. All the platters are stacked on a single shaft with just enough spacing between them for the heads. Each disk has a head for the top surface and one for the bottom. If the system has four disks, then it has eight heads. All heads are controlled by the same positioner, and they all move together. If head 1 is over track 1, sector 1, then all the other heads are over track 1, sector 1 on each disk surface.

Head actuators or positioners

There are several different types of head positioners or actuators. Some use stepper motors to move the heads in discrete steps to a certain track. Some use a worm gear or screw-type shaft that moves the heads in and out. Others use voice coil technology.

The voice coil of a loudspeaker is made up of a coil of wire that is wound on a hollow tube that is attached to the material of the speaker cone. Permanent magnets are then placed inside the coil and around the outside. Whenever a voltage is passed through the coil of wire, it causes magnetic lines of force to be built up around the coil. Depending on the polarity for the input voltage, these lines of magnetic flux are either the same as or opposite to the lines of force of the permanent magnets. If the polarity of the voltage, for instance, a plus voltage, causes the lines of force to be the same as the permanent magnet, then they repel each other and the voice coil moves forward. If they are opposite, they attract each other and the coil moves backward.

Some of the better and faster hard disks use voice coil technology with a closed-loop servo control. These types use one surface of one of the disks to store data and track locations. Most specification sheets give the number of heads on a drive. If you see one that has an odd number of heads, such as 5, 7, or 9, it probably uses the other head for servo information. The voice coil moves the heads quickly and smoothly to the track area. Feedback information from the closed loop accurately positions the head to the exact track. Voice coil drives might cost 30% to 40% more than stepper motor drives with an equivalent capacity.

Setup routine

When you install a hard disk, your BIOS must be told what kind of disk it is. The BIOS also must know the time, the number and type of floppies you have, as well as other information. It also must set or reset the clock on the motherboard. The diagnostic routine asks several questions, then configures the BIOS for that configuration. This part of the BIOS configuration is in low-power CMOS and is on at all times, even when the computer is turned off.

One of the questions that the routine asks is, What type of hard disk do you have? There were only 15 different types when the AT was introduced in 1984. There are now hundreds. Most new BIOS ROMs list 46 types. If yours is not among the 46 listed, the BIOS usually allows you to input the parameters of any that are not listed. You must tell it what type you have installed. You should have received some information from your vendor that tells you the number of heads, cylinders, and other specifications.

I already had two IDE drives installed. Neither one of them were on the list of drives, so I had to use the one type that allowed me to input the characteristics. The only way I could install a third drive was to use one that fit one of the 47 types listed. But all of the types listed are older MFM types with 17 sectors per track. The other alternative was to use a SCSI drive that does not have to be listed under the CMOS setup.

Manufacturers need to update the BIOS CMOS setup to include newer drives. I am amazed that BIOS manufacturers have not addressed this problem. I am sure that they will eventually update their BIOS chips.

CAUTION! Never boot up with a floppy disk version that is different from the version used to format the hard disk. There is a short boot record on the hard disk. If a different version is used to boot up, you might lose all of your data on the disk.

Progress

Figure 8-8 shows two hard disk platters. The large platter was developed by Ampex in the early 1970s. It is 16¼ inches in diameter and ¼ inch thick. It has the ability to store 1.5Mb of data on each side, for a total of 3Mb. This was an enormous amount at that time. The smaller platter is 5¼ inches in diameter and is ¹⁄₁₆ inch thick. It can store about 50Mb on each side, for a total of 100Mb.

8-8   Hard disk evolution. An early hard disk platter that is 16¼ inches in diameter and ¼ inch thick. It has a capacity of 1.5Mb on each side. The smaller disk is 5¼ inches in diameter and ¹⁄₁₆ inch thick. It can store about 50Mb on each side.

Sources

Local computer stores and computer swap meets are a good place to find hard disks. You can at least look them over and get an idea of the prices and what you want. Mail order is a very good way to buy a hard disk. You can find hundreds of ads in the many computer magazines. Check the list of magazines in chapter 17.

9
Backup

When you buy a software program, the very first thing you should do is write-protect the floppies. It is very easy to become distracted and write on a program disk in error. This will probably ruin the program. It takes less than a minute to write-protect a diskette, and it might save you weeks of valuable time. If a program diskette is ruined because it was not protected it might take weeks to get a replacement for the original, and you might even have to buy a new program.

How to write-protect your software

If you are using 5¼-inch floppies, you should cover the square write-protect notch with a piece of opaque tape. Don't use clear tape. The drive focuses a light through the square notch. If the light detector senses the light, it allows the disk to be written on, read, or erased. If the notch is covered with opaque tape, the diskette can be read, but cannot be written on or erased. Some vendors now distribute programs on disk without the square notch.

If you are using 3½-inch diskettes, you should move the small slide on the left rear so that the square hole is open. The 3½-inch disk write-protect system is just the opposite of the 5¼-inch disk system. The 3½-inch disk system uses a microswitch. If the square hole is open, the switch allows the diskette to be read, but not written on or erased. If the slide is moved to cover the square hole, the diskette can be written on, read, or erased.

After you have made sure that the diskettes are write-protected, the second thing you should do is to use DISKCOPY to make exact copies of your original disks. The originals should then be stored away. Only the copies should be used. If you damage a copy, you can always make another copy from the original.

Protection from dirt and dust

A simple, easy way to protect your original program disks from dirt and dust is to seal them in a plastic sandwich bag.

Unerase software

Anyone who works with computers for any length of time is bound to make a few errors. One of the best protections against errors is to have a backup. The second best protection is to have a good utility program such as Norton Utilities or PC Tools. These programs can unerase a file or even unformat a disk. When a file is erased, DOS goes to the FAT and deletes the first letter of each file name. All of the data remains on the disk unless a new file is written over it. If you have erased a file or formatted a disk in error, do not do anything to it until you have tried using a recover utility. Don't use the DOS Recover utility except as a last resort. Use Norton Utilities (213-319-2000), Mace Utilities (504-291-7221), PC Tools (503-690-8090), DOSUTILS, (612-937-1107), or any of several other recovery utilities. These utilities allow you to restore the files by replacing the missing first letter of the file name.

The early versions of DOS made it very easy to format your hard disk in error. If you happened to be on your hard disk and typed FORMAT, it would immediately begin to format your hard disk and wipe out everything. Later versions will not format unless you specify a drive letter. These versions also allow you to include a volume label, or name, on the drive when you format it by including the /v. Or you can add a label name later by using the command LABEL. If the drive has a volume label, it cannot be formatted unless the drive letter and correct volume name is specified. (You can display, delete, assign, or change the name of a volume by typing the command LABEL. The label name is also displayed when CHKDSK is run.)

Many people have erased files in error. They are only human so they will probably do it again. Some of them will not have backups and unerase software. In a fraction of a second, some of them will wipe out data that might be worth thousands of dollars, or took hundreds of hours to accumulate, and it might be impossible to duplicate it. Yet many of these unfortunate people have not backed up their precious data. Most of these people are those who have been fortunate enough not to have had a major catastrophe. Just as sure as there are earthquakes in California, if you use a computer long enough, you can look forward to at least one disaster. There are thousands of ways to make mistakes. There is no way that you can prevent them. But if your data is backed up, it doesn't have to be a disaster. It is a lot better to be backed up than sorry.

Jumbled FAT

I talked about the all-important FAT in the previous chapter. It keeps a record of the location of all the files on the disk. Parts of a file might be located in several sectors, but the FAT knows exactly where they are. If for some reason track 0 (where the FAT is located) is damaged, erased, or becomes defective, then you will not be able to read or write to any of the files on the disk.

Because the FAT is so important, programs such as PC Tools and Mace Utilities make a copy of the FAT and store it in another location on the disk. Every time you add a file or edit one, the FAT changes, and so these programs make a new copy every time the FAT is altered. If the original FAT is damaged, you can still get your data by using the backup FAT.

If you have a large-capacity hard disk and it fails, you might not be able to access or recover any of the data. But if a large disk is divided into several smaller logical drives, if one drive fails, you might still be able to recover the data on the other drives.

Head crash

The heads of a hard disk "fly" over the disk just a few microinches from the surface. They have to be close in order to detect the small magnetic changes in the tracks. The disk spins at 3600 rpm. If the heads contact the surface of the spinning disk, they can scratch it and ruin the disk.

A sudden jar or bump to the computer while the hard disk is spinning can cause the heads to crash. Of course, a mechanical failure or some other factor can also cause a crash. You should never move or bump your computer while the hard disk is running.

Most of the newer disks have a built-in park utility. When the power is removed, the head is automatically moved to the center of the disk, where there are no tracks. It is also possible for the head to crash if the power is suddenly removed, such as in a power failure.

The technology of hard disk systems has improved tremendously over the last couple of years. But they are still mechanical devices, and as such, you can be sure that eventually they will wear out, fail, or crash. Most hard disks are now relatively bug free. Manufacturers quote MTBF figures of 40,000 to 150,000 hours, but these figures are only an average. There are lots of businesses that do nothing but repair hard disks that have crashed or failed. There is no guarantee that your disk won't fail in the next few minutes.

A failure can be frustrating, time-consuming, and make you feel utterly helpless. In the unhappy event of a crash and depending on its severity, it is possible that some of your data might be recovered, one way or another.

Crash recovery

There are companies that specialize in recovering data and rebuilding hard disks. Many of them have sophisticated tools and software that can recover some data if the disk is not completely ruined. If it is possible to recover any of the data, Ontrack Computer Systems (612-937-1107) can probably do it. There are several other companies that perform data recovery including California Disk Drive Repair (408-727-2475) and Rotating Memory Service (916-939-7500).

The cost for recovery services can be rather expensive. If you have important data, it is well worth it, but it is a whole lot cheaper to have a backup.

Small logical drives are better

Early versions of DOS would not recognize a hard disk larger than 32Mb. DOS now allows you to have a drive C: or D: of 512Mb or more. Don't do it. If this large hard disk crashes, you might not be able to recover any of its data. If the same disk is divided into several smaller logical drives, and one of the logical sections fails, it might be possible to recover data in the unaffected logical drives.

Excuses for not backing up

1. *I don't have the time.* This is not a good excuse. If your data is worth anything at all, it is worth backing up. It takes only a few minutes to back up a large hard disk with some of the newer software.

2. *It's too much trouble.* It is a bit of trouble unless you have an expensive automated tape backup system. Backup can require a bit of disk swapping, labeling, and storing. But with a little organizing, it can be done easily. If you keep all of the disks together, you don't have to label each one. Just stack them in order, put a rubber band around them, and put a label on the first one of the lot.

   Yes, it is a bit of trouble to make backups. But if you don't have a backup, consider what it would take to redo the files on a disk that has crashed. The trouble that it takes to make a backup is infinitesimal.

3. *I don't have the necessary disks, software, or tools.* Depending on the amount of data to be backed up and the software used, it might require 50 to 100 360K disks. Of course it will require a lot fewer if high-density disks are used. Again, it takes only a few minutes and a few disks to make a backup of the data that has been changed or altered. In most cases, the same disks can be reused the next day to update the files. There are several discount mail-order houses that sell 360K disks for as little as $.25 each; $.39 each for 1.2Mb and 720K disks, and $.59 for 1.44Mb disks. There are several discount companies listed in chapter 6.

4. *Failures and disasters only happen to other people.* People who believe this are those who have never experienced a disaster. There is nothing you can say to convince them. They just have to learn the hard way.

A few other reasons to backup
General failure

Outside of ordinary care, there is little you can do to prevent a general failure. It could be a component in the hard disk electronics or in the controller system, or any one of a thousand other things. Even things such as a power failure during a read/write operation can cause data corruption.

Theft and burglary

Computers are easy to sell, and they are favorite targets for burglars. It is bad enough to lose your computer, but many computers have hard disks that are filled with data that is even more valuable than the computer. It might be a good idea to put your name and address on several of the files on your hard disk. It is also a good idea to scratch identifying marks on the back and bottom of your computer case. You should also write down the serial numbers of your monitor and drives.

Another good idea is to store your backup files in an area away from your computer. This way there is less chance of losing both your computer and backups in a burglary or fire. You can always buy another computer, but if you have a large database of customer orders, files, and history, how could you replace that?

Archival

Another reason to backup is for archival purposes. No matter how large the hard disk is, it will eventually fill up with data. Quite often, there are files that are no longer used, or they might be used only once in a great while. I keep copies of all the letters that I write on disk. I have hundreds of them. Rather than erase the old files or old letters, I put them on a disk and store them away.

Fragmentation

After a hard disk has been used for awhile, files begin to fragment. The data is recorded on concentric tracks in separate sectors. If part of a file is erased or changed, some of the data might be in a sector on track 20 and another part on track 40. There might be open sectors on several tracks because portions of data have been erased. Hunting all over the disk can slow the disk down. If the disk is backed up completely, then erased, the files can be restored so that they are recorded in contiguous sectors. The utility programs mentioned above can unfragment a hard disk by copying portions of the disk to memory and rearranging the data in contiguous files.

Data transfer

Often it is necessary to transfer a large amount of data from one hard disk to another. A good backup program can accomplish this quite easily and quickly. It is easy to make several copies that can be distributed to others. This method can be used to distribute data, company policies and procedures, sales figures, and other information to several people in an office or company. The data can also be shipped or mailed to branch offices, customers, or anyone that needs it.

Methods of backup
Software

There are two main types of backup: image and file oriented. An *image backup* is an exact bit-for-bit copy of the hard disk copied as a continuous stream of data. This type of backup is rather inflexible and does not allow for a separate file backup or restoration. The *file oriented* type of backup identifies and indexes each file separately. A separate file or directory can be backed up or restored. It can be very time-consuming to have to backup an entire 40Mb or more each day. But with a file oriented system, once a full backup has been made, only incremental backups of those files that have been changed or altered are needed.

DOS stores an archive attribute in each file directory entry. When a file is created, DOS turns the archive attribute flag on. If the file is backed up by using DOS BACKUP or any of the commercial backup programs, the archive attribute flag is turned off. If this file is later altered or changed, DOS turns the attribute flag back on. At the next backup, you can have the program search the files looking for the attribute flag. You can then backup only those files that have been altered or changed since the last backup. You can view or modify a file's archive attribute by using the DOS ATTRIB command.

There are several very good software programs on the market that let you use a 5¼-inch or 3½-inch disk drive to backup your data. You should already have backups of all your master software, so you don't have to worry about backing up that software every day. Because DOS stamps each file with the date and time it is created, it is easy to backup only those files that were created after a certain date and time.

Once the first backup is made, all subsequent backups need only be made of any data that has been changed or updated. Most backup programs can recognize whether a file has been changed since the last backup. Most of them can also look at the date that is stamped on each file and back up only those within a specified date range. It might take only a few minutes to make a copy of those files that are new or changed. And of course, it is not necessary to backup your program software. You have the original software disks safely tucked away, don't you?

Backup.com One of the least expensive methods of backup is to use the backup.com and restore.com that comes with MS-DOS. But there is a price to pay in that it is slow, time-consuming, and rather difficult to use. It will do the job if nothing else is available.

A few commercial backup programs are discussed below. There are many others.

Norton Backup Norton Backup, (213) 319-2000, is one of the newest and fastest backup programs on the market. It is also one of the easiest to use. It compresses data so that fewer disks are needed.

Norton Desktop for Windows Norton and Symantec have now merged. This software package has several very useful utilities, emergency unerase, manual and automatic backup, and utilities for creating batch files and managing directories and files under Windows.

Fastback Fastback Plus, (504) 291-7221, was one of the first fast backup software programs. It is now past version 3.0. It is easy to learn and use. It also compresses the data so that fewer floppy disks are needed.

Back-It 4 Back-It, from Gazelle Systems, (800) 233-0383, has recently been revised to version 4.0. This new version uses very high-density data compression, as much as 3 to 1. It is also very fast and uses a sophisticated error correction routine. Unlike some of the other systems, Back-It 4 will allow you to use different format floppies at the same time.

PC Tools PC Tools comes bundled with a very good backup program. They have now decided to sell the backup program separately to anyone who doesn't want to buy the whole bundle.

XTree XTree is an excellent shell program for disk and file management. It has several functions that make computing much easier. You can use it to copy files from one directory or disk to another. I often use it to make backups when I only have a few files to back up.

Q-DOS III Q-DOS III, from Gazelle Systems, is also an excellent shell program that is similar to XTree. It can be used to select and copy files to another hard disk or to floppies.

DOS XCOPY   The XCOPY command is a part of MS-DOS versions higher than 3.2. There are several switches that can be used with XCOPY. (A switch is a /). For instance, XCOPY C:*.*.A:/A will copy only those files that have their archive attribute set to ON. It does not reset the attribute flag. XCOPY C:*.*A:/M will copy the files, then reset the flag. Whenever a disk on drive A: is full, you merely have to insert a new floppy and hit F3 to repeat the last command. It will continue to copy all files that have not been backed up. XCOPY C:*.*A:/D:03-15-92 will copy only those files created after March 15, 1992. There are several other very useful switches that can be used with XCOPY.

Several other very good backup software packages are available. Check through the computer magazines for ads and reviews.

Tape

There are several tape backup systems on the market. Tape backup is easy, but it can be relatively expensive at $400 to $1000 for a drive unit and $5 to $20 for the tape cartridges. Most tape backup systems require the use of a controller that is similar to the disk controller, so they will use one of your precious slots. Unless the system is used externally, it will also require the use of one of your disk mounting areas. Because it is only used for backup, it will be idle most of the time.

One of the big problems with software backup is that you have to sit there and put in a new disk when one is full. One big plus for tape is that it can be set up so that it is done automatically. You don't have to worry about forgetting to backup or about wasting your time doing it.

Digital audio tape (DAT)

Several companies are offering DAT systems for backing up large hard disk systems. DAT systems offer storage capacities as high as 1.3Gb on a very small cartridge. DAT systems use a helical scan-type recording that is similar to that used for video recording. DATs are 4 millimeters wide (0.156 inches), yet they can store about twice as much data as 0.25-inch tape.

Very high-density disk drives

Several companies are now making extended high-density 2.8Mb floppies and very high-density 20Mb floppy disk drives. Insite Peripherals and Brier Technology have developed floppy drives that can store 20Mb on a 3½-inch floppy disk. The Bernoulli drive can put 90Mb on a 5¼-inch floppy disk.

Even if it costs a bit more, a high-density floppy drive can be more advantageous than a tape system. Tape drives are only used for backup, but a high-density floppy has much more utility, possibly even obviating the need for a hard disk.

Data compression

I discussed data compression in chapter 7. It can be used with any floppy or hard disk to double the storage capacity. For more details on drives and data compression, refer to chapter 7.

Second hard disk

The easiest and fastest of all methods of backup is to have a second hard disk. It is very easy to install a second hard disk. It doesn't have to be a large one, a 30Mb or 40Mb drive is fine. With a second hard disk as a backup, you do not need a backup software package. A good backup software package might cost $200 or more. You can buy a 40Mb MFM hard disk for less than $200.

An average hard disk has an access speed of about 28 ms. Floppy disks operate at about 300 ms, which can seem like an eternity when compared to the speed of even the slowest hard disk. Depending on the number of files, how fragmented the data is on the disk, and the access speed, a second hard disk can back up 20Mb in a matter of seconds. To back up 20Mb using even the fastest software requires 15 to 20 minutes. It also requires that you do a lot of disk swapping. Depending on the type of disks you use for backup and the type of software, it might require 15 to 20 disks to back up 20Mb. Some of the backup software makes extensive use of data compression, so fewer disks are needed.

Another problem with using backup software is that it is often difficult to find a particular file. Most backup software stores the data in a system that is not the same as DOS files. Usually there is no directory like that provided by DOS. Even the DOS BACKUP files show only a control number when you check the directory.

External plug-in hard drives

Several companies are now manufacturing small 20Mb to 80Mb hard disks that operate off the parallel or serial connector. Many of them are battery-powered so they can be used with a laptop. They can also be used to back up data from a large desktop system or to transfer data from one system to another. Pacific Rim Systems makes an excellent 20Mb system. By installing the Stacker compression software on this 20Mb hard disk, it can store about 40Mb.

Hard cards

You can buy a hard disk on a card for $300 to $600. Compression software can be used on these disks, so it might be worthwhile to install a card in an empty slot and dedicate it to backup.

If there are no empty slots, you might want to consider plugging in the card once a week or so to make a backup, then remove the card until it is needed again. This entails removing the cover from the machine each time, but I remove the cover from my computer so often that I only use one screw on it to provide grounding. I can remove and replace my cover in a very short time.

No matter what type of system or method is used, if your data is worth anything at all, you should be using something to back it up. You might be one of the lucky ones and never need it. But it is much better to be backed up than to be sorry.

10
Input devices

Before you can do anything with a computer you must input data to it. There are several ways to input data: from a disk, by modem, mouse, scanner, bar-code reader, voice data input, fax, or on-line from a mainframe or a network.

Keyboards

But by far the most common way to get data into a computer is by way of the keyboard. For most common applications, it is impossible to operate the computer without a keyboard.

The keyboard is a most personal connection with your computer. If you do a lot of typing, it is very important that you get a keyboard that suits you. Not all keyboards are the same. Some have a light mushy touch, some are heavy. Some have noisy keys, others are silent with very little feedback.

A need for standards

Typewriter keyboards are fairly standard. There are only 26 letters in the alphabet and a few symbols, so most QWERTY typewriters have about 50 keys. I have had several computers over the last few years and every one of them has had a different keyboard. The main typewriter characters aren't changed or moved very often, but some of the very important control keys like the Esc, Ctrl, Prtsc, \, function keys, and several others are moved all over the keyboard. IBM can be blamed for most of the changes.

The original IBM keyboard had the very important and often-used Esc key just to the left of the 1 key in the numeric row. The 84-key keyboard moved the Esc key to the top row of the keypad. The tilde (˜) and grave (`) key was moved to the original Esc position to the left of the 1. The IBM 101-key keyboard moved the Esc key back to its original position.

For some unknown reason IBM also decided to move the function keys to the top of the keyboard above the numeric keys. This is quite frustrating for WordStar users because the Ctrl key and the function keys are used quite often. The original position made them very easy to access.

There are well over 400 different keyboards available in the United States. Many people make their living by typing on a keyboard. Many large companies have systems that count the number of keystrokes that an employee makes during a shift. If the employee fails to make a certain number of keystrokes, then that person can be fired. Can you imagine the problems if a person has to frequently learn a new keyboard? I am not a very good typist in the first place and I have great difficulty using different keyboards. There definitely should be some sort of standard. Figure 10-1 shows two keyboards; each has a different key arrangement.

Innovation, creating something new that is useful and needed and makes life better or easier, is great. That type of innovation should be encouraged everywhere. But many times changes are made just for the sake of differentiation without adding any real value or functionality to a product. This applies not only to keyboards, but to all technology.

10-1   An 84-key keyboard (bottom) and a 101-key keyboard (top).

How a keyboard works

The keyboard is actually a computer in itself. It has a small microprocessor with its own ROM. The computerized electronics of the keyboard eliminate the bounce of the keys, determine when you hold a key down for repeat, store up to 20 or more keystrokes, and determine which key was pressed first if you press two keys at a time.

In addition to the standard BIOS chips on your motherboard, there is a special keyboard BIOS chip. Each time a key is pressed a unique signal is sent to the BIOS. This signal comes from a dc voltage that is turned on and off a certain number of times within a definite time frame to represent 0s and 1s. Each time a 5-volt line is turned on for a certain amount of time, it represents a 1; when it is off for a certain amount of time, it represents a 0. In the ASCII code, if the letter A is pressed, the code for 65 is generated: 1 0 0 0 0 0 1.

Reprogramming key functions

The keys can be changed by various software programs to represent almost anything you want them to. One thing that makes learning computers so difficult is that every software program uses the function and other special keys in different ways. You might learn all the special keys that WordStar uses, but if you want to use a word processor such as Word-Perfect or Microsoft Word, or any of the others, you have to learn the special commands and keys that they use.

The major word processing, spreadsheet, and other software programs will let you set up macro programs. A macro program lets you record a series of keystrokes, such as your name and address, the time and date, or other frequently used items, and types them by pressing just one or two keys.

Keyboard sources

Keyboard preference is strictly a matter of individual taste. Key Tronic (509-928-8000) makes some excellent keyboards. Their keyboards have set the standards. Key Tronic keyboards have been copied by the clone makers, even to the extent of using the same model numbers.

Key Tronic offers several models. They can let you change the little springs under the keys to produce different tensions. The standard is 2 ounces, but you can configure the key tension to whatever you like. You can install 1-, 1.5-, 2-, 2.5-, or 3-ounce springs for an extra $15. They also let you exchange the positions of the Caps Lock and Ctrl keys. Their keyboards have several other functions that are clearly described in their large manual, the most detailed of any company. There are hundreds of clone makers who offer keyboards that are very good for $35 to $90. Look through the ads in the computer magazines.

Specialized keyboards

Several companies have developed specialized keyboards. I have listed only a few of them below.

Quite often I have the need to do some minor calculations. The computer is great for calculations. Several programs, such as SideKick, Windows, and WordStar, have built-in calculators, but most of these programs require that the computer be on. Keyboards available from Shamrock (800-722-2898) and Jameco (415-592-8097) have a built-in solar-powered calculator where the number pad is located. The calculator can be used whether the computer is on or not.

Focus Electronics (818-820-0416) has a series of specialized keyboards. They have keyboards with built-in calculators, function keys in both locations, extra * and \ keys, and several other goodies. Their FK-5001 keyboard has eight cursor (arrow) keys. With these keys the cursor can be moved right or left, up or down, and diagonally up or down from any of the four corners of the screen. The speed of the cursor can be varied by using the 12 function keys. These eight cursor keys will do just about everything that a mouse can do.

The Datacomp DFK 2010 is very similar to the FK-5001. It has the function keys at the top and at the left. It also lets you switch the Ctrl key back to where it is supposed to be. It also has the diagonal arrow cursor keys like the FK-5001.

Besides their standard keyboards, Key Tronic has developed a large number of specialized ones. Instead of a keypad, one has a touch pad. This pad can operate in several different modes. One mode lets it act like a cursor pad. By using your finger or a stylus, the cursor can be moved much the same as with a mouse. It comes with templates for several popular programs such as WordStar, WordPerfect, DOS, and Lotus 1-2-3.

Another Key Tronic model has a bar-code reader attached to it. This can be extremely handy if you have a small business that uses bar codes. This keyboard would be ideal for a computer in a point-of-sale system.

Keyboard covers

There are special plastic covers that can protect your keyboard against spills, dust, and other environmental hazards. There are some areas such as the floor of a manufacturing area where a cover is absolutely essential. Most of the covers are made from soft plastic that is molded to fit over the keys. They are pliable, but they will slow down any serious typist.

Several companies manufacture custom covers, including CompuCover (800-874-6391) and Tech-Cessories (800-637-0909). Well over 400 different types of keyboards are used in the United States. If you count foreign keyboards, there are probably over 4000 different types used worldwide. These companies claim that they can provide a cover for most of them. The average cover costs about $25. This is a bit expensive for just a bit of shrink-type plastic, but one reason they are so expensive is that there are so many different keyboards.

Mouse systems

One of the biggest reasons for the success of the Macintosh is that it is easy to use. With a mouse and icons all you have to do is point and click. You don't have to learn a lot of commands and rules. A person who knows nothing about computers can become productive in a very short time. The people in the DOS world finally took note of this and began developing programs and applications such as Windows for the IBM and compatibles.

There are dozens of companies now manufacturing mice. Many software programs can be used without a mouse, but they operate much faster and better with a mouse. To be productive, a mouse is essential for programs such as Windows 3.0, CAD programs, paint and graphics programs, and many others.

You can't just plug in a mouse and start using it. The software, whether it's Windows, WordStar, or a CAD program, must recognize and interface with the mouse. So mouse companies have developed software drivers that allow their mice to operate with various programs. The drivers are usually supplied on a disk. The Microsoft mouse is the de facto standard, and most other companies emulate the Microsoft driver.

Types of mice

There is no standardization in the types of mice. Some use optics with an LED that shines on a reflective grid. As the mouse is moved across the grid the reflected light is picked up by a detector and sent to the computer to move the cursor. For a design that demands very close tolerances, the spacings of the grid for an optical mouse might not provide sufficient resolution. You might be better off with a high-resolution mouse that utilizes a ball.

The ball-type mouse has a small, round rubber ball on the underside that contacts the desktop. As the mouse is moved, the ball turns. Inside the mouse, two flywheels contact the ball, one for horizontal and one for vertical movements. You don't need a grid for the ball-type mouse, but you do need about a square foot of clear desk space to move the mouse. The ball picks up dirt so it should be cleaned often.

Some of the less expensive mice have a resolution capability of only 100 to 200 dots per inch (DPI). Logitech has developed a high-resolution mouse that has a resolution of 320 DPI. Logitech includes several utilities and software programs with their mouse. Figure 10-2 shows some of them.

IMCS (805-239-8976) has developed a mouse in a pen-like configuration. Their mouse-pen has a barrel about 6 inches long and about ½ inch square. The foot of the pen has a small ball that functions exactly like a mouse, and it has two buttons on the barrel. It is moved just as if you are writing.

Number of buttons

The Macintosh mouse has only one button. That doesn't give you much choice except to point and click. Almost all of the PC mice have at least two buttons, giving the user three choices: (1) click the left button, (2) click the right button, or (3) click both buttons at the same time. Some mice have three control buttons. With three buttons the user has seven possible choices: (1) click left, (2) click middle, (3) click right, (4) click left and middle, (5) click middle and right, (6) click left and right, or (7) click all three. Despite all these choices, most software requires that only two of the buttons be used, one at a time.

Mouse interfaces

Most of the mice require a voltage, usually 5 volts. Some come with a small plug-in transformer that should be plugged into your power strip. Some let you insert an adapter between the keyboard cable connector and the motherboard connector.

Some mice require the use of one of your serial ports for their input to the computer. This might cause a problem if you already have devices such as a serial printer using COM1 and a modem using COM2. You might have to buy a board and use one of your

10-2   A Logitech bus mouse. Shown is the bus plug-in card, the mouse, and the five different manuals that come with the mouse.

plug-in slots to provide a serial interface for the COM ports. Some motherboards have ports built into the board.

Microsoft, Logitech, and several other mouse companies have developed a bus mouse. It interfaces directly with the bus and does not require the use of one of your COM ports, but the system comes with a board that requires the use of one of your slots. Most of the mouse systems come with several software packages and drivers that allow the mouse to be used with several programs.

Mouse cost

You can buy a fairly good mouse for $50 to $100. One factor in the cost is that some companies include options of software packages and other goodies with their products. Another cost factor is the resolution. Some have a resolution of only 100 DPI. The better ones have a resolution of 200 DPI up to 350 DPI. The higher resolution is necessary for some CAD programs and critical design work that requires close tolerances.

Some mouse systems are advertised for as little as $30. These would probably be perfectly acceptable for point-and-click work with icons. Of course, the higher-resolution systems are going to cost more. It is best to call the companies for their latest price list and spec sheets. There are many companies that manufacture mouse systems. Check the ads in the computer magazines listed in chapter 17.

Trackballs

A trackball is a mouse that has been turned upside down. Like the mouse, it must have a voltage from a transformer or some other source. It also requires a serial port, or a slot if it is of the bus type.

Instead of moving the mouse to move the ball, the ball is moved by your fingers. Trackballs are usually larger than the ball in a mouse, so it is possible to have better resolution. Trackballs usually do not require as much desk space as an ordinary mouse. If your desk is as cluttered as mine, then you definitely need a trackball.

There are several companies that manufacture trackballs. Look through the computer magazines for ads.

Keyboard/trackball combination

Amtac (718-392-1703), Chicony (714-771-6151), and several other companies have keyboards with a trackball built into the right-hand area. This gives you the mouse's benefits and capabilities without using up any desk space. The trackball is compatible with standard Microsoft and mouse systems.

I bought a Chicony keyboard with a trackball for $68. This is a real bargain when you consider that several other companies offer a stand-alone trackball that costs $75 or more. Several other companies make combination trackball/keyboard systems. Check the computer magazines for ads.

Digitizers and graphics tablets

Graphics tablets and digitizers are similar to a flat drawing pad or drafting table. Most of them use some sort of pointing device that can translate movement into digitized output. Some are rather small, while some are as large as a standard drafting table. They range in price from as little as $150 to over $1500. Most of them have a very high resolution, are very accurate, and are intended for precision drawing. Some of the tablets have programmable overlays and function keys. Some work with a mouse-like device, a penlight, or a pencil-like stylus. The tablets can be used for designing circuits, CAD programs, graphics designs, freehand drawing, and even for text and data input. The most common use is with CAD-type software.

Most of the tablets are serial devices, but some of them require their own interface board. Many of them are compatible with the Microsoft and other mouse systems. Figure 10-3 shows the CalComp Wiz. The Wiz is a low-cost combination digitizer and mouse. Contact CalComp at (602) 948-6540.

Scanners and optical character readers

Most large companies have mountains of memos, manuals, documents, and files that must be maintained, revised, and updated periodically. If a document is bound, the whole manual

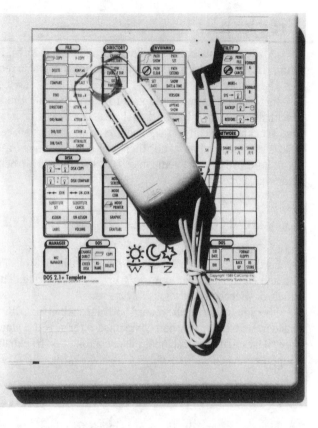

10-3   The CalComp Wiz, a combination mouse and digitizer.

or document might have to be retyped and reissued. If a manual or document is in a loose-leaf form, then only those pages that have changed need to be retyped.

Several companies now manufacture optical character readers (OCRs) that can scan a line of printed type, recognize each character, and input each character into a computer just as if it were typed in from a keyboard. Once the data is in the computer, a word processor can be used to revise or change the data and print it out again. Or the printed data can be entered into a computer and stored on floppies or a hard disk. If copies of the printed matter are stored in a computer it can be searched very quickly for any item. Many times I have spent hours going through printed manuals looking for certain items. If the data had been in a computer, I could have found the information in just minutes.

Optical character readers have been around for several years. When they first came out they cost from $6000 to more than $15,000. They were very limited in the fonts that they could recognize and they were unable to handle graphics at all. But vast improvements have been made in the last few years. Many full-page scanners are now fairly inexpensive, starting at about $650. Some hand-held scanners, which are rather limited, cost as little as $200. For $375, I bought a good hand-held scanner from Caere Corporation (408-395-7000). The more expensive models usually have the ability to recognize a large number of fonts and graphics.

Houston Instruments specializes in manufacturing plotters. They have developed a scanning head for one of their plotters that can scan a large drawing, digitize the lines and symbols, and input them to a computer. The drawing can then be changed and replotted very easily.

There are many manufacturers of input devices. Look in any of the computer magazines listed in chapter 17. You will see many ads for all types of keyboards, scanners, mice, and other input devices. Some of the magazines, such as *PC Sources* and *Computer Shopper,* have a separate product listing in the back pages. It is a great help. However, they list only those products that are advertised for that month in their magazine. Of course there are many good products from companies that can't afford the high cost of magazine ads.

Computers and devices for the handicapped

Several computer devices have been developed that can help the disabled person live a better life. There are devices that allow the blind, the deaf, the quadriplegic, and other severely disabled people to communicate. There are special braille keyboards and keyboards with enlarged keys for the blind. The EyeTyper from Sentient Systems Technology has an embedded camera in the keyboard that can determine which key the user is looking at. It then enters that key into the computer. Words Plus has a sensitive visor that can understand input from a raised brow, head movement, or eye blinks. Speaking Devices Corporation (408-727-5571) has a telephone that can be trained to recognize an individual's voice. It can then dial up to 100 different numbers when the person tells it to. The same company has a tiny earphone that also acts as a microphone. These devices are ideal for a person who can speak, but cannot use their hands.

Devices for the disabled allow many people to lead active, useful, and productive lives. They have become artists, programmers, writers, and scientists. These communication devices have allowed them a bit of freedom from the harsh prison of their disabilities.

Several organizations can help in locating special equipment and lending support. If you know someone who might benefit from the latest technology and devices for the handicapped, contact these organizations:

- AbleData   (800) 344-5405
- Accent on Information   (309) 378-2961
- Apple Computer   (408) 996-1010
- Closing the Gap, Inc.   (612) 248-3294
- Direct Link for the Disabled   (805) 688-1603
- Easter Seals Systems Office   (312) 667-8626
- IBM National Support Center   (800) 426-2133
- American Foundation for the Blind   (212) 620-2000
- Trace Research and Development Center   (608) 262-6966
- National ALS Association   (818) 340-7500

Get a tax deduction

Now that you have assembled a new 486, you might be retiring an older computer. You could probably advertise and sell it, but that might be more trouble than it is worth. It might be worth more to you to give it away to an organization like one of those listed above or any legitimate charitable organization. You can then deduct the reasonable value from your income tax. Any of these organizations will be most happy to get anything that you can give them.

11
Telecommunications

About 70 million computers are installed in homes, offices, and businesses. About 35 million of them have a modem or some sort of communications capability. A *modem* is an electronic device that allows a computer to use an ordinary telephone line to communicate with other computers that are equipped with a modem. Modem is a contraction of the words *modulate* and *demodulate.* The telephone system is analog, while computer data is usually digital. The modem modulates the digital data from a computer and turns it into analog voltages for transmission. At the receiving end, another modem demodulates the analog voltage back into a digital form.

A person can use a telephone to communicate with any one of several million persons anywhere in the world. Likewise, a computer with telecommunications capabilities can communicate with several million other computers in the world. With a modem, your computer can access over 10,000 bulletin boards in the United States. You can take advantage of electronic mail, faxes, up-to-the-minute stock market quotations, and a large number of other on-line services such as home shopping, travel agencies, and many other data services and databases.

Why modems are not being utilized

There are many excellent user-friendly software programs and hardware components that almost anyone can learn to use. But as Peter Norton pointed out in his foreword to *Dvorak's Guide to PC Telecommunications,* many people seem to have a "telecommunications phobia." Of the 35 million computers with telecommunication capability, less than 2 million are being fully utilized. That is a terrible waste of resources.

Believe me, I can understand why a person might have a fear such as this. Years ago when I bought my first modem, I can vividly recall trying to transmit an article to an editor. I tried for some time but could not connect to the editor's modem. With older systems, both modems had to be set to use the same protocols. I couldn't find the right combination. I finally gave up and drove 50 miles to hand deliver the article. I felt frustrated and dumb. It was sometime before I used the modem again. If you are one of those persons with a telecommunications phobia, maybe I can help you.

CCITT recommended standards

The communications industry is very complex and there are not many real standards. There are many different manufacturers and software developers. Of course, all of them want to differentiate their hardware or software by adding new features.

A United Nations standards committee has helped to establish some standards. It is called the Comite Consulatif Internal de Telegraphique et Telephone (CCITT). This committee has representatives from over 80 countries and several large private manufacturers. The committee makes recommendations only. A company is free to use or ignore them, but more and more companies are now adopting the recommendations.

All CCITT recommendations for small computers have a V or X prefix. The V series is for use with switched telephone networks, which is almost all of them. The X series is for systems that do not use switched phone lines. Revisions or alternate recommendations have bis (second) or ter (third) added. Here are a few CCITT recommendations:

- **V.22** — a 1200 baud standard.
- **V.22 bis** — a 2400 baud standard.
- **V.32** — a 9600 baud standard.
- **V.42** — an error-correcting protocol. It includes MNP-4 and LAP M error correction.
- **V.42 bis** — a standard for 4:1 data compression. Under ideal conditions, this standard can permit data transmission speeds four times greater than the rated baud rate. With this much compression a 14,400-bps (bits per second) modem can transmit at 57,600 bps.
- **X.25** — a protocol for packet mode communications on data networks such as Telenet and Tymnet.
- **MNP** — Microcom networking protocol. A series of 10 different protocols developed by the Microcom company. Several of the protocols are very similar to the CCITT V series.
- **LAP M and LAP B** — other protocols that are supported by AT&T and Hayes. They are similar to the CCITT V.42 error-correcting standard.

Protocols

Protocols are procedures that have been established for exchanging data, along with the instructions that coordinate the process. Most protocols can sense when the data is corrupted or lost due to noise, static, or a bad connection, and will automatically resend the affected data until it is received correctly.

There are several protocols, but the most popular ones are Kermit (named for Kermit the frog), Xmodem, and Ymodem. These protocols transmit a block of data along with an error-checking code, then wait for the receiver to send back an acknowledgement.

They then send another block and wait to see if it got through okay. If a block does not get through, it is resent immediately. Protocols such as Zmodem and HyperProtocol send a whole file in a continuous stream of data with error-checking codes inserted at certain intervals. They then wait for confirmation of a successful transmission. If the transmission is unsuccessful, then the whole file must be resent. The sending and receiving modems should both use the same protocol.

Baud rate

Telephone systems were originally designed for voice and have a very narrow bandwidth. They are subject to noise, static, and other electrical disturbances. These problems, and the state of technology at the time, limited the original modems to about 5 characters per second (cps), or a rate of 50 baud.

The term baud comes from Emile Baudot (1845–1903), a French inventor. Originally, the baud rate was a measure of the dots and dashes in telegraphy. It is now defined as the actual rate of symbols transmitted per second. For the lower baud rates, it is essentially the same as bits per second. Remember that it takes eight bits to make a character. Just as we have periods and spaces to separate words, we must use one start bit and two stop bits to separate the on/off bits into characters. A transmission of 300 baud means that 300 on/off bits are sent in 1 second. Counting the start/stop bits, it takes 11 bits for each character, or 300/11 = 27 cps. Some of the newer technologies might actually transmit symbols that represent more than one bit. For baud rates of 1200 and higher, the cps and baud rate can be considerably different.

There have been some fantastic advances in modem technology. A couple of years ago, the 2400 baud system was the standard. Today they are practically obsolete. The industry has leaped over the 4800 and 9600 baud systems to the 14.4K systems. These units also incorporate the V.42 bis standard. This allows them to use 4:1 data compression and thus they can transmit at 57.6K bps.

When communicating with another modem both the sending and receiving unit must operate at the same baud rate and use the same protocols. Most of the faster modems are downward compatible and can operate at slower speeds. Ordinarily, the higher the baud rate, the less time it takes to download or transmit a file. (This might not always be the case, because at higher speeds, more transmission errors might be encountered. In cases of errors, parts of the file, or the whole file, might have to be retransmitted.) If the file is being sent over a long-distance line, the length of telephone connect time can be costly. If your modem is used frequently your telephone bills could be very substantial, especially if you have a slow modem.

How to estimate connect time

You can estimate the approximate length of time that it will take to transmit a file. For rough approximations of cps you can divide the baud rate by 10. For instance, 1200 baud would be 120 cps; 2400 baud would be 240 cps. Look at the directory and determine the number of bytes in the file. Divide the number of bytes in the file by the cps. You then multiply that figure by 1.3 for the start/stop bits to get a final approximation. For instance, with a 1200 baud modem, to figure the time for a 40K file, divide 40K by 120 cps to get 333 seconds times 1.3 equals about 433 seconds or 7.2 minutes.

If you transmitted the same 40K file with a 2400 baud modem, it would be 40,000/ 240 = 167 × 1.3 = 217 seconds or 3.6 minutes. With a 9600 baud modem, the same 40K file could be sent in about 55 seconds. Considering the telephone rates for long distance, it might be worthwhile to spend a bit more to get a high-speed modem.

Besides the phone line charges you have to pay, the major on-line service companies such as CompuServe, Dataquest, and Dow Jones News/Retrieval charge for connect time to their service. The connect time is much less with some of the high-speed modems. But in order to keep their revenue up, some companies charge more for the higher speed modems.

Sources

I have not listed the names and manufacturers of modems because there are so many. Look in any computer magazine and you will see dozens of ads. Most of them are fairly close in quality and function.

One company that I do want to mention is USRobotics. It manufactures a large variety of modems, especially the high-end high-speed type. Call (800) 342-5877 for a free 110-page booklet that explains all you need to know about modems.

Communications software

In order to use a modem, it must be driven and controlled by software. Dozens of communications programs can be used. One of the better ones is Relay Silver from VM Personal Computing, (203) 798-3800. It also publishes Relay Gold, one of the most versatile of the high-end communications software packages. It has features that allow remote communications, accessing of mainframes, and dozens of utilities not found on the usual communications programs.

Crosstalk, (404) 998-3998, was one of the earlier modem programs. It now comes in a Windows version. It works with any Windows version which makes it very easy to learn and use. ProComm, (314) 474-8461, is one of several low-cost shareware programs. In many areas it outperforms some of the high-cost commercial programs. The registration cost is $89. Qmodem, (319) 232-4516, is another excellent shareware program with a registration cost of only $30. You can get copies of shareware programs from bulletin boards or from any of the companies that provide public domain software. Shareware is not free. You can try it out and use it, but the developers usually ask that you register the program and send in a nominal sum. For this low cost you will usually get a manual and some support.

Besides using a faster baud rate, another way to reduce phone charges is to use file compression. Bulletin boards have been using a form of data compression for years. There are several public domain programs that squeeze and unsqueeze data. The newer modems take advantage of V.42 bis 4:1 compression.

Basic types of modems

There are two basic types of modems: the external desktop and the internal. Each type has some advantages and disadvantages.

The external type requires some of your precious desk space and a voltage source. It also requires a COM port to drive it. The good news is that most external models have LEDs that light up and let you know what is happening during your call. Both the external and internal models have speakers that let you hear the phone ringing or if you get a busy signal. Some of the external models have a volume control for the built-in speaker.

The internal modem is built entirely on a board, usually a half or short board. The good news is that it doesn't use up any of your desk space, but the bad news is that it uses one of your precious slots. And it does not have the LEDs to let you know the progress of your call. Even if you use an external modem, if your motherboard does not have built-in COM ports, you will need an I/O board that will require the use of one of your slots.

Hayes compatibility

One of the most popular early modems was made by Hayes Microcomputer Products. They have become the IBM of the modem world and have established a de facto standard. There are hundreds of modem manufacturers. Except for some of the very inexpensive ones, almost all of them emulate the Hayes standard.

Installing a modem

If you are adding a modem on a board to a system that is already assembled, the first thing to do is remove the computer cover. Then find an empty slot and plug it in. The board will have jumpers or small switches that must be set to enable COM1 or COM2. If you have an I/O board in your system with external COM ports, or built-in COM ports on your motherboard, you must configure them for whichever port will be used for the modem.

If you are installing an external modem, you must go through the same procedure to make sure the COM port is accessible and does not conflict. If you have a mouse, a serial printer, or some other serial device, you will have to determine which port they are set to. You cannot have two serial devices set to the same COM port.

Often it is difficult to determine which COM port is being used by a device. You can use the AT command to determine if your modem is working. At the DOS prompt C:>, type the following using uppercase: ECHO AT DT12345>COM1:. If the modem is set properly, you will hear a dial tone, then the modem will dial 12345. If two devices are set for COM1 there will be a conflict. The computer will try for a while, then give an error message and the familiar, "Abort, Retry, Ignore, Fail?" A diagnostic program such as Check-It, from TouchStone, (714) 969-7746, can determine which ports are being used. It also does several other very helpful diagnostic tests. Port Finder from Netronic Systems; (713) 462-7687, is an excellent low-cost shareware program.

Plug in the modem board and hook it up to the telephone line. Unless you expect to do a lot of communicating, you don't need a separate dedicated line. The modem might have an automatic answer mode. In this mode it will always answer the telephone. Unless you have a dedicated line, this mode should be disabled. Check your documentation. There should be a switch or some means to disable it. Having your modem and telephone on the same line should cause no problems unless someone tries to use the telephone while the modem is using it.

There should be two connectors at the back of the board. One is labeled for the line in and the other for the telephone. Unless you have a dedicated telephone line, you should unplug your telephone, plug in the extension to the modem and line, and plug the telephone into the modem. If your computer is not near your telephone line, you might have to go to a hardware store and buy a telephone extension line.

After you have connected all of the lines, turn on your computer and try the modem before you put the cover back on. Make sure you have software. Call a local bulletin board. Even if you can't get through, or have a wrong number, you should hear the dial tone and hear it dial the number.

An external modem is connected to one of the COM ports with a cable. If you did not get a cable with your unit, you will have to buy one. If you have built-in COM ports, the cable will cost about $5. If you have to use the bus to access the ports, you will need a cable and an I/O board with serial ports.

Bulletin boards

If you have a modem, you have access to several thousand computer bulletin boards. There are over 100 in the San Francisco area and about twice that many in the Los Angeles area. Many of them are free. You only have to pay the phone bill if they are out of your calling area. But some of them charge a nominal fee to join, and some just ask for a tax deductible donation.

Some of the bulletin boards are set up by private individuals and some by companies and vendors as a service to their customers. Some are set up by user groups and other special interest organizations. There are over 100 boards nationwide that have been set up for doctors and lawyers. There is even a gay bulletin board in the San Francisco area. There are also X-rated boards and several for dating.

Most of the bulletin boards are set up to help individuals. They usually have lots of public domain software and a space where you can leave messages for help, for advertising something for sale, or for just plain old chit-chat. If you are just getting started you probably need some software. There are public domain software packages that are equivalent to almost all of the major commercial programs, and the best part is that they are free.

Viruses

A few individuals have hidden "viruses" in some public-domain and even in some commercial software. The software might appear to work as it should for a time, but eventually it contaminates or destroys many of your files. The viruses often cause the files to become larger.

Most bulletin boards also have public-domain software to check for viruses. One of the better virus detectors is the McAfee ShareWare Scan program. It is available for downloading from the BBS at (408) 988-4004. If you download bulletin board software, check it with a virus software. It is best not to install unknown software on your hard disk. Run it from a floppy disk until you are sure it is not sick.

Illegal activities

Some of the bulletin boards have been used for illegal and criminal activities. Stolen credit card numbers and telephone charge numbers have been left on the bulletin boards. Because of this, many of the bulletin board sysops (system operators) are now carefully checking any software that is uploaded onto their systems. Many of them are now restricting access to their boards. Some of them have had to start charging a fee because of the extra time it takes to monitor the boards.

Where to find the bulletin boards

Several computer magazines devote a lot of space to bulletin boards and user groups. In California, *MicroTimes* and *Computer Currents* have several pages of bulletin boards and user groups each month. *Computer Shopper* has the most comprehensive listing of bulletin boards and user groups of any national magazine. *Computer Shopper* alternates each month, with a listing of user groups one month and bulletin boards the next.

If you don't have a copy of *Computer Shopper*, you can call Allen Bechtold of the BBS Press Service at (913) 478-3157. He can arrange to have a copy of the bulletin boards and user groups listings sent to you.

CD-ROM

New information is being published and disseminated at an ever-increasing rate. We are being inundated in a flood of information that makes Noah's flood seem like an April shower. I subscribe to over 50 computer magazines, and I have a difficult time just trying to keep up.

I have recently subscribed to the Ziff-Davis *Computer Library* on CD-ROM (212-503-3500). Subscribers get a new CD-ROM disk filled with articles from over 140 magazines. One big advantage to having the articles on CD-ROM is that I can search for items that are of interest very quickly. I can also cut and paste items into another file on my hard disk. The subscription is rather expensive at over $700.

Several other vendors provide hundreds of educational and scientific programs, data, and information on CD-ROM disks. One is the Bureau of Electronic Publishing at (201) 808-2700. Several companies sell public domain software on CD-ROM. One is PC-SIG (800-245-6717); another is the Alde Publishing Company (612) 835-5240. A CD-ROM might contain over 3000 different programs, just about everything that you would ever need.

CD-ROM drives are now very reasonable and cost from $250 to $500. There are external types that sit on your desk and internal types that can be installed in a standard half-height bay.

On-line services

There are several large national bulletin board, information, and reference services, such as CompuServe, Dataquest, Dow Jones, and Dialog. These companies have huge databases of information. A caller can search the databases and download information as easily as pulling the data off his own hard disk. The companies charge a fee for the connect time.

Prodigy is unlike the other on-line services. Prodigy does not charge for connect time. It charges only a very nominal monthly rate. It has phone service to most areas, so there is not even a toll charge. Prodigy has an impressive list of services, including home shopping, home banking, airline schedules and reservations, and stock market quotations, among others. In San Francisco, you can even order your groceries through Prodigy and have them delivered to your door. It is a real bargain. One of its faults is that it is relatively slow, but because it is so inexpensive, I can live with it. Contact Prodigy at (800) 759-8000.

E-mail

Many of the national bulletin boards offer electronic mail (E-mail) along with their other services. These services can be of great value to some individuals and businesses.

E-mail subscribers are usually given a "post office box," usually a file on one of the large hard disk systems. When a message is received, it is recorded in this file. The next time the subscriber logs on to the service, he or she is alerted that there is "mail" in the box.

E-mail is becoming more popular every day and there are now several hundred thousand subscribers. The cost for an average message is about $1. The cost for overnight mail from the U.S. Post Office, Federal Express, and UPS is $11 to $13.

Some of the companies that provide E-mail at the present time include

- AT&T Mail   (800) 367-7225
- CompuServe   (800) 848-8990
- DASnet   (408) 559-7434
- MCI Mail   (800) 444-6245
- Western Union   (800) 527-5184

LAN E-mail

Most of the larger LAN programs also provide an E-mail utility in their software. For those packages that do not provide this utility, programs that work with installed LANs are available.

The CCITT has recommended that X.400 be the standard for LAN E-mail. This standard provides the gateway to installed LANs. Another gateway system supported by Novell and Lotus is the message handling system (MHS). Some of the companies that provide LAN E-mail include

- Action Technologies   (800) 624-2162
- Inbox Plus   (415) 769-9669
- Lotus Express   (800) 345-1043

- MS-Mail   (206) 882-8080
- PCC Systems   (415) 321-0430
- Quickmail   (515) 224-1995

Banking by modem

Many banks offer systems that let you do all your banking with your computer and a modem from the comforts of your home. You will never again have to drive downtown, hunt for a parking space, and stand in line for a half hour to do your banking.

Telephone technology advances

There have been some advances in telephone technology. A box can be attached to your telephone that will display the number of the caller. If you know the number of someone you don't want to talk to, you can look at the displayed number and choose whether to answer the phone or not. Certain numbers can be excluded so that the phone will not ring. Because the caller's number is displayed by this box, it should help to reduce computerized, unwanted, and obscene calls. It will also be an enormous help to police and fire departments, and to pizza and fast-food delivery stores.

Some people have objected to the caller ID system. A court in Pennsylvania has declared it unconstitutional on the grounds that it is an invasion of privacy. It is difficult to understand the judge's ruling. How is it violating a person's rights if you want to know who is calling before you answer? Phonevision is another new technology that will soon be in all homes.

ISDN

ISDN is an acronym for integrated services digital network. Eventually the whole world will have telephone systems that use this concept. It is a system that transmits voice, data, video, and graphics in digital form rather than the present analog form. When this happens, we can scrap our modems. We will then need only a simple interface to communicate. ISDN is already installed in several cities. But don't throw your modem away just yet. The new service will be rather expensive and might not be available at all locations for some time.

Facsimile boards and machines

Facsimile (fax) machines have been around for quite a while. Newspapers and businesses have used them for years. The early machines were similar to the early acoustic modems. Both used foam rubber cups that fit over the telephone receiver and mouthpiece for coupling. They were very slow and subject to noise and interference. Fax machines and modems have come a long way since those early days.

Modems and facsimile machines are quite similar and are related in many respects. A modem sends and receives bits of data. A fax machine or board usually sends and receives scanned whole-page letters, images, signatures, etc. A computer program can be sent over a modem, but not over a fax. A fax sends and receives the information as digitized data. A page of text or a photo is fed into the facsimile machine and scanned. As the scanning beam moves across the page, white and dark areas are digitized as 1s and 0s, which are transmitted over the telephone lines. A modem converts the digital information that represents characters into analog voltages, sends it over the line, and converts it back to digital information.

There are millions of facsimile machines in use today. They can be used to send documents, handwriting, signatures, seals, letterheads, graphs, blueprints, photos, and other types of data around the world, across the country, or across the room to another fax machine.

I mentioned earlier that it costs $11 to $13 to send an overnight letter, but that E-mail only costs about $1. A fax machine can deliver the same letter for about $.40 and do it in less than 3 minutes. Depending on the type of business and the amount of mail that must be sent out, a fax system can pay for itself in a very short time.

Stand-alone fax units

There are still several facsimile machines that are stand-alone devices that attach to a telephone. They have been vastly improved in the last few years. Most of them are as easy to use as a copy machine. In fact most of them can be used as a copy machine. Some overseas companies are making stand-alone units that are fairly inexpensive, some for as little as $400. You might not be happy with a low-cost unit. You are better off to spend a bit more and get one with a paper cutter, high resolution, a voice/data switch on the system, a document feeder, automatic dialer, automatic retry, delayed transmission, transmission confirmation, polling, built-in laser printer, and large memory. You might not need or be able to afford all of these features, but try to get a machine with as many as possible. Of course, the more features, the higher the cost.

Fax computer boards

Several companies have developed fax machines on circuit boards that can be plugged into computers. Many of the newer models have provisions for a modem on the same board. Follow the same procedure to install a fax board as outlined for installing an internal modem.

Special software allows the computer to control the fax boards. Using the computer's word processor, letters and memos can be written and sent out over the phone lines. Several letters or other information can be stored or retrieved from the computer hard disk and transmitted. The computer can even be programmed to send the letters out at night when the rates are lower.

But computer fax boards have one disadvantage. They cannot scan information unless a scanner is attached to the computer. Without a scanner the information that can be sent is usually limited to that which can be entered from a keyboard or disk. As we pointed out above, stand-alone units scan pages of information, including such things as handwriting, signatures, images, blueprints, and photos. However, the computer can receive and store any fax that is sent. The digitized data and images can be stored on a hard disk and printed on a printer.

Hundreds of companies manufacture fax boards and products. Look for ads in the computer magazines.

Scanners

Scanners were discussed briefly in chapter 10. They are not absolutely essential to the operation of a PC-based fax, but there might be times when it is necessary to transmit photographs, blueprints, documents, or handwritten signatures on contracts, and a host of other things. A scanner is needed to get the most utility from a fax. In any business that does a lot of communicating, a good fax and modem system will pay for itself in a very short time.

Installing a fax board

Most fax boards are very easy to install and easy to operate. If your computer is already assembled, just remove the five screws that hold the cover on. Check your documentation and set any switches that are necessary. Plug the board into an empty slot. Replace the computer cover and connect the telephone line. You should have received some software to control the fax. This should be installed on your hard disk and you should be up and ready to send and receive faxes.

If you use a word processing program, such as WordStar, to create letters or text for a fax transmission, the text must be changed into an ASCII file before it can be sent. Most word processors have this capability.

Telecommuting

One reason I took early retirement from my job at Lockheed was because I hated being stuck in traffic. Of course, another reason was that my books were selling well.

Millions of people risk their lives and fight traffic every day. Many of these people have jobs that could allow them to stay home, work on a computer, and send the data to the office over a modem or a fax. Even if the person had to buy a computer, modem, and fax, it still might be worth it. You could save the cost of gasoline and auto maintenance, as well as lower your insurance. Being able to work at home is ideal for those who have young children, for the handicapped, or for anyone who hates traffic.

12
Monitors

The monitor is your primary link to your computer. Most of the time you spend working on a computer will be spent looking at the monitor. You can buy a monochrome monitor for as little as $65. But life is so very short, and it can be a lot more enjoyable if you have a good high-resolution color monitor. Even if you do nothing but word processing, color makes the job a lot easier and more pleasant. But alas, like so many other things in life, the better the color and the higher the resolution, the higher the cost. Also the larger the screen, the higher the cost.

There have been several improvements in the design and development of monitor electronics. New chip sets and VLSI chips have helped reduce manufacturing costs. But there is not much that can be done to reduce the cost of manufacture of the main component, the cathode-ray tube (CRT). A good color CRT requires a tremendous amount of labor-intensive, precision work. The larger the screen, the more costly it is to manufacture.

We are very fortunate in that there are many manufacturers. They make many, many different types, sizes, and kinds of monitors. This helps to keep the prices fairly reasonable.

Many available options

Because there are so many types of monitors and so many options, you have some difficult decisions to make when you buy your system. You have a wide choice as to price, resolution, color, size, and shape. You can buy a 12-inch monochrome monitor for as little as $65. But unless I absolutely could not afford anything else, I wouldn't even consider a monochrome, CGA, or EGA monitor. VGA and Super VGA monitors cost from $200 to $5000 depending on such things as size, resolution, scan rate, bandwidth, brand, and adapter chosen.

The monitor is a very important part of your system, and it can represent a large percentage of the cost of your system. You should make sure that you get the best that you can afford. If you are buying by mail, or even at a store, try to get a copy of the manufacturer's specifications and study them. Look at the ads in magazines like *Computer Shopper, Computer Buyer's Guide,* and others to get an idea of the cost of different monitors. But be aware that ads cost a lot of money, so a lot of good information is sometimes left out. Ask questions.

Monitors are usually long-lived. I have an early NEC Multiscan model that is more than 5 years old. I have gone through several computers and hard disks, but this monitor is still going strong.

What to buy if you can afford it

Buy the biggest and best multisync color Super VGA that you can afford. A 14-inch NEC 2A costs about $400 and has 800 × 600 resolution. An adapter to drive it can cost from $100 to $1000. You can buy off-brand monitors and adapters for a little less. You need a good adapter to drive the monitor if you want good color. Figure 12-1 shows an unusual adapter that can be used by ISA or MCA. Figure 12-2 shows a good high-resolution monitor from Princeton.

If you decide to buy an off-brand system, you should try to check it out first. Check for dot pitch, multiscanning, bandwidth, controls, noninterlacing, special drivers, glare, swivel, cables, and connectors. Get the vendor spec sheets and read them carefully.

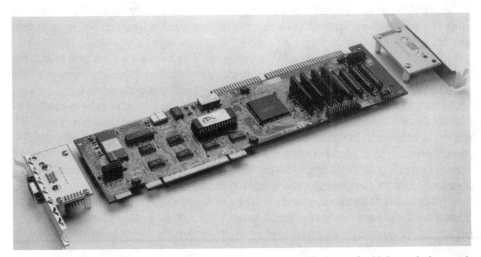

12-1 The 8514/Ultra from ATI Technologies. A very unusual adapter for high-resolution monitors. It has a connector on one side for the IBM PS/2 MCA system. It also has a connector on the other side so that it can be used in the standard AT- or ISA-type system.

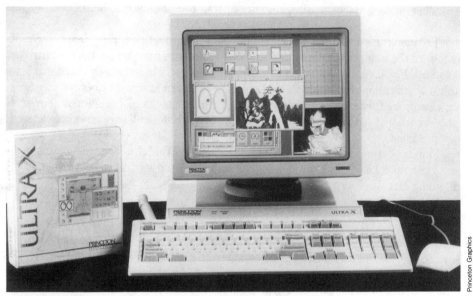

Princeton Graphics

12-2 The Ultra X, a high-resolution monitor from Princeton Graphics.

Monitor basics

A few monitor specifications, terms, and acronyms are discussed below. If you know the basics you can make a more informed decision as to which monitor to buy.

In IBM language, a monitor is a display device. This is probably a better term, because the word *monitor* is from the Latin meaning *to warn*. But despite IBM, most people still call it a monitor.

Basically a monitor is similar to a television set. The face of a TV set or a monitor is the end of a CRT. These are vacuum tubes and they have many of the same elements that made up the old vacuum tubes that were used before the advent of the semiconductor age. CRTs have a filament that boils off a stream of electrons. These electrons have a potential of about 25,000 volts. They are "shot" from an electron gun toward the front of the CRT where they slam into the phosphor on the back of the screen, causing it to light up. Depending on the type of phosphor used, once the pixels are lit up, they continue to glow for a period of time. The electron beam moves rapidly across the screen, but because the phosphor continues to glow, we see the images that are created.

When you watch a movie, you are seeing a series of still photos flashed one after the other. Due to our persistence of vision, it appears to be continuous motion. It is this same persistence of vision that allows us to see motion and images on our television and video screens.

In a magnetic field, a beam of electrons reacts very much like iron. Like iron, a beam of electrons can be attracted or repelled by the polarity of a magnet. In a CRT, a beam of electrons must pass between a system of electromagnets before it reaches the back of the CRT face. In a basic system there is an electromagnet on the left, one on the right, one at the top, and one at the bottom. Voltage through the electromagnets can be varied, causing the magnetic force to be greater or less. The beam of electrons is repulsed by one side and attracted by the other, or pulled to the top or forced to the bottom. With this electromagnetic system, a beam of electrons can be bent and directed to any spot on the screen. It is much like holding a hose and directing a high-pressure stream of water.

Scan rates

When you look at the screen of a TV set or a monitor, you see a full screen only because of the persistence of vision and the type of phosphor used on the back of the screen. Actually, the beam of electrons starts at the top left corner of the screen, and under the influence of the electromagnets, it is pulled across to the right top corner, lighting up the pixels as it sweeps across. It is then returned to the left side, dropped down one line, and swept across again. On a TV set, this is repeated so that 525 lines are written on the screen in about 1/30 of a second. This is one frame, so 30 frames are written to the screen in 1 second.

The time that it takes to fill a screen with lines from top to bottom is the vertical scan rate. Some of the newer multiscan, or multifrequency, monitors can have variable vertical scan rates from 1/40 to 1/100 of a second.

The horizontal scanning frequency of a standard TV set is 15.75 kHz. This is also the frequency used by CGA systems. The horizontal scanning frequency used by EGA systems is about 22 kHz, while that used by VGA systems is 31.5 kHz and up. The higher resolutions require higher frequencies. Multiscan monitors can vary from 15.5 kHz up to 100 kHz.

Controlling the beam

The CRT has control grids, much like the old vacuum tubes, for controlling the signal. When an image is scanned, light areas cause a small voltage to be generated, while dark areas cause no voltage change. If these on/off voltages are fed to the control grid of the CRT it causes the beam of electrons to turn on and off as it is swept across the back of the screen. As the electrons pass through the electromagnetic system, the electron beam is pulled up and down or from side to side. The beam can be made to light up the screen to make a copy of the input signal.

Resolution

If you look closely at a black-and-white photo in the newspaper, you can see that the photo is made up of small dots. There are a lot of dots in the darker areas and fewer dots in the light areas. The text or image on a monitor or television screen is also made up of dots very similar to a newspaper photo. You can easily see these dots with a magnifying glass. If you look closely you can see spaces between the dots. These are much like the dots of a dot matrix printer. The more dots and the closer together they are, the better the resolution. A good high-resolution monitor has solid, sharply defined characters and images.

An ideal resolution would look very much like a high-quality photograph, but it will be some time before we reach the resolution of film.

Pixels

Resolution is also determined by the number of picture elements (pixels) that can be displayed. The following figures relate primarily to text, but graphics resolution is similar to text. A standard color graphics monitor (CGA) can display 640 × 200 pixels. It can display 80 characters in one line with 25 lines from top to bottom. If you divide 640 by 80 you find that one character is 8 pixels wide. There can be 25 lines of characters, so 200 ÷ 25 = 8 pixels high. The entire screen has 640 × 200 = 128,000 pixels.

Most monitor adapters have text character generators built onto the board. When you send an A to the screen, the adapter goes to its library and sends the signal for the A to the screen. Each character occupies a cell made up of a number of pixels depending on the resolution of the screen and the adapter. In the case of the CGA monitor, if all the dots within a cell were lit up, there would be a solid block of dots 8 pixels (or dots) wide and 8 pixels high. When the A is placed in a cell, only the dots necessary to form an outline of an A are lit up. It is very similar to the dots formed by a dot matrix printer when it prints a character.

A graphics adapter, along with the proper software, allows you to place lines, images, photos, normal and various text fonts, and almost anything you can imagine on the screen. An enhanced graphics system (EGA) can display 640 × 350, or 640/80 = 8 pixels wide and 350/25 = 14 pixels high. The screen can display 640 × 350 = 224,000 pixels. Enhanced EGA and VGA systems can display 640 × 480 = 307,200 pixels; each character is 8 pixels wide and 19 pixels high.

The Video Electronics Standards Association (VESA) has chosen 800 × 600 to be the Super VGA standard, which is 800/80 = 10 pixels wide and 600/25 = 24 pixels high. Many of the newer systems are now capable of 1024 × 768, 1280 × 1024, 1664 × 1200, and more. With a resolution of 1664 × 1200, you have 1,996,800 pixels that can be lit up. We have come a long way from the 128,000 pixels possible with CGA systems.

Interlaced versus noninterlaced

For CGAs the horizontal system sweeps the electron beam across the screen from top to bottom 200 times in 1/60 of a second to make one frame, or 60 frames in 1 second. For VGAs it sweeps from top to bottom 480 times in 1/60 of a second. For Super VGAs it sweeps 600 times, and for 1024 × 768 it sweeps 768 times in 1/60 of a second. As you can see, the higher the resolution, the more lines, the closer they are together, and the faster they have to be painted on the screen. Higher resolution also causes the electron beam to light up more pixels on each line as it sweeps across.

The higher horizontal frequencies demand more precise and higher-quality electronics, which of course, requires higher costs to manufacture. To avoid this higher cost, IBM designed some of its VGA systems with an interlaced horizontal system. Instead of increasing the horizontal frequency, the system paints every other line across the screen from top to bottom, then returns to the top and paints the lines that were skipped. Theoretically, this sounds like a great idea. But it doesn't work too well because it causes a flicker that can be very irritating to some people who have to work with this type of monitor for very long. This flicker is not readily apparent, but some people have complained of eyestrain, headaches, and fatigue after prolonged use of an interlaced monitor.

If the monitor is only used for short periods of time, then the interlaced type is probably okay.

Some companies make models that use interlacing in some modes and noninterlacing in other modes. Most companies don't advertise the fact that their monitors use interlacing. The interlace models are usually a bit lower in price than the noninterlaced models. You might have to ask the vendor what system is used. If you get a chance, compare the interlaced and noninterlaced models. You might not be able to tell the difference. If cost is a prime consideration, the interlaced type is usually a bit less expensive.

The adapter that you buy should match your monitor. Use an interlaced adapter with an interlaced monitor. An adapter that can send only interlaced signals might not work with a noninterlaced monitor. Some of the high-end adapters are able to adjust and operate with both interlaced and noninterlaced monitors.

Drivers

Most of the software being developed today has built-in hooks that allow it to take advantage of the high-resolution goodies. Some vendors supply as many as two or three disks full of drivers. Depending on the software you intend to use, the drivers supplied with the adapter you purchase might be an important consideration.

Monochrome

A monochrome monitor has a single electron gun and a single color phosphor. It writes directly on the phosphor and can provide very high resolution for text and graphics. It is even possible to get monochrome analog VGAs that can display in as many as 64 different shades. Large monochrome monitors might be ideal for some desktop publishing (DTP) systems and even some CAD systems, but these large monochrome monitors can be almost as expensive as the equivalent-size color monitor.

Color graphics

Color TVs and color monitors are much more complicated than monochrome systems. During the manufacture of color monitors, three different phosphors — red, green, and blue — are deposited on the back of the screen. Usually a very small dot of each color is placed in a triangular shape. They have three electron guns, one for each color. By lighting up the three different colored phosphors selectively, all the colors of the rainbow can be generated.

The guns are called red, green, and blue (RGB), but the electrons they emit are all the same. They are called RGB because each gun is aimed so that it hits the red, the green, or the blue dots on the back of the monitor screen. These guns are very accurately aimed so that they will converge or impinge only on their assigned color.

Dot pitch

The distance from a dot of one color to the next dot of the same color is called the dot pitch. Dots per inch determines the resolution. A high-resolution monitor might have a dot pitch of 0.31 millimeter (mm). (1 mm = 0.0394 inches; 0.31 mm = 0.0122 inches, or about the thickness of an average business card.) A monitor with very high resolution might have a dot pitch of 0.26 mm or even less. The smaller the dot pitch, the more precise and more difficult the monitor is to manufacture. (Some Sony monitors use stripes instead of dots. Their specifications indicate stripe pitch, which might be about the same as the better dot pitch specs, or 0.25 mm to 0.31 mm.)

Some low-cost monitors have a dot pitch of 0.42 mm to as great as 0.52 mm. The 0.52-mm monitors might be suitable for playing some games, but it would be difficult to do any productive computing on such a system.

Adapter basics

It won't do you much good to buy a high-resolution monitor unless you buy a good adapter to drive it. You can't just plug a monitor into your computer and expect it to function. Just as a hard disk needs a controller, a monitor needs an adapter to interface with the computer. Also, like the hard disk manufacturers, many of the monitor manufacturers do not make adapter boards. Just as a hard disk can operate with several different types of controllers, most monitors can operate with several different types of adapters.

The original IBM PC came with a green monochrome monitor and a monochrome display adapter (MDA) that could display text only. The Hercules Company immediately saw the folly of this limitation. They developed the Hercules monographic adapter (HMGA) and set a new standard. It wasn't long before IBM and a lot of other companies were selling similar MGA cards that could display both graphics and text. These adapters provide a high resolution of 720 × 350 on monochrome monitors.

IBM then introduced its color monitor and CGA. It provides only 640 × 200 resolution. The CGA is a digital system that allows a mix of the red, green, and blue. The cable has four lines, one each for red, green, and blue, and one for intensity. This allows two different intensities for each color: on for bright or off for dim. So there are four objects, each of which can be in either of two states (2^4); therefore, CGAs have a limit of 16 colors. CGA monitors have very large spaces between the pixels so that the resolution and color are terrible. It is similar to the nine-pin dot matrix printer.

An EGA can drive a high-resolution monitor to display 640 × 350 resolution. The EGA system has six lines and allows each of the primary colors to be mixed together in any of four different intensities, so there are 2^6 (64) different colors that they can display.

Analog versus digital

Up until the introduction of the PS/2 with VGA, most displays used the digital system. But digital systems have severe limitations. Digital signals are of two states, either on or off. The signals for color and intensity require separate lines in the cables. As pointed out above, it takes six lines for an EGA to display 16 colors out of a palette of 64. Digital systems are obsolete.

The analog signals that drive the color guns are voltages that are continuously variable. It takes only a few lines for the three primary colors. The intensity voltage for each color can then be varied almost infinitely to create as many as 256 colors out of a possible 262,144. To display more than 256 colors requires a true color adapter.

Very high-resolution graphics adapters

Many of the high-resolution adapters have 1Mb or more of video RAM (VRAM) on board. VRAM chips are slightly different than DRAM chips. They have two ports and can be accessed by one port while being written to in the other. VRAM chips look very much like DRAM DIP chips, but they are not interchangeable with DRAM. Many adapter boards are sold with only 512K or less. They often have empty sockets for adding more memory. VRAM chips are rather inexpensive and are easy to install. Check your adapter board and add more memory if necessary.

A single complex graphics drawing might require 1Mb or more memory to store it. By having the memory on the adapter board, it saves having to go through the bus to the conventional RAM. Some adapter boards even have a separate plug-in daughterboard. Many of them have their own coprocessor on board, such as the Texas Instruments 34010 or the Hitachi HD63483.

Local bus adapters

Many of the true color adapters are special boards with an extra set of contacts on the board, similar to the MCA connector. At the present time, several manufacturers are developing local bus system motherboards. They add an extra slot on the motherboard for the special pure color adapters. If you expect to do a lot of graphics work with your computer, you might want to check out these systems. Depending on the resolution capabilities and the goodies that it has, a very high-resolution adapter board can cost from $200 to $3400.

True color

Most of the standard low-cost VGA cards are capable of only 16 colors. True color or pure color requires video boards with lots of fast memory, a coprocessor, and complex electronics. *True color* means that a video board can drive a monitor to display a large number of shades in separate, distinct hues, or pure colors. True color also means that the board will be expensive. A good adapter for true color can cost more than the monitor (see Table 12-1).

Table 12-1. Pure color

Bits	Shades	Depth
4 or 2^4	16	
8 or 2^8	256	
15 or 2^{15}	32,768	5:5:5
16 or 2^{16}	65,536	5:6:5 or 6:6:4
24 or 2^{32}	16.7 million	8:8:8

Depth

True color usually refers to displays with 15-, 16-, or 24-bit depths. Depth means that each of the individual red, green, or blue color pixels has a large amount of information about each color. The 15-bit system has 5 bits of information for each of the three colors. The 16-bit system might have 6 for red, 6 for green, and 4 for blue, or a combination of 5:6:5. The 24-bit system has 8 bits for each color.

Dithering

If a board doesn't have enough power to display true colors, it might use dithering to mix the colors to give an approximation. Dithering takes advantage of the eye's tendency to blur colors and view them as an average. A printed black-and-white photo uses all black dots, but several shades of gray can be printed depending on the number of black dots per inch. A mixture of red dots with white ones can create a pink image. Gradual color transitions can be accomplished by using dithering to intersperse pixels of various colors.

VGA-to-video adapters

Several companies have developed special VGAs that can transform VGA output to a television signal. This National Television Standards Committee (NTSC) signal can then be recorded on a VCR or displayed on a TV screen. These adapters can be used to create excellent presentations or computerized special effects.

The US Video Company, (203) 964-9000, has several adapters. Their TVGA card can drive a monitor up to 1024 × 768 pixels and also output NTSC signals. They also have several other cards for special effects. Other companies that have similar products are Jovian Logic at (415) 651-4823 and Willow Peripherals at (212) 402-0010.

Multiscan

The multiscan monitors can accept a wide range of vertical and horizontal frequencies. This makes them quite versatile and flexible. Most of the early multiscans could accept both digital and analog signals. If you had an older EGA or even a CGA card, it would work with it. Many of the new monitors will only accept VGA analog signals.

VGA, introduced by IBM on its PS/2 systems in 1987, was not a multiscan monitor. It operated at a fixed frequency. A multiscan design costs more to build, and many of the low-cost VGAs are designed to operate at a single fixed frequency. They are not as versatile or flexible as the multiscan design, but the resolution can be as good as multiscan.

Many companies are manufacturing monitors with multifixed frequencies (two or more fixed frequencies). Again, they are not quite as flexible as true multiscans, but they cost less. I am using a 19-inch Sampo TriSync, which has three different frequencies. I paid $1000 for it, which was very reasonable. It does everything that I need. Multiscan monitors sell for as little as $300 up to as much as $4000 for some of the large 19- to 30-inch sizes.

Landscape versus portrait

Most monitors are wider than they are tall. These are called landscape styles. There are others that are taller than they are wide. These are called portrait styles. You will find many of the portrait style used for DTP and other special applications.

Screen size

The stated screen size is very misleading and almost fraudulent. The size is supposed to be a diagonal measurement. There is a border on all four sides of the screen. The usable viewing area on a 14-inch monitor is about 9.75-inches wide and about 7.75-inches high. One reason for this difference is that the screen is markedly curved near the edges. This curve causes distortion so the areas are masked off and not used.

What you should buy

The primary factors in choosing a monitor should be what it is going to be used for and the amount of money you have to spend. If money is no object, buy a 19-inch analog monitor with super high resolution and a good VGA board to drive it for about $2000. If you expect to do any kind of graphics or CAD/CAM design work, you definitely need a good large-screen color monitor with very high resolution. A large screen is almost essential for most types of design drawings.

It takes a lot of time for the computer to redraw an image on the screen. In a large company, it might cost $100 or more an hour for an engineer to use a computer. With a small monitor, the engineer might have to spend a large amount of time just staring into space while the computer redraws a portion of the image. With a large screen, more of the drawing is displayed and less time is spent redrawing. At $100 or more an hour, it wouldn't take long to recover the extra cost of a large-screen monitor.

You also need a high-resolution monitor for close-tolerance designs. For instance, if you draw two lines to meet on a low-resolution monitor, they might look as if they are perfectly lined up, but when the drawing is magnified or printed out, the lines might not be anywhere close to one another.

Most DTP is done in black and white. A high-resolution, monochrome monitor might be all you need for these applications. These monitors can usually display several shades of gray. Many of these monitors are the portrait type; that is, they are higher than they are wide. Many of them have a display area of 8½ inches by 11 inches. Instead of 25 lines, they have 66 lines, which is the standard for an 11-inch sheet of paper. Many have a phosphor that lets you have black text on a white background so that the screen looks very much like the finished text. Some of the newer color monitors have a mode that lets you switch to pure white with black type.

Some of the 19-inch and larger landscape monitors, which are wider than they are high, can display two pages of text side by side. For databases, spreadsheets, accounting, or word processing, a monochrome monitor is probably sufficient.

Software for monitor testing

If you are planning to buy an expensive high-resolution monitor, you might want to buy a software program called DisplayMate from Sonera Technologies (908-747-6886). It is a collection of utilities that can perform several checks on a monitor. It lets you measure the resolution, the clarity of the image, and distortion, and has gray and color scales and a full range of intensities and colors. It also comes with a large, very comprehensive manual. The program lists for $149, but if you plan to spend $1500 or so for a monitor, it could be well worth it to test the monitor first.

What to look for

If possible, go to several stores and compare various models. Turn the brightness up and check the center of the screen and the outer edges. Is the intensity the same in the center and on the outer edges? Check the focus, brightness, and contrast with text and graphics. There can be vast differences even in the same models from the same manufacturer. I have seen monitors that displayed graphics programs beautifully, but were lousy when displaying text in various colors. If possible, try the monitor with both text and graphics.

Ask the vendor for a copy of the specs. Check the dot pitch. For good high resolution it should be no greater than 0.31 mm, and 0.28 mm or 0.25 mm is even better. Check the horizontal and vertical scan frequency specs. For a multiscan, the wider the range, the better. A good system should have a horizontal range from 30 kHz to 40 kHz or better. The vertical range should be from 45 Hz to 70 Hz or better.

Bandwidth

The bandwidth of a monitor is the range of frequencies that its circuits can handle. A multiscan monitor can accept horizontal frequencies from 15.75 kHz to about 40 kHz and vertical frequencies from 40 Hz to about 90 Hz. To get a rough estimate of the bandwidth required, multiply the resolution pixels times the vertical scan or frame rate. For instance, a Super VGA or VESA standard monitor should have $800 \times 600 \times 60$ Hz = 28.8 MHz. The systems require a certain amount of overhead, such as for retrace — the time needed to move back to the left side of the screen, drop down one line, and start a new line. So the bandwidth should be at least 30 MHz. If the vertical scan rate is 90 Hz, then it is $800 \times 600 \times 90$ = 43.2 MHz or at least 45 MHz. A very high-resolution monitor requires a bandwidth of $1600 \times 1200 \times 90$ = 172.8 MHz or at least 180 MHz counting the overhead. Many of the very high-resolution units are specified at 200 MHz video bandwidth. Of course, the higher the bandwidth, the more costly and difficult the monitor is to manufacture.

Controls

You might also check for available controls to adjust the brightness, contrast, and vertical and horizontal lines. Some manufacturers place them on the back or in some other area that is difficult to get to. It is much better if they are accessible from the front so that you can see what the effect is as they are adjusted.

Glare

If a monitor reflects too much light it is like a mirror, and can be very distracting. Some manufacturers have coated their screens with a silicon formulation to cut down on the reflectance. Some etch the screen for the same purpose. Some screens are tinted to help cut down on glare. If possible, you should try the monitor under various lighting conditions. If you have a glare problem, several supply companies and mail-order houses offer glare shields that cost from $20 to $100.

Cleaning the screen

Because about 25,000 volts of electricity hits the back of the monitor face, it creates a static attraction for dust, causing distortion and making the screen difficult to read. Most manufacturers include instructions with their monitors suggesting the best way to clean the screen. If you have a screen that is coated with silicon to reduce glare, you should not use any harsh cleansers on it. In most cases, plain water and a soft paper towel will do fine.

Tilt and swivel base

Most people put their monitor on top of their computer. If you are short or tall, have a low or high chair, or have a nonstandard desk, the monitor might not be at eye level. A tilt and swivel base allows you to position the monitor to best suit you. Many monitors now come with this base. If yours does not have one, many specialty stores and mail-order houses sell them for $15 to $40.

Several supply and mail-order houses also offer an adjustable arm that clamps to the desk. Most have a small platform for the monitor to sit on. The arm swings up and down and from side to side and frees a lot of desk space. They cost from $50 to $150.

Cables

Some monitors come without cables, which are sold separately for $25 to $75 extra. Even those monitors that have cables might not have the type of connectors that fit your adapter. At this time there is little or no standardization for cable and adapter connectors. Make sure that you get the proper cables to match your adapter and monitor.

Monitor and adapter sources

I subscribe to *PC Magazine, PC Week, Byte, Personal Computing, InfoWorld, PC World, Computer Shopper, Computer Buyer's Guide,* and about 50 other computer magazines. Most of these magazines have test labs that do extensive tests of products for their reviews. Because I can't personally test all of these products, I rely heavily on these reviews. I can't possibly list all of the monitor and adapter vendors. I suggest that you look at the magazines listed above and in chapter 17. Check the reviews and advertisements in these magazines for other vendors.

List price versus street price

Note that the prices quoted from manufacturers in most magazine reviews are list prices. Often the "street price" of a product is as little as one-half the list price. I don't know why vendors insist on using a list price. Very few people pay list price for computer products.

13
Printers

Johannes Gutenberg (1390 – 1468) started the printing revolution way back in 1436 when he developed movable type and began printing the Bible. Though he started printing the Bible, he did not complete it. He had borrowed money from a man named Johannes Fust, and when Gutenberg could not repay the loan, Fust took over the press and types and completed the work started by Gutenberg. So it was Fust who was first to print the Bible, not Gutenberg.

All you need to know to buy a printer

A short time ago choosing a printer was a difficult task because so many options were available. Even more types of printers and manufacturers are around today, but the task of selecting one is considerably easier. Buy a laser printer. If Gutenberg were around today, you can bet that he would be using a laser printer.

Printer evolution

I bought my first printer in 1983. It was a seven-pin dot matrix printer. The printing was terrible. Just as soon as I could afford it, I bought a Brother daisywheel printer. It used a carbon film ribbon and had excellent letter-quality output. But it was slower than molasses in January. It took 2 to 3 minutes to print a single page.

I finally bought a Star NB24-15 dot matrix printer. It has 24 pins and has fairly good near-letter-quality (NLQ) printing. It is also fairly fast, especially in the draft mode. It even does some simple graphics, if you have the time to wait. I often receive faxes on my Intel Connection coprocessor board. It might take 5 to 10 minutes to print a fax with line drawings. I use several graphics programs that I like to print out occasionally. My Star 24-pin printer was just not able to keep up. Besides, I do a lot of letter writing and was a bit ashamed of the Star output. I really wanted a laser printer.

I had three printers in my office, all in good working order, so it was difficult to justify the cost of another one. I kept waiting for my Star dot matrix to break down, but after 5 years of hard work it was still going strong. When my daughter decided she needed a printer, I was glad to give it to her.

I decided to buy an HP LaserJet III. It cost a bit more than some of the other laser printers, but it was well worth it. Figure 13–1 is a photo of the HP LaserJet III. Moving up to the LaserJet III from the 24-pin Star was like moving up from an XT to a 486. The XT and the dot matrix can both accomplish the tasks they were designed for, but there are many tasks that neither can accomplish. There is no comparison between the dot matrix and the laser as to speed, quality, and added functionality.

13-1   My HP Laserjet III.

Low-cost laser printers

Hundreds of laser printers are now on the market. The competition has been a great benefit to consumers. It has driven prices of both laser and dot matrix printers down. It has also forced many new improvements. Several new low-cost laser models have been introduced that print 8 to 10 pages per minute instead of the 4 to 6 pages of the original models. Also, they are smaller and can easily sit on a desktop. Most have 512K of memory with an option to add more. The discount price for some of these models is now down to less than $600. I recently bought a Panasonic KX-P4410 for $589 (see Fig. 13–2).

The original 4- to 6-page models have dropped from about $3500 down to around $2000. If you can afford to wait a few seconds, the 4- to 6-page models will do almost everything the 8 to 10 pagers will do. For some applications, the 4 page per minute models

13-2 A low-cost Panasonic laser.

seem to be almost as fast as the 8 page per minute units. The prices will drop even more as the competition increases and the economies of scale in the manufacturing process become greater.

If you have used one of the high-end laser printers such as the HP LaserJet IIIP, you might be disappointed with the limited fonts provided in many of the low-cost lasers. But you can add font cartridges to them or use font software. Most of them will let you use Adobe Type Manager (ATM), which comes bundled with OS/2 2.0, or TrueType, which comes with Windows 3.1 as an extra option. Most of them also operate with Bitstream FaceLift fonts. With these fonts you can scale the type on low-cost lasers. This gives almost all of the benefits of the HP LaserJet IIIP at about one-third the cost.

Do you need a laser?

For many applications a dot matrix printer is all that is needed to accomplish the task. The type of printer you need depends on what your computer is used for.

If at all possible, before you buy a printer, visit a computer store or a computer show and try some out. Get several spec sheets for printers in your price range and compare them. You should also look for reviews of printers in the computer magazines.

Dot matrix printers

Most of the dot matrix printers sold today are 24 pin. They are fairly reasonable in price and are sturdy and reliable. The 24-pin printer forms characters from a single vertical row of 24 pins in the print head. There are small electric solenoids around each of the wire pins in the head. By pressing various pins as the head moves across the paper, any character can be formed. It is also possible to do some graphics.

Some dot matrix printers use a multicolored ribbon to print in color. By mixing the colors on the ribbon, all of the colors of the rainbow can be printed. It is a bit slow, but if you need color to jazz up a presentation, or for accent now and then, they are great.

Some things can be done with a dot matrix printer that can't be done with a laser printer. For instance, a dot matrix can have a wide carriage; the lasers are limited to 8½ inches by 11 inches. A dot matrix can use continuous sheets or forms; the laser uses cut sheets, fed one at a time. A dot matrix printer can also print carbons and forms with multiple sheets.

A dot matrix printer can be very noisy. There are enclosures that help to reduce the noise, but they are a bit expensive. I used some foam rubber under mine to reduce the noise.

If you can get by with a dot matrix, you should be able to find some at very good prices. The low cost of the lasers is forcing the dot matrix people to lower their prices. In addition to lower prices, many dot matrix companies are also adding features, such as more memory and several fonts, in order to attract buyers.

Daisywheel printers

The daisywheel has excellent letter quality. It has a wheel with all the letters of the alphabet on flexible "petals." If the letter A is pressed, an electric solenoid hammer hits the A as it spins by and presses it against a ribbon onto the paper. Daisywheel printers are very slow and cannot print graphics. They are also quite noisy. They are practically obsolete.

Hewlett-Packard DeskJet Plus

The DeskJet Plus is a small printer that has quality almost equal to that of a laser. It uses a matrix of small inkjets instead of pins. As the head moves across the paper, ink is sprayed from the jets to form the letters. The inkjet wells are good for about 300 pages of text. They must then be replaced or refilled. This is relatively inexpensive and is easy to do. Its letter quality approaches that of a laser. It comes with the Courier font, but it can use several more fonts that are available on plug-in cartridges. It has a speed of 1 to 2 pages per minute. It is small enough to sit on a desktop and is very quiet. It is relatively inexpensive with a street price of about $500.

Bubblejets

Canon also manufactures a couple of printers based on the inkjet technology, but the company calls it bubblejet. Its BJ-10e is a small portable. It is advertised for $309. The desktop model, the BJ-330e, is advertised for $610. Canon's CJ-10 is a color scanner, printer, and copier all in one.

The Diconix division of Kodak also makes a small portable inkjet-type printer. It is advertised for $341. These two portables are ideal for attaching to laptops, providing excellent letter-quality print on the road.

Inkjet color

Hewlett-Packard has two models, the HP PaintJet for $8\frac{1}{2}$ inches by 11 inches and the HP PaintJet XL, which can handle paper as large as 11 inches by 17 inches. They provide color by using ink cartridges with four different colored inks — black, cyan, yellow, and magenta. They offer a low-cost method for good quality color. A few laser-type color printers rely on a thermal wax transfer method to create color, but they are four to five times more expensive than an inkjet. The color inkjet printers are ideal for creating colored transparencies, graphs, and schematic plottings and drawings.

Laser printer features

Lasers have excellent print quality. They are a combination of copy machine, computer, and laser technology. On the down side, they have lots of moving mechanical parts and are rather expensive. Laser printers use synchronized, multifaceted mirrors and sophisticated optics to write the characters or images on a photosensitive rotating drum. The drum is similar to the ones used in copy machines. The laser beam is swept across the spinning drum and is turned on and off to represent white and dark areas. As the drum spins the laser writes one line across the drum, then rapidly returns and writes another. It is quite similar to the electron beam that sweeps across the face of the monitor one line at a time.

The drum is sensitized by each point of light that hits it. The sensitized areas act like an electromagnet. The drum rotates through the carbon toner and the sensitized areas are covered with toner. The paper is then pressed against the drum and the toner that was picked up by the drum leaves an imprint of the sensitized areas on the paper. The paper is then sent through a heating element where the toner is heated and fused to the paper.

Except for the writing to the drum, this is the same thing that happens in a copy machine. Instead of using a laser to sensitize the drum, a copy machine takes a photo of the image to be copied. A photographic lens focuses the image onto the rotating drum.

Some companies have developed other systems to write on or sensitize the drum. Some use light-emitting diodes (LEDs) and others use liquid crystal shutters (LCSs). Essentially, they do the same thing that the laser beam does, but there are some differences. The laser beam is a single beam that is swept across the drum by a complex system of rotating mirrors. The LED system has a single row of tiny LEDs at a density of 300 per inch. The LCS system has a strip, or tiny wall, of liquid crystal substance near the drum. Behind the liquid crystal substance is a halogen light. The individual pixels in the liquid crystal are turned on to let light shine through and sensitize the drum or are left off to block the light. The end result from an LED or LCS machine is about the same as that from a laser, but many more companies use the laser engine and it has become the standard.

Engine

The drum and its associated mechanical attachments are called an engine. Canon is one of the foremost makers of engines. It manufactures them for its own laser printers and copy machines and for dozens of other companies such as Hewlett-Packard and Apple. Several other companies manufacture laser engines.

The Hewlett-Packard LaserJet was one of the first low-cost lasers. It was a fantastic success and became the de facto standard. Now hundreds of laser printers are on the market. Most of them emulate the LaserJet standard. Hewlett-Packard is the IBM of the laser world. Almost all of the laser printers emulate the Hewlett-Packard LaserJet series. Even IBM's laser printer emulates the Hewlett-Packard standard.

Extras for lasers

Don't be surprised if you go into a store to buy a laser printer that was advertised for $1000 and end up paying a lot more than that. The laser printer business is much like the automobile business. I have seen laser printers advertised in the Los Angeles area for a very low price. But somewhere in the ad, in very small print, it says "without toner cartridge and cables." You might be charged up to $150 for the toner cartridge and up to $50 for a $5 cable. Extra fonts, memory, special controller boards, and software all cost extra. Some printers have small paper bins. A large size one might cost $200 or more.

Memory

If you plan to do any graphics or desktop publishing, you need to have at least 1Mb of memory in your machine. Of course, the more memory, the better. The laser memory chips are usually in SIMM packages. Not all lasers use the same configuration, so check before you buy. Several companies offer laser memories including ASP (800-445-6190) and Elite (800-942-0018).

Page-description languages

If you plan to do any complex desktop publishing you might need a page-description language (PDL) of some kind. Text characters and graphics are two different species of animal. Monitor controller boards usually have all of the alphabetical and numerical characters stored in ROM. When you press the letter A on the keyboard, it dives into the ROM chip, drags out the A, and displays it in a precise block of pixels wherever the cursor happens to be. These are called bit-mapped characters. If you want to display an A that is twice as large, you have to have a complete font set of that type in the computer.

Printers are very much like monitors and have the same limitations. They have a library of stored discrete characters for each font that they can print. My Star dot matrix printer has an internal font and two cartridge slots. Several different font cartridges can be plugged into these slots, but it is limited to those fonts that are plugged in.

With a good PDL, the printer can take one of the stored fonts and change it or scale it to any size you want. These are scalable fonts. With a bit-mapped font, you have one typeface and one size. With scalable fonts, you have one typeface with an infinite number of sizes. Most of the lasers printers accept ROM cartridges that have as many as 35 fonts. You can print almost anything that you want with these fonts if your system can scale them.

Speed

Laser printers can print from 6 to 10 pages per minute depending on the model and what is being printed. Some very expensive high-end printers can print over 30 pages per minute.

A dot matrix printer is concerned with a single character at a time. The laser printers compose and then print a whole page at a time. With a PDL, many different fonts, sizes of type, and graphics can be printed, but the laser must determine where every dot that makes up a character or image is to be placed on the paper before it is printed. This composition is done in memory before the page is printed. More memory is required and more time is needed to compose the page with more complex pages. It might take several minutes to compose a complex graphic. Once composed, it prints out very quickly.

A PDL controls the laser and tells it where to place the dots on the sheet. Adobe's PostScript is the best known PDL. Several companies have developed their own PDLs. Of course, none of them are compatible with the others. This has caused a major problem for software developers because they must try to include drivers for each one of these PDLs. Several companies are attempting to clone PostScript, but it is doubtful that they can achieve 100% compatibility. Unless you need to move your files from a machine that does not have PostScript to one that does, you do not need to be compatible. Hewlett-Packard includes its PCL 5, a scalable system, on its LaserJet IIIs. It is working on kits that will upgrade the earlier LaserJets to the PCL 5 system.

PostScript printers

Printers sold with PostScript installed, such as the Apple LaserWriter, cost as much as $3000 more than one without PostScript. Hewlett-Packard is offering a PostScript option for their LaserJet IID (the IID duplexes, or prints on both sides of the paper) for a list price of $995. The PostScript option for the IIP and III printers is about $695.

PostScript on disk

Several software companies have developed PostScript software emulation. One of the better ones is LaserGo's GoScript. QMS offers UltraScript and the Custom Applications Company has Freedom of the Press.

Resolution

Almost all of the lasers have a 300 × 300 DPI resolution, which is very good, but not nearly as good as the 1200 × 1200 DPI typesetting used for standard publications. Several companies have developed systems to increase the number of dots to 600 × 600 DPI or more.

At 300 × 300 DPI, it is possible to print 90,000 dots in 1 square inch. On an 8½-inch-by-11-inch page of paper, if you deduct a 1-inch margin from the top, the bottom, and both sides, then you have 58.5 square inches × 90,000 dots = 5,265,000 possible dots.

Paper size

Most laser printers are limited to 8½-inch-by-11-inch paper (A size). The QMS PS2200 and the Unisys AP 9230 can print 11-inch-by-17-inch paper (B size), as well as the A size.

Maintenance

Most of the laser printers use a toner cartridge that is good for 3000 to 5000 pages. The original cost of the cartridge is about $100. Several companies refill the spent cartridges for about $50 each.

Of course there are other maintenance costs. These machines are very similar to copy machines and have a lot of moving parts that can wear out and jam up. Most of the larger companies give MTBFs of 30,000 to 100,000 pages. But remember, these are only average figures and not a guarantee.

Most of the lasers are expected to have a lifespan of 300,000 pages. You will have to replace the toner cartridge about every 3000 pages. At this time, a new toner cartridge for a Hewlett-Packard LaserJet costs almost $100. Several companies advertise refilled cartridges for as little as $29.95.

Paper

There are many different types and weights of paper. Almost any paper will work in your laser printer. If you use a cheap paper in your laser, it could leave lint inside the machine and cause problems in print quality. Generally speaking, any bond paper or a good paper made for copiers will work fine. Colored paper made for copiers will also work fine.

Many laser printers are equipped with trays to print envelopes. Hewlett-Packard recommends envelopes with diagonal seams and gummed flaps. Make certain that the leading edge of the envelope has a sharp crease.

Some companies make address labels that can withstand the heat of the fusing mechanism of the laser. There are also other specialty supplies that can be used with your laser. The Integraphix Company, (800) 421-2515, carries several different items that you might find useful. Call them for a catalog.

Sources

There are just too many laser companies to list them all. Look for ads in your local paper and in any computer magazine for the nearest dealer.

Color

A few color printers are available. They cost from $4000 to $15,000. These printers are often referred to as laser color printers, but they don't actually use laser technology. They use a variety of thermal transfer technologies using a wax or rolls of plastic polymer. The wax or plastic is brought into contact with the paper and heat is applied. The melted wax or plastic material adheres to the paper. Very precise points, up to 300 dots per inch, can be heated. By overlaying three or four colors, all of the colors of the rainbow can be created. The cost of color prints ranges from about $.05 a sheet up to about $.50.

Most of the color printers have PostScript or they emulate PostScript. The Tektronix Phaser CP can also use the Hewlett-Packard graphics language (HPGL) to emulate a plotter. These color printers can print out a page much faster than a plotter. Several other color printers will be on the market soon. A few of the companies that have color printers available include

- CalComp   (800) 225-2627
- Howtek Pixelmaster   (603) 882-5200
- NEC Technologies   (508) 264-8000

- QMS ColorScript   (800) 631-2692
- Seiko Instruments   (408) 922-5800
- Tektronix   (800) 835-6100

Plotters

Plotters are devices that can draw almost any shape or design under the control of a computer. Plotters are ideal for printing such things as circuit board designs, architectural drawings, transparencies for overhead presentations, graphs, charts, and many CAD/CAM drawings. A plotter has from one to eight or more different colored pens. There are several different types of pens for various applications, such as writing on different types of paper or on film or transparencies. Some pens are quite similar to ballpoint pens, others have a fiber-type point. The points are usually made to a very close tolerance and can be very small so that the thickness of the lines can be controlled. Line thickness can be very critical in some precise design drawings.

The plotter arm is directed to choose any one of the various pens. The arm is attached to a sliding rail and is moved from one side of the paper to the other. A solenoid lowers the pen at predetermined points on the paper so it can write.

While one motor is moving the arm horizontally from side to side, a second motor moves the paper vertically up and down beneath the arm. This motor moves the paper to predetermined points and the pen is lowered to write on that spot. The motors are controlled by predefined X-Y coordinates. The motors move pen and paper in very small increments so that almost any design can be drawn.

Values are assigned for the Y (vertical) elements and the same values are assigned for the X (horizontal) elements. The computer directs the plotter to move the pen to any point or coordinate on the sheet.

There are several different size plotters. Some desktop units are limited to only A- and B-size plots. There are other large floor-standing models that can accept paper as wide as 4 feet and several feet long. A desk model can cost as little as $200 up to $2000. A floor-standing model can cost from $4000 up to $10,000. If you are doing very precise work, such as designing a transparency that will be photographed and used to make a circuit board, you will want one of the more accurate and more expensive machines.

Just like with printers, each plotter manufacturer has developed its own drivers. Again, this is very frustrating for software developers who must try to include drivers in their programs for all of the various brands. Hewlett-Packard has been one of the major plotter manufacturers. Many of the other manufacturers now emulate the Hewlett-Packard drivers. Almost all of the software that requires plotters includes a Hewlett-Packard driver. If you are in the market for a plotter, try to make sure that it can emulate Hewlett-Packard. Houston Instruments is another major manufacturer of plotters. Their plotters are somewhat less expensive than the Hewlett-Packard models.

One of the disadvantages of plotters is that they are rather slow. There are now some software programs that allow laser printers to act as plotters. Of course, lasers are much faster than plotters, but except for the colored printers, they are limited to black and white.

Plotter sources

A few plotter manufacturers are listed below. Call them for a product list and their latest prices.

- Alpha Merics   (818) 999-5580
- Bruning Computer Graphics   (415) 372-7568
- CalComp   (800) 225-2667
- Hewlett-Packard   (800) 367-4772
- Houston Instrument   (512) 835-0900
- Ioline   (206) 775-7861
- Roland DG   (213) 685-5141

Plotter supplies

It is important that a good supply of plotter pens, special paper, film, and other supplies be kept on hand. Plotter supplies are not as widely available as printer supplies. A very high-priced plotter might have to sit idle if the supplies are not on hand. Most of the plotter vendors provide supplies for their equipment. One company that specializes in plotter pens, plotter media, accessories, and supplies is Plotpro, P.O. Box 800370, Houston, TX 77280, (800) 223-7568.

Installing a printer or plotter

Most IBM compatible computers allow for four ports—two serial and two parallel. No matter whether it is a plotter or a dot matrix, daisywheel, or laser printer, it will require one of these ports. If you have a 286 or 386 computer, these ports might be built into the motherboard. (See the previous chapter and the discussion about installing modems.) If you have built-in ports, you will still need a cable from the motherboard to the outside. You will then need another cable to your printer. If you don't have built-in ports, you will have to buy interface boards.

Almost all laser and dot matrix printers use the parallel ports. Some of them have both serial and parallel interfaces. Many of the daisywheel printers and most of the plotters use serial ports. For the serial printers, you need a board with an RS232C connector. The parallel printers use a Centronics-type connector. When you buy your printer, buy a cable from the vendor that is configured for your printer and your computer.

Printer sharing

Ordinarily a printer sits idle most of the time. Some days I don't even turn my printer on. Most large offices and businesses have several computers. Almost all of them are connected to a printer in some fashion. But it is a waste of money to have each one connected to a separate printer. It is fairly simple to make arrangements so that a printer or plotter can be used by several computers.

If there are only two or three computers, and they are fairly close together, it is not much of a problem. Manual switch boxes that cost from $25 to $150 allow any one of two or three computers to be switched on-line to a printer. But with a simple switch box, if the computers use the standard parallel ports, the cables from the computers to the printer should be no more than 10 feet long. Parallel signals begin to degrade if the cable is longer than 10 feet. A serial cable can be as long as 50 feet.

If an office or business is fairly complex, then there are several electronic switching devices available. Some of them are very sophisticated and allow a large number of different types of computers to be attached to a single printer or plotter. Many of them have built-in buffers that allow for cable lengths of 250 feet or more. The costs range from $160 to $1400. Several networks are also available to connect computers and printers together. Many of them can be very expensive to install.

One of the least expensive methods of sharing a printer is for each person to generate the text to be printed out on his or her own computer, record it on a floppy diskette, and walk over to a computer that is connected to a printer. If it is a large office, a single low-cost XT clone could be dedicated to a high-priced printer.

Printer sharing device sources

The names of some of the companies that provide switch systems are listed below. Call them for their product specs and current price list.

- Altek   (301) 572-2555
- Arnet   (615) 834-8000
- Belkin Components   (213) 515-7585
- Fifth Generation   (800) 225-2775
- Server Technology   (800) 835-1515
- Buffalo Products   (800) 345-2356
- Black Box   (412) 746-5530
- Crosspoint Systems   (800) 232-7729
- Digital Products   (800) 243-2333
- Extended Systems   (208) 322-7163
- Western Telematic   (800) 854-7226
- Quadram   (404) 564-5566
- Rose Electronics   (713) 933-7673

If Gutenberg were around today, I am sure that he would be quite pleased with the progress that has been made in the printing business. We have come a long way in the past 557 years.

14
Using your computer
in a small business

Thousands of new businesses are started every year, but a large percentage of them fail. There are all kinds of reasons why they don't succeed. The lack of adequate and proper planning is one major reason.

Ten things to do before you start a business

If you are thinking about starting a business, here are a few reminders of some basic things that you should do first.

- Study and learn as much about business, especially your planned business, as you possibly can. It might even be worthwhile to hire a consultant.
- You have a better chance of success if you start a business in which you have some hands-on experience.
- Do a survey to try to determine whether your type of business can make it in your chosen location. If you have a store front, is there a lot of foot traffic in the area from which to draw your customers?
- Have you done a demographic study of the people in the area; that is, have you determined the size, density, expected growth, distribution, and vital statistics of the population?
- Do the people in your area need your service?
- What is the economic level of the area? Can the people afford your service?
- Have you checked the area, especially the yellow pages, for competing services?
- Have you checked with the chamber of commerce for any advice it might offer?
- Have you checked with the city about permits and licenses?
- Do you have adequate finances to last until you become established?

These are just a few of the things that should be considered before you decide to become your own boss.

Home office

Many businesses can be operated from a home office. Several advantages in having a home office include no commuting, no high office rent, no need for day care if you have young children, and setting your own hours.

Deducting the cost of your computer

If you have a home office, you might be able to deduct part of the cost of your computer from your income taxes. You might even be able to deduct a portion of your rent, telephone bills, and other legitimate business expenses.

Some IRS rules

I can't give you all of the IRS rules for a home office, but several deductions are available if you use a portion of your home exclusively and regularly to operate your business. These deductions include portions of your real estate taxes, mortgage interest, operating expenses (such as home insurance premiums and utility costs), and depreciation allocated to the area used for business. You might even be able to deduct a portion of the cost of painting the outside of your house or repairing the roof.

I recommend that you buy the latest tax books and consult with the IRS or a tax expert. There are many, many rules and regulations, and they change frequently. For more information, call the IRS and ask for publication 587, *Business Use of Your Home.* Look in your telephone directory for the local or 800 number for the IRS.

Home office as a tax preparer

Congress and the IRS change the tax rules every year. Every year the rules become more and more complicated. It is almost impossible for the ordinary person to be aware of, comprehend, and understand all of the rules and regulations. Some of the rules are even difficult for the IRS to understand. If you call several IRS offices with complicated questions, about 50% of the answers you get will be wrong.

If a person works at a single job and has a single source of income, the forms are fairly simple. But if you have several sources of income or a small business, preparing your taxes can be a nightmare. It is an impossible task for many people and they must hire a tax preparer. Many tax preparers charge from $50 to $100 an hour.

Being a tax preparer is almost like having a guaranteed income. If you have any aptitude for accounting and tax preparation, then you might consider taking a course. Many community colleges offer courses in accounting, but H&R Block is probably the best place to learn tax preparation. They conduct several classes throughout the year in various locations.

Tax programs

Because you have a computer, it might not be necessary for you to pay a tax preparer to do your taxes. Several tax programs can do the job for you. Unless you have a very complicated income, it can be done quickly and easily. In many cases, the cost of the program is less than the cost of having a tax preparer do your taxes.

Besides doing your own taxes, most of these programs allow you to set up files and do the taxes of others. Of course, the software vendors would like each person to buy a separate copy of the program. Many software programs are available for professional tax businesses, but they usually cost more.

All of the programs operate much like a spreadsheet in that the forms, schedules, and worksheets are linked together. When you enter data at one place, other affected data is automatically updated. Some of the programs are simply templates for Lotus 1-2-3 or Symphony, and they require those programs to run. Most of the programs have a built-in calculator so that you can do calculations before entering figures. Many of them allow "what if" calculations to show what your return would look like with various inputs. Some of them offer modules for state taxes for some of the larger states such as New York and California. Most of them allow you to print out IRS-accepted forms.

Brief reviews of some of the better known programs are presented in the following paragraphs.

- Andrew Tobias' Tax Cut, Meca Ventures, 325 Riverside Avenue, Westport, CT 06880; (203) 222-9150. This program will handle most average returns. It can be interfaced with Andrew Tobias' Managing Your Money, which is an excellent personal financial program.

- TurboTax, ChipSoft Inc., 5045 Shoreham Place #100, San Diego, CA 92122-3954; (619) 453-8722. This program is unique in that it offers modules for 41 states. It has an excellent manual and is fairly easy to install and learn. It starts out with a personal interview about your financial situation for the past year. It then lists forms that you might need. Based on the present year's taxes, it can estimate what your taxes will be for next year.

- J.K. Lasser's Your Income Tax, 1 Gulf + Western Plaza, New York, NY 10023; (800) 624-0023, (800) 624-0024 in New York. This program has several state modules. It has a scratch pad, calculator, and a next-year tax planner. The popular *J.K. Lasser's Tax Guide* is included with the package.

- TaxView, SoftView, Inc., 4820 Adohr Lane, Suite F, Camarillo, CA 93010; (805) 388-2626 or (800) 622-6829. TaxView is the PC version of MacinTax, the foremost tax program for the Macintosh. It runs under Windows (a run-time version is included), and it is recommended that it be used with a mouse. It is very easy to learn and use. It has a calculator, allows "what ifs," and supports a large number of IRS forms.

- EasyTax, Valley Management Consultants, 3939 Bradford Road, Huntingdon Valley, PA 19006; (215) 947-4610. This program has modules for several states.

Electronic filing

The IRS is now accepting electronic filing from certain tax preparers and companies. Eventually you should be able to complete your taxes with one of the above listed programs and use your modem to send it directly to the IRS. This, of course, saves you a lot of time and will save the IRS even more. Ordinarily the IRS has to input the data from your return into their computers by hand. Can you imagine the amount of time saved if they can receive it directly into their computers. Electronic filing also offers advantages to you including:

- faster refunds (up to three weeks faster),
- direct deposit of refunds,
- more accurate returns resulting in fewer errors,
- IRS acknowledges receipt of the return,
- reduction of paperwork, and
- saves the IRS labor and taxpayers money.

There are still some limitations. For more information call (800) 829-1040 and ask for the electronic filing coordinator. Or check with your local IRS office to see if electronic filing is possible in your area.

With all the time that is saved, the IRS might have time to examine returns a bit closer and do more individual audits. This might not be too good for the taxpayer who fudges a bit here and there.

A caveat

You probably already know that there are a lot of people in the world who are trying to get their hands in your pockets. Many of them use outright fraud and deception. Several magazines run ads and articles that promise instant success and riches. The articles and ads make it sound so easy to go into business for yourself and become rich almost overnight.

It is not easy to be successful and become rich, especially in an honest and legal business. If success and riches were as easy as some would have you believe, then everybody would be rich. You have probably heard this before (I am certainly not the first to say it), but if something seems too good to be true, then it probably is.

Other tools of the trade

The following items are some other tools that work very well with a 486 for business use.

Point-of-sale terminals

Point-of-sale terminals are a combination of a cash drawer, a computer, and special software. They provide fast customer checkout, credit card handling, audit and security, reduced paperwork, and provide efficient accounting. By keying in codes for various items, the computer can keep a running inventory of everything that is sold. The store owner immediately knows when to reorder certain goods. A point-of-sale system can provide instant sales analysis data as to which items sell best, buying trends, and, of course, the cost and the profit or loss.

There are several point-of-sale systems available. A simple cash drawer with a built-in 40-column receipt printer costs as little as $500. More complex systems cost $1500 or more. Software costs from $175 to $1000, but it can replace a bookkeeper and an accountant. In most successful businesses that sell goods, a point-of-sale system can pay for itself. A few of the point-of-sale hardware and software companies include:

- Alpha Data Systems   (404) 499-9247
- CA Retail   (800) 668-3767
- Computer Time   (800) 456-1159
- CompuRegister   (314) 365-2050
- Datacap Systems   (215) 699-7051
- Indiana Cash Drawer   (317) 398-6643
- Merit Digital Systems   (604) 985-1391
- NCR   (800) 544-3333
- Printer Products   (617) 254-1200
- Synchronics   (901) 761-1166

Bar codes

Bar codes are a system of black-and-white lines that are arranged in a system much like the dots and dashes of Morse code. By using combinations of wide and narrow bars and wide and narrow spaces, any numeral or letter of the alphabet can be represented.

Bar codes were first adopted by the grocery industry. A central office was set up that assigned a unique number, a universal product code (UPC), for just about every manufactured and prepackaged product sold in grocery stores. Different sizes of the same product have a different and unique number assigned to them. The same type products from different manufacturers also have unique numbers. Most large grocery stores today sell everything from automobile parts and accessories to drugs and medicines. Each item has its own bar-code number.

When the clerk runs an item across the scanner, the dark bars absorb light and the white bars reflect light. The scanner decodes the bars and sends this number to the main computer. The computer then matches the input number to the number stored on its hard disk. Linked to the number on the hard disk is the price of the item, the description, the number in inventory, and several other pieces of information about the item. The computer sends back the price and a description of the item to the cash register, where it is printed out. The computer then deducts that item from the overall inventory and adds the price to the overall cash received for the day.

A store might have several thousand items with different sizes and prices. Without a bar-code system the clerk must know most of the prices and enter them in the cash register by hand. Many errors are committed. With bar codes, the human factor is eliminated. The transactions are performed much faster and with almost complete accuracy.

At the end of the day the manager can look at the computer and immediately know such things as how much business was done, what inventories need to be replenished, and what items were the biggest sellers. With the push of a button, he or she can change the price of any item in the store.

Bar codes can be used to increase productivity, to keep track of time charged to a particular job, to track inventory, and in many other ways. There are very few businesses, large or small, that cannot benefit from the use of bar codes.

There are several different types of bar-code readers or scanners. Some are actually small portable computers that can store data and download it into a larger computer. Some systems require their own interface card that must be plugged into one of the slots on the computer motherboard. Some companies have devised systems that can be inserted in series with the keyboard so that no slot or interface is needed. Key Tronic has a keyboard that includes a bar-code reader.

If you are interested in bar-code and automatic identification technology, there are two magazines that are sent free to qualified subscribers — *ID Systems*, 174 Concord St., Peterborough, NH 03458, (603) 924-9631, and *Automatic I.D. News*, P.O. Box 6158, Duluth, MN 55806-9858. Write for subscription qualification forms. Almost everyone who has any business connections can qualify.

Bar-code printers

There are special printers designed for printing bar-code labels. Labels can also be printed on the better dot matrix printers and on laser printers. There are several companies who specialize in printing labels to your specifications.

Radio frequency ID

Another system of identification is the use of small tags on materials that can be read by a radio frequency identification (RFID) system. These systems can be used on production lines and many places that are difficult to access.

An RFID system is being used in California for toll bridge collection. You buy a small tag that is good for a month of tolls. The tag is placed in the window of the auto and is read as it passes through the toll gate. You don't even have to slow down for the tag to be read and fed to the computer.

RFID-type systems can also be used in stores, libraries, and other places. Many clothing stores use a system that has detectors at the exits. If someone tries to walk through with an item that has not had the tag removed, an alarm is set off.

Voice data input

Another way to input data into a computer is to talk to it with a microphone. Of course, you need electronics that can take the signal created by the microphone, detect the spoken words, and turn them into a form of digital information that the computer can use.

The early voice data input systems were very expensive and limited. One reason was that voice technology requires lots of memory. But the cost of memory has dropped considerably in the last few years and the technology has improved in many other ways.

Voice technology involves "training" a computer to recognize a word spoken by a person. When you speak into a microphone, the sound waves cause a diaphragm, or some other device, to move back and forth in a magnetic field, creating a voltage that is analogous to a sound wave. If this voltage is recorded and played through a good audio system, the loudspeaker will respond to the amplified voltages and reproduce a sound that is identical to the one input to the microphone.

When a person speaks a word into a microphone, it creates a unique voltage for that word and that particular person's voice. This voltage is fed into an electronic circuit where the pattern is digitized and stored in the computer. If several words are spoken, the circuit will digitize each one of them and store them. Each word has a distinct and unique pattern. Just as no two leaves from trees are the same, no two patterns are the same. Later when the computer hears a word, it searches through the patterns that it has stored to see if the input word matches any of its stored words.

Once the computer is able to recognize a word, you can have it perform some useful work. You can command it to load and run a program or perform any of several other tasks.

Because every person's voice is different, the computer will not recognize the voice of anyone who has not trained it. Training the computer might involve saying the same word several times so that the computer can store several patterns of the person's voice.

Voice data input is very useful whenever you must use both hands for doing a job but still need a computer to perform certain tasks. A person who is disabled can have a computer do hundreds of jobs by just telling it what he or she wants done. Voice data is also useful on production lines where a person does not have time to enter data manually. It can be used in a laboratory where a scientist looking through a microscope cannot take his eyes off the subject to write down the findings or data. There are other instances when a person might have to be several feet from the computer and still be able to input data through the microphone lines. The person might even be miles away and still be able to input data over a telephone line.

In most of the systems in use today, the computer must be trained to recognize a specific word, so the vocabulary is limited. But every word that can be spoken can be derived from just 42 phonemes. Several companies are working on systems that will take a sample of a person's voice that contains these phonemes. Using the phonemes from this sample, the computer could then recognize any word that the person speaks.

Local area networks

If you have a small business where there are several other computers, you might consider connecting them together into a network. The 486 is excellent as a server for LANs. You can attach several terminals or smaller computers to your 486. This gives the less-expensive computers most of the benefits of the 486. The 486 can have databases, files, information, and software that can be accessed and shared by these terminals. A LAN allows multitasking, multiusers, security, centralized backup, and shared resources such as printers, modems, fax machines, and other peripherals.

There are three main types of LAN systems: Ethernet, token ring, and ARCnet. In addition, there are several proprietary systems. A good network system might support as many as 100 terminals or stations. Those terminals can be very inexpensive PCs, or a combination of PCs, 286s, and 386s. On a good system, the terminals will have almost all of the benefits that the powerful 486 has. A good network can multiply by several times the power and utility of a server.

Of course, the larger the network and the more complex it is, the more expensive it is. If you have a small business you might not need a large network or one that is very sophisticated. There are many types of LANs with many levels of complexity. Two or more computers tied together so that they can share and process the same files is called a *shared CPU* system because all the terminals share the same CPU. This can work well if there are only a few terminals on-line. If there are several terminals vying for attention at the same time, there will usually be some delay.

Some systems use diskless terminals. One reason is for security reasons to prevent the copying of data and software. These terminals are usually low-cost PCs with a monitor.

Equipment needed for LANs

Besides the terminals, other types of equipment needed to form a LAN are plug-in boards, cables, and software. Most systems require a plug-in board in each terminal and a master board in the server. The boards cost from $100 to $1000 each.

Several types of cable can be used such as the inexpensive twisted telephone cable, coaxial shielded cable, and fiber-optic cable. The type of system installed dictates the type of cable needed. A simple system might require only standard telephone cable. A fast sophisticated system might need shielded coaxial or fiber-optic cable.

Besides the plug-in boards, the system needs special drivers and LAN software to control and manage the network. Some companies supply special software to match their hardware. Many companies such as Novell and Microsoft develop network software for several types of network hardware. Most software is sold with the explicit understanding and agreement that it will be used on a single computer by a single user. If it is to be used on a network it usually costs more.

Low-cost switches and LANS

You might have just a couple of computers and want them to share a printer or switch from a laser printer to a dot matrix printer. This can be done very easily with mechanical switch boxes. Some switch boxes can handle the switching needs for as many as four or five systems. These boxes cost from $50 to $500. Check the ads in the computer magazines.

Some electronic switch boxes are a bit more sophisticated and have more capabilities and functions. Some offer buffers and spooling. Computone Products has an ATCC cluster controller that can control up to 64 terminals (see Fig. 14-1). Vendors of switches, buffers, and controllers include:

- Aten Research   (714) 992-2836
- Computone Products   (800) 241-3946
- Interex Computer   (316) 524-4747
- Protec Microsystems (800) 363-8156
- Rose Electronics   (713) 933-7673
- Total Technology   (714) 241-0406
- Western Telematic   (714) 586-9950

Zero-slot LANs

Several companies provide low-cost LANs that use the RS232 serial port and don't require the use of a slot including:

- Applied Knowledge   (408) 739-3000
- Amica   (800) 888-8455

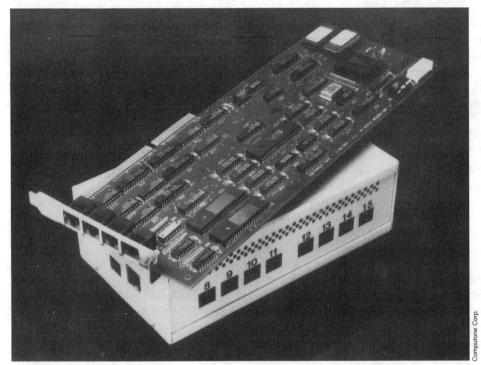

14-1 The Computone ATCC Cluster Controller which can control up to 64 terminals.

- Artisoft   (602) 293-6363
- Fifth Generation System   (800) 873-4384
- GetC   (800) 663-8066 or (604) 684-3230
- Traveling Software   (800) 662-2652 or (206) 483-8088

LAN magazines

Most of the computer magazines carry articles on networking from time to time. There are several magazines devoted entirely to LANs. Check the list of magazines in chapter 17.

Books on LANs

If you would like to learn more about networks, you might buy the book *Build Your Own Network And Save A Bundle* by Aubrey Pilgrim. I highly recommend it. There are also several other books on networking from Windcrest/McGraw-Hill:

- *TOPS: The IBM/Macintosh Connection,* S. Cobb and M. Jost, #3210
- *Networking with the IBM Token-Ring,* C. Townsend, #2829
- *Networking with Novell NetWare — A LAN Manager's Handbook,* Paul Christiansen, Steve King, and Mark Munger, #3283
- *Networking with 3 + Open,* Stan Schatt, #3437

You can order them from TAB McGraw-Hill, Blue Ridge Summit, PA 17294-0850; (800) 822-8138. Call them for a catalog.

Desktop publishing

Desktop publishing (DTP) covers a lot of territory. A system could be just a PC with a word processor and a dot matrix printer. Or it could be a full-blown system that uses laser printers with PostScript and lots of memory, scanners, 286 or 386 computers with many megabytes of hard disk space, sophisticated software, and other goodies. As always, the type of system needed depends on what you want it to do (and of course, how much money you want to spend).

Desktop publishing can be used for newsletters, ads, flyers, brochures, sales proposals, manuals, and all sorts of printed documents. I have a friend who has written and published several books with a fairly simple and relatively inexpensive DTP system.

Desktop publishing software

If your project isn't too complex, you can probably do a fairly good job with a laser printer and a good word processing program. WordStar 7.0 has page preview, scalable fonts, and several other functions that can be used in desktop publishing. Microsoft Word, WordPerfect, AMI, and several other programs can also be used. Most of the more sophisticated word processors will let you add graphics and flow the text around them.

If you are doing a more complicated and professional type of desktop publishing, with a lot of graphics and different types and fonts, then you should use the more advanced software packages. The premier high-end packages are Ventura from Xerox and PageMaker from Aldus. There are many other software packages ranging from $89 up to $15,000.

A few of the companies that supply page layout software include

- Aldus, PageMaker — (206) 622-5500
- Digital Research, GEM DTP — (800) 443-4200
- Haba/Arrays, Front Page — (818) 994-1899
- IMSI, InteGraphics — (415) 454-8901
- Microsoft, Publisher 1.0 — (800) 426-9400
- Power Up Software, Express Publisher — (800) 851-2917
- Serif, PagePlus — (603) 889-8650
- Timeworks, Publish It 2.0 — (800) 323-7744
- Unison World Software, Avagio — (800) 444-7553
- Xerox, Ventura — (800) 832-6979

Clip art

Several software packages contain images that you can import and place in your page layout. The software lets you move, rotate, size, or revise them. The images include humans, animals, business, technical, industrial, borders, enhancements, etc.

Most of the companies have the images set up in modules on floppies. Most have several modules with hundreds and even thousands of images. The cost of each of the modules ranges from $15 to $200. Contact the companies listed below for more information.

- Antic Cyber Design, Architecture   (800) 234-7001
- Artware System Artware, Varied   (800) 426-3858
- CD Design Graphics, Varied   (800) 326-5326
- EMS Shareware DTP Library, Varied   (301) 924-3594
- Kinetic Corporation, Maps   (502) 583-1679
- Metro ImageBase PicturePak, Varied   (800) 525-1552
- Micrografx Clip Art, Varied   (800) 272-3729

Micrografx has four different packages that allow you to create almost any kind of art or line drawing for your desktop publishing.

Printers for DTP

If you are going to be doing primarily text, then you can probably get by with a good 24-pin dot matrix printer. You will need a laser printer if you expect to be doing a lot of graphics and using different type styles and fonts.

Most of the low-cost lasers have only a few bitmapped fonts, but most of them will work with Adobe Type Manager (ATM), Bitstream FaceLift, and TrueType. OS/2 2.0 comes bundled with ATM. TrueType is available for Windows 3.1 at extra cost. These fonts allow you to scale a large variety of sizes. You can buy a laser printer for less than $600. You can get OS/2 2.0 or Windows 3.1 for about $50.

Books for DTP

If you are serious about desktop publishing, there are several good books on the subject. A few from TAB McGraw-Hill include

- *Mastering PageMaker*, G. Keith Gurganus, #3176
- *Ventura Publisher*, Elizabeth McClure, #3012
- *The Print Shop Companion*, P. Seyer and H. Leitch, #3218
- *IBM Desktop Publishing*, G. Lanyi and J. Barrett, #3109
- *Desktop Publishing and Typesetting*, M.L. Kleper, #2700

You can order these books from TAB McGraw-Hill, Blue Ridge Summit, PA 17294-0850, or call (800) 822-8138.

Microsoft Press also publishes books on desktop publishing and many other phases of the computer industry. Write to them for a catalog at Microsoft Press, One Microsoft Way, Redmond, WA 98052-6399; or call (800) 888-3303.

DTP magazines

There are also several magazines that are devoted to desktop publishing. Almost every computer magazine carries articles about desktop publishing. Check the list of magazines in chapter 17.

15
Accessories and adjuncts

Once you have your computer and peripherals set up, a few other items can make using it more enjoyable.

UPS

No, this doesn't refer to the delivery service. UPS in this case means uninterruptible power supply. You probably know that if the power to a computer is interrupted, even for a fraction of a second, any data that is being worked on can be lost forever. UPS systems are designed to prevent losses due to power interruptions.

If you live on the East Coast, or in an area where there are lots of lightning storms, you are probably familiar with UPS systems. You don't see too many of them in the San Francisco and Los Angeles areas because they seldom have lightning storms. But a lot of people have found out the hard way that there are other causes of power failures besides lightning. Drunk drivers knock over power poles and kids release metallic helium-filled balloons that short out power lines. And the power company itself has unexpected failures occasionally.

There are many other causes for power failures. Once my 3-year-old granddaughter walked into the room where I was working. I didn't pay much attention to her, so she walked over to the wall and unplugged my computer. I lost about 2 hours of hard work. I love my granddaughter, but I put a lock on the door.

I was using WordStar 3.3 when my granddaughter successfully got my attention. WordStar 5.0 and later versions have an option that automatically saves your files to disk at specified intervals. After a specified length of time when no typing is detected from the keyboard, it automatically saves a backup of the file. It has saved me hours of work.

I worked in a large office at one time. Most of us were diet- and health-food conscious. Instead of donuts and jelly rolls for our coffee breaks, we had popcorn. It is surprising how much power is consumed by electric popcorn poppers and coffee makers. If somebody turned on both machines at the same time, it would cause the circuit breaker to trip. If anyone happened to be working on a computer, all data was lost. The boss could have made us take out all the popcorn and coffee machines, but because he was a good guy and he also liked popcorn, he called maintenance and had a new electric circuit installed.

Not all power problems are as easy to solve as the two above. That is why several large companies manufacture UPS systems.

How the power supply operates

Your system probably has a power supply in a chrome-plated enclosure. It is supplied with 100-volts ac at 60 Hz. The power supply must convert the 110-volts ac to the 5-volts and 12-volts dc needed by the computer. The power supply rectifies the 60-Hz ac voltage and turns it into dc. This dc is then chopped up by switching power transistors at a rate of 50,000 to 100,000 Hz. It is effectively turned back into a high-frequency ac voltage. This ac voltage is then fed into a transformer that reduces the voltage. At this point it is still ac voltage. It is then rectified again, and the final output is 5 volts and 12 volts dc.

The UPS system takes the 110-volts ac and sends it through a transformer to reduce it to 12 volts. It then rectifies this voltage and uses it to charge and maintain a charge on a 12-volt battery.

On-line UPS

There are two main systems in use today: on-line and standby systems. Both systems invert the 12-volts dc from the battery and change it to 110-volts ac. Transistors chop up the 12-volts dc from the battery and send it through a transformer to step it up to 110-volts ac for the computer power supply.

On-line systems are in series with the voltage to the computer. The 110 volts is used to charge the battery that feeds the computer at all times. If there is a power failure, or a brownout where the voltage drops very low, the battery continues to supply voltage. But because it is no longer being charged, it will eventually become discharged.

Standby UPS

The standby system is in parallel with the 110 volts to the computer. It also uses a 12-volt battery that is continuously charged. But the standby system switches on-line only in the event of a power failure. Its sensors detect power failures and immediately switch on. It takes 2 ms or more for the system to switch.

Advantages and disadvantages

There are advantages and disadvantages to both systems. The on-line system operates all the time, which can reduce the life of the battery. But because it is on-line all the time, it offers the best protection. The standby system is less expensive and the battery might last a bit longer, but some people worry that the switching time might allow the loss of data.

The cost of these systems depends on the amount of power that you want from them. A single computer should require no more than 300 or 400 watts, which can provide power for 5 to 20 minutes so the system can be shut down. Some systems can provide power for up to 1 hour for a single computer, or provide power for three or four computers long enough to save any open files. The cost of these systems ranges from $500 to $1500.

UPS plug-in boards

Depending on the wattage required, some of the UPS systems can be very large and heavy. Emerson (800-222-5877) has developed a plug-in board with a battery on it. They call it the AccuCard. The small half-card size board plugs into any slot on the motherboard. The small 12-volt battery is kept charged up by the bus voltage. In the event of a power outage, the 12-volt battery supplies voltage to the bus long enough to shut the system down. It even remembers which file you were working on and automatically reloads it when the power comes back. It costs only $249. Other than having to give up a slot, it is a fantastic idea. Emerson also manufactures several other large UPS systems up to several kilovolt-amps (kVA).

Dakota Microsystems (800-999-6288) manufactures a UPS on a plug-in full-size card. It lists for $299.

A built-in UPS

If you remove the cover of your power supply, you will find that there is a lot of empty space in it. The PC Power & Cooling Company (619-723-9513) has taken advantage of the extra space and developed a power supply with a built-in UPS. They have installed a battery inside the power supply. It is a standby type and provides dc power for the computer and 110 volts for the monitor for as long as 8 minutes.

UPS sources

Companies that manufacture UPSs:

- Alpha Technologies   (206) 647-2360
- American Power Conversion   (401) 789-5735
- Best Power Technology   (800) 356-5794
- Clary Corporation   (818) 287-6111
- Dynatech Computer Power   (800) 638-9098
- SL Waber   (800) 634-1485
- Taesung   (800) 874-3160
- Unison   (714) 855-8700

Power panel

Your system probably has five or six power cords to be plugged in. A single power source is a lot neater and there is less chance of having grounding problems. Many people use a power strip with five or six outlets. These power strips are available at most hardware and discount stores.

I have a power panel that is about 12 inches wide, 13 inches deep, and 2 inches high. It has five power outlets for the computer, the monitor, the printer, and two auxiliary devices. It has lighted switches in the front so that I can switch any device on or off. The panel sits on top of my computer and the monitor sits on top of the panel. It is very handy. They range in cost from $15 to $30. Most of them claim to have surge protection, but it is only minimal. They are available at most computer supply stores and from several mail-order stores. Check the mail-order catalogs listed in chapter 17.

Furniture and office supplies

If you are setting up your computer at home or in a business, you probably need a desk, chairs, filing cabinets, shelves, furniture, and supplies. Most of the mail-order catalogs listed in chapter 17 carry everything that you might need in an office. They have air purifiers, coffee makers, cables, furniture, paper, work stations, and lots more. The catalogs are free and most of them have toll-free numbers. But you should be aware that most of the items from the catalog stores are very expensive. Everything is sold at list or above. Most of them have no discount prices.

Several discount computer supply stores advertise in the *Computer Shopper* and other computer magazines. The prices are considerably less at these stores. If you live near a large city, there are probably several discount stores nearby such as Sears, Montgomery Ward, K-Mart, CostCo, and others. Most of them carry some computer supplies. In the Los Angeles area, several new discount stores have opened that specialize in office and computer supplies and furniture.

Most larger cities also have stores that sell used office furniture, such as desks, chairs, tables, filing cabinets, and other supplies. They usually have some very good bargains.

Lighting in your office can be very important. Improper lighting can cause reflection and glare from the screen. There are antiglare products listed in the computer supply catalogs. Some of them even claim to reduce or eliminate video display terminal (VDT) radiation. Several studies have been done on VDT radiation, but absolute evidence of health damage has not yet been found. The shields do help eliminate the glare and they might help eliminate some VDT radiation.

Supply sources

The following mail-order firms send out catalogs that cover office supplies, paper, ribbons, diskettes, cartridges, toner, pens, hardware, software, and electronic supplies.

- Altex Electronics   (800) 531-5369
- Businessland Direct   (800) 551-2468
- Damark   (800) 729-9000
- Data Dynamics   (800) 999-1172
- Dartek   (800) 832-7835
- Devoke   (800) 822-3132
- Digi-Key   (800) 344-4539
- 800-SOFTWARE   (800) 227-4587

- Fidelity Graphic Arts   (800) 328-3034
- Global   (800) 227-1246
- Inacomp Computer   (800) 999-9898
- Inmac   (800) 547-5444
- Jameco Electronics   (415) 592-8097
- JDR Microdevices   (800) 538-5000
- Jensen   (602) 968-6231
- Lyben Computer   (313) 589-3440
- MISCO   (800) 876-4726
- Moore   (800) 323-6230
- National Computer   (916) 441-1568
- Nebs Computer Forms   (800) 225-9550
- Power Up!   (800) 851-2917
- Priority One   (818) 709-5464
- Selective Software   (800) 423-3556
- Tenex   (800) 776-6781

This is not a complete listing, but it will give you an idea of what is available. Thumbing through catalogs is a great way to be aware of what is available and do some price comparing without leaving home. You should be aware that most of the catalogs listed above are not for discount houses. They might have considerably higher prices than those you see advertised in some of the computer magazines.

16
Essential software

There is more software already written and immediately available than you can use in a lifetime. Except for very unusual applications, the ordinary user should never have to do any programming. There are off-the-shelf programs that can do almost everything that you could ever want to do with a computer. For most general applications, there are certain basic programs that you will need.

Speaking of basic, BASIC is one program that is needed. GW-BASIC from Microsoft is more or less the standard. Before MS-DOS 5.0, GW-BASIC was included with all versions of DOS. It has been changed and is now called QBASIC. To run old BASIC programs, you have to convert them to QBASIC. Many applications still use BASIC. Even if you are not a programmer, it is simple enough that anyone can design a few special applications with it.

There are several categories of programs that you will need such as a disk operating system, word processors, databases, spreadsheets, utilities, shells, communications, windows, graphics, and computer-aided design. Depending on what you intend to use your computer for, there are hundreds of other programs for special needs.

Software can be more expensive than the hardware. The prices vary from vendor to vendor. Few people pay the list price. It pays you to shop around. I have seen software with a list price of $700 advertised by a discount house for as little as $350. Also remember that public domain programs are free and they can do almost everything that the high-priced commercial programs can do. Check your local bulletin board, user group, or the ads for public domain software in most computer magazines. There are also some excellent shareware programs that can be registered for a very nominal sum.

I can't possibly list all of the thousands of software packages available. Again, subscribe to the magazines listed in chapter 17. Most of them have detailed reviews of software in every issue.

Operating system software
MS-DOS

DOS to a computer is like gasoline is to an automobile. Without it, it won't operate. DOS is an acronym for disk operating system, but it does much more than just operate the disks. In recognition of this, OS/2 has dropped the D.

If you are new to computers, DOS should be the first thing that you learn. DOS has over 50 commands, but chances are you will never need to know more than 15 or 20 of them. You can use any version of DOS on your 486. I don't know why anyone would want to, but you can even use version 1.0. Of course, you would be severely limited in what you could do. I recommend that you buy the latest version of MS-DOS, DR DOS, or OS/2.

When the operating system, config.sys, buffers, drivers, TSRs, and other files are loaded into the 640K of available RAM, there is often not enough memory left to load other programs. OS/2, DR DOS 6.0, and MS-DOS 5.0 can take the operating system, TSRs, buffers, drivers, and other files out of low memory and place them in memory above 640K. The older versions of DOS loaded everything into low memory. Quite often there was not enough RAM left over to run any programs.

There are many good commands in DOS, but there are some that if not used properly, can be disastrous. Be very careful when using commands such as FORMAT, DEL, ERASE, COPY, and RECOVER. When invoked, RECOVER renames and turns all of the files into FILE0001.REC, FILE0002.REC. . . . The disk will no longer be bootable and critical files might be garbled. Many experts say that you should erase the RECOVER command from your disk files and leave it only on your original diskettes. It should only be used as a last resort. Norton Utilities, Mace Utilities, PC Tools, or one of the other utilities is much better to unerase or restore a damaged file.

COPY can cause problems if you copy a file onto a disk that has another file with the same name. The file with the same name is replaced and gone forever. If you erase or delete a file, you can possibly recover it. But if it has been copied over or written over, it is history.

DR DOS 6.0

The DR is for Digital Research, not doctor. The Digital Research Corporation was founded by Gary Kildahl, the developer of CP/M, the first operating system for personal computers. DR DOS 6.0 is completely compatible with MS-DOS. You could say that it is a clone of MS-DOS 5.0, except that DR DOS 5.0 preceded MS-DOS 5.0 by a couple of years.

DR DOS 6.0 is the latest version. It has several good features. One is FileLINK, which allows you to connect and transfer files over a serial cable. It also has ViewMAX to view, organize, and execute files and commands using only one or two keystrokes or a mouse. It has comprehensive on-line help, supports hard disk partitions up to 512Mb, has disk cache, a full-screen text editor, password protection, and many features not found in MS-DOS.

If you work in a large office you might want to keep some of your nosy neighbors from snooping into your personal files. DR DOS 6.0 allows you to use a password to protect them.

The ViewMAX shell feature lets DR DOS use icons to operate very much like Windows 3.0. You can use a mouse to quickly open files, copy, delete, and perform many other commands and functions. ViewMAX also has a clock that can run in a window of the screen. Another feature is a calculator for on-screen calculations. DR DOS is very easy to install on a hard disk by just copying it onto the disk. There is no need to reformat your disk. If you have a previous version of DOS on your disk, it will copy over and replace the older DOS. It has the same commands and is fully compatible with DOS.

DR DOS also comes bundled with SuperStor, a file compression program that allows you to double the capacity of your disks. If you bought the SuperStor program separately, it would cost over $100. The discount price for DR DOS 6.0 plus SuperStor is less than $100. It is a real bargain!

Digital Research has merged with Novell, the network company. At the present time they are developing new and more powerful versions of DR DOS for both single users and for high-end networks.

OS/2 2.0

OS/2 was originally designed to overcome some of the limitations of DOS. It was a joint effort by IBM and Microsoft, though Microsoft did all of the program development. OS/2 1.x was rather expensive and there were not too many applications that could take advantage of its capabilities. IBM asked Microsoft to revise the program and they began the project.

In May 1990, Microsoft introduced Windows 3.0. It was a fantastic hit. They sold nine million copies between May 1990 and the introduction of Windows 3.1 in April 1992. Microsoft was so busy with Windows 3.0 that they abandoned the work on OS/2. Several deadlines passed with no results. Finally IBM decided to take over the project and do the work themselves.

OS/2 2.0 was introduced at the Spring Computer Dealers Exposition (COMDEX) in April 1992. It comes complete with MS-DOS 5.0 and Windows 3.0. (They have promised to update to Windows 3.1 shortly.) OS/2 also has Adobe Type Manager that allows scalable fonts for Windows and for printing. It has several other excellent utilities and goodies.

OS/2 2.0 breaks the 640K barrier and can seamlessly address over 4Gb of RAM. It can do true multitasking and run several programs at the same time. If one program crashes, the other programs are not affected. It can run all DOS software and any of the software that has been developed for Windows. IBM claims that OS/2 runs Windows applications better than Windows under MS-DOS. A few games such as Solitaire and Chess have been included if you have nothing else to do.

Many people bought Macintosh computers because they are easy to use and learn. IBM's OS/2 has many similarities with the Macintosh. For some applications it might even be easier to use than the Macintosh. But Apple is not complaining because IBM is now a partner.

At the present time there is not much software that can take advantage of OS/2's 32-bit capabilities. But at the Spring 1992 COMDEX introduction, over 800 companies pledged to develop 32-bit software for OS/2.

One disadvantage of OS/2 is that it requires over 25Mb of hard disk space and about 6Mb of RAM. But hard disk and memory prices are dropping every day. The advantages of its vast capabilities far outweigh the disadvantages of it being a memory hog.

An advantage is that it is very inexpensive. IBM gave away thousands of copies at COMDEX. They have priced it from $49 to $149. For this price you get MS-DOS 5.0, Windows 3.0, Adobe Type Manager, and many other utilities. My copy came on twenty-one 1.44Mb floppy disks. The 21 disks alone, even if they were blank, are worth $49.

Windows 3.1

Windows 3.0 was one of the most phenomenal successes of all time, but it had some flaws. Microsoft has extensively revised Windows and has added several new features. One added option is TrueType scalable fonts for the screen and for printing. This gives you a true what-you-see-is-what-you-get (WYSIWYG) screen. An extensive list of printer drivers has also been added. It can print faster and has a better SMARTDrive with read and write caching.

One flaw in 3.0 was that it often got hung up with unrecoverable application errors (UAEs). The whole system would then have to be rebooted. If you had work that was not saved to disk or had two or more windows open, everything was lost.

The new 3.1 does away with UAEs. If there is an error, the program analyzes it and gives you several options. Dr. Watson, a diagnostic utility, asks you to describe the details of what happened. These comments are saved as a record and might be useful in helping Microsoft or other developers eliminate the problems. If the program does crash, only that operation goes down without affecting any other open window. They have also added an object linking and embedding (OLE) utility. This allows data or graphics in one file to be imported and embedded in another.

Sound capabilities have been built into 3.1 by using sound boards such as Sound Blaster, (408) 986-1461; Pro AudioSpectrum, (800) 638-2807; Soundcards, (213) 685-5141; and MultiSound, (717) 843-6916.

Windows NT

Several other improvements have been made in 3.1, but it is still a 16-bit system. At this moment Microsoft is working overtime to complete Windows NT (New Technology). It is a 32-bit system that will compete head-to-head with OS/2 2.0. The outcome will be interesting.

New Wave 4.0

Hewlett-Packard's New Wave adds several important features that make Windows 3.1 even better. It lets you use more than 11 characters to name a file. It lets you create objects, put them in folders, and manage them. You can use it to create multiple views of objects and to create macros to automate tasks. It has several other very good utilities not found in Windows 3.1 and is an essential adjunct to 3.1.

Norton Desktop for Windows 2.0

Norton Desktop for Windows has all of the utilities found in Norton Utilities for DOS plus several others including Norton Backup. It too is an essential adjunct to 3.1.

DESQview

This is similar to Windows in that it runs on top of DOS. It allows multitasking and multiusers. You can have up to 50 programs running at the same time and have as many as 250 windows open. It runs all DOS software and is simple to learn and use.

DESQview is one of the better programs for managing DOS memory. It can load TSRs and other memory resident software into memory above 640K. DESQview seems to be able to find little niches and spaces above 640K that most other memory managers can't find or use.

DOS help programs

Learning DOS can be very difficult, but there are several help programs that have been developed. One such program is Doctor DOS from VMG. Phoenix, one of the first developers of a clone BIOS, has an excellent help program for learning DOS. There are many others including some public domain programs. Look for ads in the computer magazines.

Word processors

Word processors are the most used of all software. There are literally hundreds of word processing packages, each one slightly different from the others. It amazes me that they can find so many different ways to do the same thing. Most word processing programs come with a spelling checker and some of them have a thesaurus. They usually also include utilities for such things as communications programs for your modem, outlining, desktop publishing, print merging, and many others.

WordStar

I started off with WordStar 3.0 on my little CP/M Morrow with a hefty 64K of memory and two 140K single-sided disk drives. It took me some time to learn it. I have tried several other word processors since then and have found that most of them would require almost as much time to learn as WordStar did originally. WordStar does all I need. I have been using it for so long that it is like second nature to me. I can do most of the commands with my eyes closed and one hand tied behind my back. I am presently using version 7.0 which has many added features. It allows the use of a mouse so that you can point and click and easily control the position of the cursor. Version 7.0 is available for DOS and for Windows 3.1.

WordStar has an educational division that offers discounts to schools, both for site licenses and for student purchases.

WordPerfect

This is one of the hottest selling word processors, so it must be doing something right. One thing they are doing right is giving free, unlimited, toll-free support. WordPerfect can select fonts by a proper name, has simplified printer installation, has the ability to do columns and most desktop publishing functions, as well as many other useful functions and utilities. It also works with Windows.

Microsoft Word for Windows

This package was developed by the same people who gave us MS-DOS and is one of the best-selling softwares in the country. It lets you take advantage of all of the features and utilities of Windows. If you have previously learned a different word processor, Word for Windows includes a manual that lists the differences between the most popular word processors. It can help you quickly become accustomed to Word for Windows.

PC-Write

This is the least expensive of all the word processors; it is shareware and is free if copied from an existing user. Quicksoft, (800) 888-8088, asks for a $16 donation. Full registration with manual and technical support is $89. It is easy to learn and is an excellent personal word processor.

There are many other good word processors. Look for ads and reviews in the computer magazines.

Grammar checkers

You might be the most intelligent person alive, but you might not be able to write a simple intelligible sentence. There are several grammar checking programs such as Right Writer from Que Corp. and Grammatik from Reference Software that work with most of the word processors. They analyze your writing and suggest ways to improve it.

Database programs

Database packages are very useful for business purposes. They allow you to manage large amounts of information. Most programs allow you to store information, search it, sort it, do calculations, make up reports, and several other very useful features.

There are almost as many database programs as there are word processors. Few of them are compatible with each other. There is a strong effort in the industry to establish some standards under the structured query language (SQL) standard. Several of the larger companies have announced their support for this standard.

dBASE IV

Ashton-Tate, with dBASE II, was one of the first to produce a database program for the personal computer. dBASE is a very powerful program with hundreds of features. It is a highly structured program and can be a bit difficult to learn. dBASE IV is much faster than dBASE III, has a built-in compiler, SQL, and an upgraded user interface along with several other enhancements. Ashton-Tate is now a division of Borland.

askSAM

The funny looking name is an acronym for access knowledge via stored access method. It is a free-form, text-oriented database management system that is almost like a word processor. Data can be typed in randomly, sorted, and accessed. Data can also be entered in a structured format for greater organization. It is not quite as powerful as dBASE IV, but it is much easier to use. It is also much less expensive and is ideal for personal use and for the majority of business needs.

Seaside Software has a discount program for students. Students can buy the $295 program for only $45 when the order is placed by an instructor. Any instructor who places an order for 10 or more copies gets a free copy. This is a fantastic bargain.

R:BASE 3.1

R:BASE has been around for a long time and has recently been revised and updated. It now has pull-down menus, mouse support, is fully relational for multitable tasks, and has an English-like procedural language. It is one of the most powerful and versatile of the database programs. Microrim is so sure that you will like the program that they offer an unlimited, no questions asked, 90-day money back guarantee.

FoxPro

FoxPro is very easy to use. It has windows and can be controlled by a mouse or the keyboard. Of course, using it with a mouse saves several keystrokes. A view window is the master control panel to create databases, open files, browse, set options, and perform other functions. You don't have to be a programmer to type commands into the command window to operate FoxPro. The browse window lets you view, edit, append, or delete files. It also has memo fields and a built-in editor, allows you to create macros, and has extensive context-sensitive help and much more. The Fox company is now a part of Microsoft.

Paradox

Paradox is fairly easy to learn and use and is fast and powerful. It is designed for both beginners and expert users. It is a full-featured relational database that can be used on a single PC or on a network. The main menu has functions like view, ask, report, create, modify, image, forms, tools, scripts, and help. Choosing one of these items brings up options that are associated with that item. Extensive use is made of the function keys. The query by example is very helpful for beginners and experts alike. Paradox has a very powerful programming language — PAL. Experienced programmers can easily design special applications.

Paradox is one of the Borland family of products. Philippe Kahn is the founder and president of Borland. He is young, about the same age as Gary Kildahl, Bill Gates, and Steve Jobs, and several of the other young computer pioneers. He was penniless when he came to this country from Belgium. His first product was Sidekick, then Turbo Pascal, and pretty soon dozens of products. His company has recently acquired Ashton-Tate and dBASE IV.

Spreadsheets

Spreadsheets are primarily number crunchers. They have a matrix of cells in which data is entered. Data in a particular cell is acted on by formulas and mathematical equations. If the data in the cell that is acted on affects other cells, recalculations are done on them. Several of the tax software programs use a simple form of spreadsheet. Income and deductions are entered. If an additional deduction is discovered, it can be entered and all the calculations are done again automatically. In business, spreadsheets are essential for inventory, expenses, accounting, forecasting, making charts, and dozens of other vital business uses.

Lotus 1-2-3

Lotus was one of the first and most popular spreadsheets. It is now available in a Windows version.

Microsoft Excel

Excel is a very powerful spreadsheet program with pull-down menus, windows, and dozens of features. It can even perform as a database.

Quattro

The Quattro spreadsheet looks very much like Lotus 1-2-3, but it has better graphics capabilities for charts, calculates faster, has pull-down menus, can print sideways, and has several other features not found in Lotus 1-2-3. One of the better features is the suggested list price of $195—$148 from many discount houses.

SuperCalc5

SuperCalc, introduced in 1981, was one of the pioneer spreadsheets. It has never enjoyed the popularity of Lotus, though it has features not found in Lotus. It is compatible with Lotus 1-2-3 files and can link to dBASE and several other files. It is an excellent spreadsheet. Computer Associates has also developed several excellent accounting packages costing from $595 to $695.

There are many other spreadsheet programs. Check the ads and reviews in the computer magazines.

Utilities

Utilities are essential tools that can unerase a file, detect bad sectors on a hard disk, diagnose, unfragment, sort, and do many other things. Norton Utilities was the first and is still foremost in the utility area. Mace Utilities has several functions not found in Norton. Mace Gold is an integrated package of utilities that includes POP—a power-out protection program—a backup utility, TextFix, and dbFix for data retrieval. PC Tools has even more utilities than Norton or Mace.

Ontrack, the people who have sold several million copies of Disk Manager for hard disks, also has a utility program called DOSUTILS. It provides tools to display and modify any physical sector of a hard disk, to scan for bad sectors, and to diagnose and analyze the disk.

Steve Gibson's SpinRite, Prime Solution's Disk Technician, and Gazelle's OPTune are excellent hard disk tools for low-level formatting, defragmenting, and detecting potential bad sectors on a hard disk.

Norton Utilities

Λ program that everybody should have. Norton also has Norton Commander, a shell program, and Norton Backup, a very good hard disk backup program. Norton has recently merged with Symantec, (213) 453-2361.

Mace Utilities

Mace Utilities was developed by Paul Mace. It was recently acquired by Fifth Generation Systems, (504) 291-7221, the people who developed FastBack, the leading backup program.

PC Tools

PC Tools, from Central Point Software, (503) 690-8090, is an excellent program that just about does it all. It has data recovery utilities, hard disk backup, a DOS shell, a disk manager, and more.

SpinRite II

This software can check the interleave and reset it for the optimum factor. It can do this without destroying your data. It can also test a hard drive and detect any marginal areas. SpinRite, (714) 362-8800, can maximize hard disk performance and prevent hard disk problems before they happen.

Steve Gibson, the developer of SpinRite, writes a very interesting weekly column for *InfoWorld*.

Disk Technician

Disk Technician, from Prime Solutions, (619) 274-5000, does essentially the same thing that SpinRite does, and a bit more. It has several automatic features and can now detect most viruses.

OPTune

OPTune is another utility that can maximize hard disk performance. It is similar to SpinRite and Disk Technician. Gazelle Systems, (800) 233-0383, has also developed QDOS 3, an excellent shell program, and Back-It 4, a very good hard disk backup program.

CheckIt

CheckIt, from Touchstone Software, (714) 969-7746, quickly checks and reports on your computers configuration, type of CPU, amount of memory, and installed drives and peripherals. It runs diagnostic tests of the installed items and can do performance benchmark tests.

Directory and disk management programs

There are dozens of disk management programs that can help you keep track of files and data on your hard disk, as well as find, rename, view, sort, copy, delete, and many other useful utilities. They can save an enormous amount of time and make life a lot simpler.

XTreePro Gold

Executive Systems, (800) 634-5545, XTree was one of the first and is still one of the best disk management programs. It has recently been revised and is now much faster and has several new features.

QDOS III

A disk management program from Gazelle Systems, (800) 233-0383, that is similar to XTree. It does not have quite as many features as XTree, but it is less expensive.

Tree86 3.0

This low-cost disk management program from Aldridge Company, (713) 953-1940, is similar to XTree.

Wonder Plus 3.08

Wonder, or 1DIR, was one of the early disk management shells. Bourbaki, Inc., (208) 342-5849, has recently revised and updated it.

Search utilities

I have about 3000 files on my hard disk in several subdirectories. You can imagine how difficult it is to keep track of all of them. I sometimes forget in which subdirectory I filed something. There are a couple of programs that can go through all of my directories and look for a file by name, but because only eight characters are allowed for a file name, it is difficult to remember what is in each file. Several programs are available that can search through all my files and find almost anything that I tell them to. I don't even have to know the full name of what I'm looking for. The programs will accept wild cards and tell me where there are matches.

Magellan 2.0

Magellan 2.0, from Lotus, is a very sophisticated program that can navigate and do global searches through files and across directories. It finds text and lets you view it in a window. It will let you compress files, backup, compare, undelete, and several other excellent utilities.

Several other search programs are available that are not quite as sophisticated as Magellan. There are also public domain and shareware search programs.

Computer-aided design
AutoCAD

AutoCAD, from Autodesk, is a high-end, high-cost design program. It is quite complex with an abundance of capabilities and functions. It is also rather expensive at about $3000. Autodesk is the IBM of the CAD world and has more or less established the standard for the many clones that have followed.

Generic CADD

Autodesk has several modules and other programs that cost less than AutoCAD. One of them is Generic CADD 6.0.

Home Series

Autodesk has a set of five low-cost programs they call the Home Series. These programs are home, kitchen, bathroom, deck, and landscape. The programs let you design your dream home, an up-to-date kitchen, a bathroom, a deck, or plan your landscape. Each of the five programs has a list price of $59.95. The programs come with a library of professional symbols such as doors, outlets, furniture, fixtures, and appliances that you can import and place in your drawing. The program tracks the materials specified in your drawing and automatically creates a shopping list. I recommend these programs for anyone who plans to design their own home or do any remodeling on an older home. They can save you hours of time and lots of money.

DesignCAD 2D and DesignCAD 3D

These CAD programs, from American Small Business Computers, (918) 825-4844, will do just about everything that AutoCAD will do at about one-tenth of the cost. DesignCAD 3D allows you to make three-dimensional drawings.

There are several other companies that offer CAD software. Check the computer magazines.

Tax programs

Because you have a computer, it might not be necessary for you to pay a tax preparer to do your taxes. Several tax programs are available that can do the job for you. Unless you have a very complicated income, your taxes can be done quickly and easily. In many cases, the cost of the program will probably be less than the cost of having a tax preparer do your taxes.

Besides doing your own taxes, most of these programs allow you to set up files and do the taxes of others. Many companies offer programs for professional tax businesses, but usually at a much higher price. I mentioned several tax software programs in chapter 15.

Miscellaneous

Programs are available for accounting, statistics, finance, and many other applications. Some are very expensive, some are very reasonable.

Money Counts

This is a very inexpensive program from Parsons Technology that can be used at home or in a small business. With it you can set up a budget, keep track of all your expenses, balance your checkbook, and several other functions. It costs about $40.

It's Legal

Another program from Parsons Technology, (800) 223-6925, this software helps you create wills, leases, promissory notes, and other legal documents.

WillMaker 4.0

A low-cost program, from Nolo Press, (800) 992-6656, that can help you create a will. A will is an important document. Everyone should have a will, no matter what your age or how much you own. Many people put it off because they don't want to take the time or they don't want to pay a lawyer a large fee. This inexpensive software can help you create a legal will.

The Random House Encyclopedia

Microlytics, (716) 248-9150, has placed a whole encyclopedia on disk, enabling you to find any subject very quickly.

ACT!

ACT!, from Contact Software, (800) 228-9228, lets you keep track of business contacts, schedules, and expenses, write reports, and about 30 other features.

Form Express

Most businesses have dozens of forms that must be filled out. Quite often the information is then transferred to a computer. Forms Express, (415) 382-6600, lets you easily design and fill in almost any kind of form on a hard disk. If necessary, the form can then be printed out.

Summary

I can't possibly mention all of the fantastic software that is available. There are thousands and thousands of ready-made software programs that will allow you to do almost anything with your computer. Look through any computer magazine for the reviews and ads. You should be able to find programs for almost any application.

17
Component sources

How much you save by building your own computer depends on what components you buy and who you buy them from. You have to shop wisely and be fairly knowledgeable about the components in order to take advantage of good bargains.

Computer swaps

I have done almost all of my buying at computer shows and swap meets. There is at least one computer show or swap almost every weekend in large cities. If you live in or near a large city, check your newspaper for ads. In California several computer magazines, such as *MicroTimes* and *Computer Currents*, list the coming events.

One of the best features of swap meets is that almost all of the components that you will need are on display in one place. Several booths have the same components. I usually take a pencil and pad with me to the shows so I can write down the prices of the items that I want to buy and compare prices at the various booths. There can be quite a wide variation in prices. I bought a good printer at one show. One dealer was asking $995, and about 50 feet away, another dealer was offering the same printer for $695.

You can also haggle with most of the dealers at these shows, especially when it gets near closing time. Rather than pack up the material and lug it back to their stores, many sell it for a lower price.

The Interface Company puts on the biggest computer shows in the country. They have a Spring COMDEX in Atlanta or Chicago and a Fall COMDEX in Las Vegas. They usually attract over 120,000 visitors for the Las Vegas show.

Support your local store

I consider myself to be fairly knowledgeable about electronics and computers. I hate to admit it, but a few times in the past I have been sold inferior and shoddy merchandise at computer swaps. Times have changed and most of the boards and components today have been around long enough that most of the bugs have been found and eliminated. Most of the vendors at the swaps are local business people. They want your business and will not risk losing you as a customer. There might be a few vendors from other parts of the country. If you buy something from a vendor who does not have a local store, be sure to get a name and address. Most components are reliable, but there is always a chance that something might not work. You might need to exchange it or get it repaired, or you might need to ask some questions or need some support to get it working.

Again, computers are very easy to assemble. Once you have all of the components, it will take less than an hour to assemble your computer. But it is possible to make a mistake. Most components are now fairly reliable, but there is still a possibility that a new part that you buy and install could be defective. Most dealers will give you a warranty of some kind and will replace defective parts. If there is something in the system that prevents it from operating, you might not be able to determine just which component is defective. Besides that, it can sometimes take a considerable amount of time to remove a component like a motherboard and return it to someone across town — or even worse, someone across the country. So if at all possible, try to deal with a knowledgeable vendor who will support you and help you if you have any problems.

Mail order

Every computer magazine carries pages and pages of ads for compatible components and systems that can be sent to you through the mail. If you live in an area where there are no computer stores or shows, you can buy by mail. Another reason to use mail order is that it is usually less expensive than local vendors. Most local vendors have to buy their stock from a distributor. The distributor buys it from the manufacturer or a wholesaler. By the time you get the product, it has passed through several companies who have each made some profit. One reason an IBM or Apple computer is more expensive is that they have several middlemen. Most of the direct marketers who advertise by mail have cut out the middlemen.

Most mail-order businesses are honest. Ads are the lifeblood of magazines. The subscription price of a magazine does not even pay the mailing costs — they must have ads. A few bad advertisers can ruin a magazine so the magazines have formed the Microcomputer Marketing Council (MMC) of the Direct Marketing Association. They have an action line at (212) 297-1393. If you have problems with a vendor that you cannot resolve, they might be able to help. They police their advertisers fairly closely.

You should be sure of what you need and what you are ordering. Some of the ads aren't written very well and might not tell the whole story. If possible, call the company before ordering and make sure. Ask what their return policy is for defective merchandise. Also ask how long before the item will be shipped, and ask for the current price. The ads are usually placed about two months before the magazines are delivered or hit the stands. The way prices change, there could be quite a difference in price at the time you place your order. A $2 or $3 phone call could save you a lot of time, trouble, grief, and maybe even some money.

Ten rules for ordering by mail

1. Look for a street address. Make sure the advertiser has a street address. In some ads, they give only a phone number. If you decide to buy from this vendor, call and verify that there is a person on the other end with a street number. But before you send any money, do a bit more investigation. If possible, look through past issues of the same magazine for previous ads. If he has been advertising for several months, then he is probably okay.

2. Compare other vendors prices. Check through the magazines for other vendors' prices for this product. The prices should be fairly close. If it appears to be a bargain that is too good to be true, then . . . you know the rest.

3. Buy from MMC members. Buy from a vendor who is a member of the Microcomputer Marketing Council of the Direct Marketing Association or other recognized association. About 10,000 members now belong to marketing associations. They have agreed to abide by the ethical guidelines and rules of the associations. Except for friendly persuasion and the threat of expulsion, the association has little power over its members. But most association members realize what is at stake and put a great value on their membership. Most who advertise in the major computer magazines are members. The United Stated Post Office, the Federal Trade Commission, the magazines, and the legitimate businessmen who advertise have taken steps to try to stop the fraud and scams.

4. Do your homework. Read the ads carefully. Many ads use abbreviations or might not be entirely clear. If in doubt, call and ask. A $2 telephone call might save you time and prevent a lot of frustration. Know exactly what you want — state precisely the model, make, size, component, and any other pertinent information. Tell them which ad you are ordering from and ask them for the current price, if the item is in stock, and when you can expect delivery. If the item is not in stock, indicate whether you will accept a substitute or want your money refunded. Ask for an invoice or order number. Ask the person's name. Write down all of the information, the time, the date, the company's address and phone number, a description of the item, and the promised delivery date. Write down and save any information about telephone conversations, including the time, the date, and the person's name. Save any and all correspondence.

5. Ask questions. Ask if the advertised item comes with all the necessary cables, parts, accessories, software, etc. Ask what the warranties are. Ask about the seller's return and refund policies and who you should correspond with if there is a problem.

6. Don't send cash. You will have no record of it. If possible, use a credit card. If you have a problem, you can possibly have the bank refuse to pay the amount. A personal check might cause a delay of three to four weeks while the vendor waits for it to clear. A money order or credit card order should be filled and shipped immediately. Keep a copy of the money order.

7. Ask for a delivery date. If you have not received your order by the promised delivery date notify the seller.

8. Try the item out as soon as you receive it. If you have a problem, notify the seller immediately, by phone, then in writing. Give all details. Don't return the merchandise unless the dealer gives you a return material authorization (RMA). Make sure to keep a copy of the shipper's receipt or packing slip or some evidence that the material was returned.

9. If you believe a product is defective or you have a problem, reread your warranties and guarantees. Reread the manual and any documentation. It is very easy to make an error or misunderstand how an item operates if you are unfamiliar with it. Before you go to a lot of trouble, try to get some help from someone else. At least get someone to verify that you do have a problem. There are many times when a problem will disappear and the vendor will not be able to duplicate it. If possible, when you call, try to have the item in your computer and be at the computer so you can describe the problem as it happens.

10. Try to work out your problem with the vendor. If you cannot, then write to the consumer complaint agency in the seller's state. You should also write to the magazine and to the DMA, 6 E. 43rd St., New York, NY 10017.

Federal Trade Commission rules

1. The seller must ship your order within 30 days unless the ad clearly states that it will take longer.

2. If it appears that the seller cannot ship when promised, he must notify you and give a new shipping date. He must give you the opportunity to cancel the order and refund your money if you desire.

3. If the seller notifies you that he cannot fill your order on time, he must include a stamped self-addressed envelope or card so that you can respond to his notice. If you do not respond, he may assume that you agree to the delay. He still must ship within 30 days of the end of the original 30 days or cancel your order and refund your money.

4. Even if you consent to a delay, you still have the right to cancel at any time.

5. If you cancel an order that has been paid for by check or money order, the seller must refund your money. If you paid by credit card, your account must be credited within one billing cycle. Store credits or vouchers in place of a refund are not acceptable.

6. If the item you ordered is not available, the seller may not send you a substitute without your express consent.

On-line services

If you have a modem, several bulletin board and on-line companies offer all kinds of shopping services. You can call from your computer and buy such things as airline tickets, furniture, clothing, toys, electronics, computers, and just about everything else you can imagine.

The on-line services offer some advantages over mail order. The prices quoted in some magazines might be two or three months old by the time the magazine is published. The prices quoted by the on-line services are the latest up-to-the-minute prices.

A few of the bulletin boards that offer on-line buying include

First Capitol Computer
16 Algana
St. Peters, MO 63376
(314) 928-9889
BBS line (314) 928-9228

Leo Electronics
Box 11307
Torrance, CA 95124
(213) 212-6133
BBS line (213) 212-7179

JDR Microdevices
2233 Branham Ln.
San Jose, CA 95124
(408) 559-1200
BBS line (408) 559-0253

Swan Technologies
3075 Research Dr.
State College, PA 16801
(814) 234-2236
BBS line (814) 237-6145

On-line companies include

- CompuServe   (800) 848-8990
- Delphi   (800) 544-4005
- Prodigy   (800) 776-3449
- Genie   (800) 638-9636

Sources of knowledge

Several good magazines can help you gain the knowledge needed to make sensible purchases and to learn more about computers. These magazines usually carry some very interesting and informative articles and reviews of software and hardware. They also have many ads for computers, components, and software. Some of the better magazines that you can subscribe to are *Computer Shopper, PC Sources, Byte, Computer Buying World, Computer Monthly, PC World,* and *PC Magazine.* Most of these magazines are available on local magazine racks. But you will save money with a yearly subscription and they will be delivered to your door.

If you need a source of components, you only have to look in any of the magazines listed above to find hundreds of them. If you live near a large city, there will no doubt be several vendors who advertise in your local paper.

Many of the magazines have a section that lists all of the products advertised in that particular issue. The components and products are categorized and listed by page number. It makes it very easy to find what you are looking for.

Another source of computer information can be found in the many good computer books published by TAB McGraw-Hill and others.

Recommended computer magazines

A few of the magazines that will help you keep abreast of the many changes in the computer field include

Byte
P.O. Box 558
Highstown, NJ 08520

Micro Times
5951 Canning St.
Oakland, CA 94609

Compute!
P.O. Box 3244
Harlan, IA 51593-2424

PC Magazine
P.O. Box 51524
Boulder, CO 80321-1524

Computer Currents
5720 Hollis St.
Emeryville, CA 94608

PC Computing
P.O. Box 50253
Boulder, CO 80321-0253

Computer Graphics World
P.O. Box 122
Tulsa, OK 74101-9966

PC Sources
P.O. Box 50237
Boulder, CO 80321-0237

Computer Monthly
P.O. Box 7062
Atlanta, GA 30357-0062

PC Today
P.O. Box 85380
Lincoln, NE 68501-9815

Computer Shopper
P.O. Box 51020
Boulder, CO 80321-1020

PC World
P.O. Box 51833
Boulder, CO 80321-1833

Data Based Advisor
P.O. Box 3735
Escondido, CA 92025-9895

Personal Workstation
P.O. Box 51615
Boulder, CO 80321-1615

Home Office Computing
P.O. Box 51344
Boulder, CO 80321-1344

Publish!
P.O. Box 51966
Boulder, CO 80321-1966

LAN
P.O. Box 50047
Boulder, CO 80321-0047

Unix World
P.O. Box 1929
Marion, OH 43306

Free magazines to qualified subscribers

The magazines listed as free are sent only to qualified subscribers. The subscription price of a magazine usually does not cover the costs of publication, mailing, distribution, and other costs. Most magazines depend almost entirely on advertisers for their existence. The more subscribers a magazine has, the more it can charge for its ads. Naturally a magazine can attract a lot more subscribers if the magazine is free.

PC Week and *InfoWorld* are excellent magazines. They are so popular that the publishers have to limit the number of free subscribers. They cannot possibly accommodate all the people who have applied. They have set standards which have to be met in order to qualify. They do not publish the standards, so even if you answer all of the questions on the application, you still might not qualify.

To get a free subscription, you must write to the magazine for a qualifying application form. The form will ask several questions, such as how you are involved with computers, the company you work for, whether you have any influence in purchasing the computer products listed in the magazines, and several other questions that give them a very good profile of their readers.

The list of magazines below is not nearly complete. There are hundreds of trade magazines that are sent free to qualified subscribers. The Cahners Company alone publishes 32 different trade magazines. Many of the trade magazines are highly technical and narrowly specialized.

Automatic I.D. News
P.O. Box 6170
Duluth, MN 55806-9870

California Business
P.O. Box 70735
Pasadena, CA 91117-9947

Communications Week
P.O. Box 2070
Manhasset, NY 11030

Computer Buying World
401 Edgewater Pl. #630
Wakefield, MA 01880

Computer Design
P.O. Box 3466
Tulsa, OK 74101-3466

Computer Products
P.O. Box 14000
Dover, NJ 07801-9990

Computer Reseller News
P.O. Box 2040
Manhasset, NY 11030

Computer Systems News
600 Community Dr.
Manhasset, NY 11030

Computer Technology Review
924 Westwood Blvd., Suite 65
Los Angeles, CA 90024

Designfax
P.O. Box 1151
Skokie, IL 60076-9917

Discount Merchandiser
215 Lexington Ave.
New York, NY 10157

EE Product News
P.O. Box 12982
Overland Park, KS 66212

Electronic Manufacturing
P.O. Box 159
Libertyville, IL 60048

Electronic Publishing & Printing
650 S. Clark St.
Chicago, IL 60605-9960

Electronics
P.O. Box 985061
Cleveland, OH 44198

Federal Computer Week
P.O. Box 602
Winchester, MA 01890

ID Systems
P.O. Box 874
Peterborough, NH 03458

Identification Journal
2640 N. Halsted St.
Chicago, IL 60614-9962

InfoWorld
1060 Marsh Rd.
Menlo Park, CA 94025

LAN Times
122 East, 1700 South
Provo, UT 84606

Lasers & Optronics
301 Gibraltar Dr.
Morris Plains, NJ 07950

Machine Design
P.O. Box 985015
Cleveland, OH 44198-5015

Manufacturing Systems
P.O. Box 3008
Wheaton, IL 60189-9972

Medical Equipment Designer
29100 Aurora Rd., Suite 200
Cleveland, OH 44139

Mini-Micro Systems
P.O. Box 5051
Denver, CO 80217-9872

Modern Office Technology
1100 Superior Ave.
Cleveland, OH 44197-8032

Office Systems 90
P.O. Box 3116
Woburn, MA 01888-9878

Office Systems Dealer 90
P.O. Box 2281
Woburn, MA 01888-9873

PC Week
P.O. Box 5920
Cherry Hill, NJ 08034

Photo Business
1515 Broadway
New York, NY 10036

The Programmer's Shop
5 Pond Park Rd.
Hingham, MA 02043-9845

Quality
P.O. Box 3002
Wheaton, IL 60189-9929

Reseller Management
Box 601
Morris Plains, NJ 07950

Robotics World
6255 Barfield Rd.
Atlanta, GA 30328-9988

Scientific Computing
301 Gibraltar Dr.
Morris Plains, NJ 07950

Unix Review
P.O. Box 7439
San Francisco, CA 94120

Surface Mount Technology
P.O. Box 159
Libertyville, IL 60048

Public domain and shareware software

There are several companies that provide public domain, shareware, and low-cost software. They also publish catalogs listing their software. Some might charge a small fee for the catalog.

- PC-Sig 1030D   (800) 245-6717
- MicroCom Systems   (408) 737-9000
- Public Brand Software   (800) 426-3475
- Software Express/Direct   (800) 331-8192
- Selective Software   (800) 423-3556
- The Computer Room   (703) 832-3341
- Softwarehouse   (408) 748-0461
- PC Plus Consulting   (818) 891-7930
- Micro Star   (800) 443-6103
- International Software Library   (800) 992-1992
- National PD Library   (619) 941-0925
- Computers International   (619) 630-0055
- Shareware Express   (800) 346-2842

Computer books

Several companies publish computer books. One of the larger companies is TAB Books, a division of McGraw-Hill. Write to them for a catalog listing the many books that they publish at TAB Books, Blue Ridge Summit, PA 17294-0850, or call (800) 822-8138.

18
Troubleshooting

If you assembled your computer properly, it should work perfectly. You should have a record of the switch and jumper settings for each of your boards. You should know what components are inside your computer and how they are configured.

The number one cause of problems

If your network is not up and running, there is always the possibility that something was not plugged in correctly or some minor error was made in the installation. I have a friend who works for a large computer mail-order firm. His job is to check and repair all of the components that are returned by customers. I asked him what the biggest problem was, and his answer was, "People just don't read and follow the instructions or they make errors and don't bother to check their work."

By far the greatest problem in assembling a unit, adding something to a computer, or installing software is not following the instructions. Quite often it is not necessarily the fault of the person trying to follow the instructions. I am a member of Mensa and have worked in the electronic industry for over 30 years, but sometimes I have great difficulty trying to decipher and follow the instructions in some manuals. Sometimes a very crucial instruction or piece of information is inconspicuously buried on page 300 of a 450-page manual.

If you have just assembled a computer or added something to it, recheck all the cables and any boards. Make sure the boards are configured properly and that they are properly seated. Read the instructions again, then turn on the power. If it works, put the cover on and button it up.

What to do if it is completely dead

Several diagnostic software programs are available. They are great in many cases, but if the computer is completely dead, the software won't do you any good. If the computer is completely dead, the first thing to do is check the power. If you don't have a voltmeter, plug a lamp into the socket and see if it lights. Check your power cord. Check the switch on the computer. Check the fan in the power supply. Is it turning? Check the monitor, its power cord, its fuses, and its adapter.

If you have added a board or some accessory and your computer doesn't work, remove the item and try the computer again. If the computer works without the board, then you know that it must be the board. If it is still dead, then you probably have some serious problems. You probably need some high-level troubleshooting.

Levels of troubleshooting

There are many levels of troubleshooting. Advanced troubleshooting requires much sophisticated equipment such as oscilloscopes, digital meters, logic probes, signal generators, and lots of training. But most of the problems that you will encounter are rather minor, so you don't need all that equipment and training. Most problems can be solved with just a little common sense and the use of our five senses of sight, hearing, touch, smell, and taste. Actually, you probably won't be using taste very often.

Electricity — the life blood of the computer

Troubleshooting is a little easier if you know just a little of the electronic basics. Computers are possible because of electricity. An electronic charge is formed when there is an imbalance or an excess number of electrons at one pole. The excess electrons flow through whatever path they can find to get to ground or to the other pole. It is much like water flowing downhill to find its level.

Most electric or electronic paths have varying amounts of resistance so that work or heat is created when the electrons pass through them. For instance, if a flashlight is turned on, electrons pass through the bulb, which has a resistive filament. The heat generated by the electrons passing through the bulb causes the filament to glow red hot and create light. If the flashlight is left on for a period of time, all of the excess electrons from the positive anode of the battery will pass through the bulb to the negative pole of the battery. At this time the amount of electrons at the negative and positive poles will be the same. There will be a perfect balance and the battery will be dead.

A computer is made up of circuits and boards that have resistors, capacitors, inductors, transistors, motors, and many other components. These components perform useful functions when electricity passes through them. The circuits are designed so that the paths of the electric currents are divided, controlled, and shunted to do the work that we want done.

Occasionally, too many electrons find their way through a weakened component and burn it out, or for some reason the electrons are shunted through a different path. This might cause an intermittent, a partial, or a complete failure.

The basic components of a computer

The early IBM PC had an 8088 CPU and four other basic support chips: the 8259 interrupt controller, the 8237 DMA controller, the 8253/8254 programmable interval timer, and the 8255 programmable input/output controller. These same chips are found in the 8086, 286, 386, and 486. You will find two DMA and two interrupt controllers in the 286, 386, and 486. You might not be able to see these chips on the modern motherboards because they are usually contained in a very large-scale integrated (VLSI) package.

The CPU is the brains of the computer. It controls the basic operation by sending and receiving control signals and memory addresses. It sends and receives data along the bus to and from other parts of the system. It carries out computations, numeric comparisons, and many other functions in response to software programs.

The 8259 programmable interrupt controller responds to interrupt requests (IRQs) generated by system hardware components. These requests come from such components as the keyboard, disk drive controller, and system timer.

The 8237 DMA controller is able to transfer data to and from the computer's memory without passing it through the CPU. This allows input and output from the disk drives without CPU involvement.

The 8253/8254 programmable interval timer generates timing signals for various system tasks.

The 8255 programmable input/output controller provides an interface between the CPU and the I/O devices.

Of course, several other chips are interrelated to each of these main chips and all of the main chips are interrelated. Because they are all so intimately interrelated, a failure in any main chip, and some minor chips, can cause the whole circuit to fail. The actual defect can be very difficult to pinpoint.

Fewer bugs today

In the early days there were lots of bugs and errors in the clone computers. The Far East manufacturers didn't spend a lot of money on quality control and testing. But most of the computer manufacturers have been making the parts long enough now that the designs have been firmed up and most of the bugs have been eliminated.

Document the problem

The chances are if a computer or network is going to break down, it will do it at the most inopportune time. This is one of the basic tenets of Murphy's immutable and inflexible laws.

If if breaks down, try not to panic. Ranting, cussing, and crying might make you feel better, but it won't solve the problem. Instead, get out a pad and pencil and write down everything as it happens. It is very easy to forget. Write down all the particulars, how the cables are plugged in, the software that is running, and anything that might be pertinent. You might get error messages on your screen. Use the PrtSc (print screen) key to print out the messages.

If you can't solve the problem, you might have to call someone or your vendor for help. If you have all the written information before you, it helps. If possible, try to call from your computer, as it is acting up.

Power on self-test (POST)

Every time a computer is turned on, or booted up, it does a power on self-test (POST). It checks the RAM, the floppy drives, the hard drives, the monitor, the printer, the keyboard, and other peripherals that you have installed. If everything is okay, it gives a short beep then boots up. If it does not find a unit, or if the unit is not functioning correctly, it will beep and display an error code. It might beep two or more times depending on the error, or if the power supply or motherboard is defective, it might not beep at all.

The codes start with 100 and can go up to 20,000. Ordinarily the codes will not be displayed if there is no problem. If there is a problem, the last two digits of the code will be something other that 00. Each BIOS manufacturer develops their own codes so there are some slight differences, but most of them are similar to those shown in the following list:

101	Motherboard failure
109	Direct memory access test error
121	Unexpected hardware interrupt occurred
163	Time and date not set
199	User-indicated configuration not correct
201	Memory test failure
301	Keyboard test failure or a stuck key
401	Monochrome display and/or adapter test failure
432	Parallel printer not turned on
501	Color graphics display and/or adapter test failure
601	Diskette drives and/or adapter test failure
701	Math coprocessor test error
901	Parallel printer adapter test failure
1101	Asynchronous communications adapter test failure
1301	Game control adapter test failure
1302	Joystick test failure
1401	Printer test failure
1701	Fixed disk drive and/or adapter test failure
2401	Enhanced graphics display and/or adapter test failure
2501	Enhanced graphics display and/or adapter test failure

The listing of codes is very brief. If you would like to see an extensive listing of these codes, I recommend that you get Scott Mueller's *Upgrading and Repairing PCs,* 2nd Edition, published by QUE.

POST cards

Several companies have developed diagnostic cards or boards that can be plugged into a slot on the motherboard to display the POST codes. If there is a failure in the system, it can tell you immediately what is wrong.

Micro 2000, (818) 547-0125, has a POST-probe diagnostic card. Their card not only checks and displays the POST codes, it also checks for the correct power supply voltages. It can be used on all ISA, EISA, and even MCA computers.

DOS error messages

DOS has several error messages if you try to make the computer do something it can't do. But many of the messages are not very clear. The DOS 5.0 manual has over 650 pages, and according to the index, there are only two very brief mentions of *error* in the whole manual.

Power supply

Most of the components in your computer are fairly low power and low voltage. The only high voltage in your system is in the power supply, and it is pretty well enclosed, so there is no danger of shock if you open your computer and put your hand inside it. But you should NEVER EVER connect or disconnect a board or cable while the power is on. Fragile semiconductors might be destroyed if you do so.

Most of the power supplies have short-circuit protection. If too much of a load is placed on them, they will drop out and shut down, similar to what happens when a circuit breaker is overloaded. Most power supplies are designed to operate only with a load. If you take one out of a system and turn it on without a load, most of them will not work. You can plug in a floppy drive to act as a load if you want to check the voltages out of a system.

Semiconductors have no moving parts. If the circuit is designed properly, the semiconductors should last indefinitely. Heat is an enemy and can cause semiconductor failure. The fan in the power supply should provide adequate cooling. All of the openings on the back panel that correspond to the slots on the motherboard should have blank fillers. Even the holes on the bottom of the chassis should be covered with tape. This forces the fan to draw air in from the front of the computer, pull it over the boards and exhaust it through the opening in the power supply case. Nothing should be placed in front of or behind the computer that will restrict air flow. If you don't hear the fan when you turn on a computer, or if the fan isn't running, then the power supply might be defective.

The pin connections and wire colors from the power supply are shown in Table 18-1.

The 8 slotted connectors on the motherboard have 62 contacts — 31 on the A side and 31 on the B side. The black ground wires connect to B1 of each of the eight slots. B3 and B29 have +5-V dc, B5 has −5-V dc, B7 has −12-V dc, and B9 has +12-V dc. These voltages go to the listed pins on each of the eight plug-in slots.

Instruments and tools

For high levels of troubleshooting, you need some rather sophisticated and expensive instruments to do a thorough analysis of the system. You need a good high-frequency oscilloscope, a digital analyzer, a logic probe, and several other expensive pieces of equipment. You need a test bench with a spare power supply, disk drives, and a computer with some empty slots so that you can plug in suspect boards and test them. You need a volt-ohmmeter, some clip leads, side-cutting dikes, long-nose pliers, various screwdrivers, nut

Table 18-1. Power supply conections

Disk drive power supply connections

Pin	Color	Function
1	Yellow	+12 Vdc
2	Black	Ground
3	Black	Ground
4	Red	+5 Vdc

Power supply connections to the motherboard

P8 Pin	Color	Function
1	White	Power good
2	No connection	
3	Yellow	+12 Vdc
4	Brown	−12 Vdc
5	Black	Ground
6	Black	Ground

P9 Pin	Color	Function
1	Black	Ground
2	Black	Ground
3	Blue	−5 Vdc
4	Red	+5 Vdc
5	Red	+5 Vdc
6	Red	+5 Vdc

drivers, a soldering iron, and solder. You need plenty of light over the bench and a flashlight or a small light to light up the dark places in the computer case. And most importantly, you need quite a lot of training and experience.

Common problems

For most of the common problems you don't need a lot of test gear. Often a problem can be solved by using your eyes, ears, nose, and touch.

If you look closely, you might see a cable that is not plugged in properly, or a board that is not completely seated, or a switch that is not set right, or many other obvious things.

You can use your ears to listen for any unusual sounds. The only sound from your computer should be the noise of your drive motors and the fan in the power supply.

If you have ever smelled a burned resistor or a capacitor, you never forget it. If you smell something unusual, try to locate where it is coming from.

If you touch a component and it seems to be unusually hot, that could be the cause of your problem. Except for the insides of your power supply, there should not be any voltage above 12 volts in your computer. It should be safe to touch the components.

Electrostatic discharge

When you walk across a carpet and then touch a brass doorknob you can sometimes see a spark fly and often get a shock. Before you touch any of the components or handle them, you should ground yourself and discharge any static voltage that you have built up. You can discharge yourself by touching an unpainted metal part on any device that is plugged in. It is possible for a person to build up a charge of 4000 volts or more of electrostatic voltage. On electronic assembly lines, the workers wear a ground strap whenever they are working with any components that might be sensitive to electrostatic discharge.

Recommended tools

Some tools that you should have around, even if you never have any computer problems, are discussed in the following paragraphs.

You should have several sizes of screwdrivers. A couple of them should be magnetic for picking up and starting small screws. You can buy magnetic screwdrivers, or you can make them yourself. Just take a strong magnet and rub it on the blade of the screwdriver a few times. The magnets on cabinet doors, or the voice coil magnet of a loudspeaker will do. Be very careful with any magnet around your floppy diskettes. It can erase them.

You should also have a small screwdriver with a bent tip that can be used to pry up ICs. Some of the larger ICs are very difficult to remove. One of the blank fillers for the slots on the back panel makes a good prying tool.

You should have a couple of different types of pliers. You should have at least one long-nose pliers and side-cutting dikes for clipping component leads and cutting wire. You might buy cutters that also have wire strippers.

You should have a soldering iron and some solder. You shouldn't have to do much soldering but you never know when you might need to repair a cable or do some other minor job. You should also have some cable crimpers if you build your own cables.

By all means buy a volt-ohmmeter. There are dozens of uses for a volt-ohmmeter. It can be used to check the wiring continuity in your cables, phone lines, switches, etc. You can also use a volt-ohmmeter to check for proper voltages in your computer. You can buy a relatively inexpensive volt-ohmmeter at any Radio Shack or electronics store. You should also have several clip leads. You can buy them at the local Radio Shack or electronics store.

You should have a flashlight for looking into the dark places inside your computer or at the cable connections behind your computer.

How to find the problem

If a computer is down and you suspect a board, if you have a spare that is the same, swap it out. If you don't have a spare, maybe you can borrow one from another computer.

If you suspect a board, but don't know which one, take the boards out to the barest minimum. Then add them back until the problem develops.

CAUTION!! Always turn off the power when plugging in or unplugging a board or cable.

Wiggle the boards and cables to see if it is an intermittent problem. Many times a board might not be seated properly. A wire or cable can be broken and still make contact until it is moved.

Check the ICs and connectors for bent pins. If you have installed memory ICs and get errors, check to make sure that they are seated properly and that all the pins are in the sockets. If you swap an IC, make a note of how it is oriented before removing it. There should be a small dot of white paint or a U-shaped indentation at the end that has pin 1. If you forget to note the orientation, look at the other ICs. Most of the boards are laid out so that all of the ICs are oriented the same way. The chrome fillers that are used to cover the unused slots in the back of the case make very good tools for prying up ICs.

You might also try unplugging a cable or a board and plugging it back in. Sometimes the pins can be slightly corroded or not seated properly. Before unplugging a cable, you should put a stripe on the connector and cable with a marking pen or nail polish so that you can easily see how they should be plugged back in. Recently I turned on one of my computers that hadn't been used for about a month. I got a message that the FDC had an error. This board also controls my hard disks, so I was a bit concerned. I unplugged the controller board and cleaned the contacts and plugged it back in. (The copper contacts on a plug-in board can become corroded. You can clean them with an ordinary pencil eraser.) But I still got the FDC error message. I got out another FDC and prepared to plug it in, but I had to change the setting of a shorting bar on the controller board. On a hunch, I slipped the shorting bar on and off a few times, then tried the board again. The floppy drives worked perfectly. The shorting bar and the pins had become corroded during the time it was not used.

The problem could be in a DIP switch. You might try turning it on and off a few times.

CAUTION!! Again, always write down the switch positions before touching them. Make a diagram of the wires, cables, and switch settings before you disturb them. It is easy to forget how they were plugged in or set before you moved them. You could end up making things worse. Make a pencil mark before turning a knob or variable coil or capacitor so that it can be returned to the same setting when you find out that it didn't help. Better yet, resist the temptation to reset these types of components. Most were set using highly sophisticated instruments. They don't usually change enough to cause a problem.

If you are having monitor problems, check the switch settings on the motherboard. There are several different motherboards. Some have DIP switches or shorting bars that must be set to configure the system for the type of monitor you are using, such as monochrome, CGA, EGA, or VGA. Most monitors also have fuses. You should check them. Also check the cables for proper connections.

Printer problems, especially the serial type, are so many that I do not even attempt to list them here. Many printers today have both parallel and serial connectors. The IBM compatible ISA systems default to the parallel system. If at all possible, use the parallel port. There are very few problems with parallel as compared to serial. If you use the serial port, you will probably have to use the DOS Mode command to change from the LPT port to the serial port. The commands might be something like this:

MODE COM1 : 9600,N,8,P

then

MODE LPT1 : = COM1.

In the command above, the 9600 sets the baud rate, the N means no parity, the 8 means 8 bits, and the P means send the output to the printer. The printer has to be set to match these settings.

Everytime the computer is booted up, it automatically defaults to the LPT port, so each time you want to use the serial port to print, you have to invoke the above commands. If you use the serial printer all the time, you can put the above commands in your autoexec.bat file so that they will be loaded each time you boot up.

Most printers have a self-test. It might run this test fine, but then completely ignore any efforts to get it to respond to the computer if the cables, parity, and baud rate are not properly set.

Sometimes the computer will hang up. You might have told it to do something that it could not do. You can usually do a warm reboot of the computer by pressing Ctrl-Alt-Del. Of course, this wipes out any file in memory that you might have been working on. Occasionally the computer will not respond to a warm boot. You can pound on the keyboard all day long and it will ignore you. In that case, you will have to switch off the main power, let it sit for a few seconds, and power up again. Always wait for the hard disk to wind down and stop before turning the power on again.

Finding fault

It is a good idea to have a few spare computer components on hand. It might be very difficult to determine the cause of a floppy disk drive failure, but it is very easy to plug in a spare disk drive to check it. A floppy drive costs about $50.

A keyboard can be ruined by a cup of spilled coffee. You can buy a spare for about $35. You might be wise to have spares of all the major components. The money spent for a spare component might be a real bargain if it keeps your computer up and running.

Diagnostic and utility software

Most BIOS chips have many diagnostic routines and other utilities built-in. These routines allow you to set the time and date and tell the computer what type of hard drive and floppies are installed, the amount of memory, the wait states, and several other functions. The AMI and DTK BIOS chips have a very comprehensive set of built-in diagnostics. They allow hard and floppy disk formatting, checking of disk drives, rotation speed performance testing of hard drives, and several other tests.

I mentioned some utility software programs in chapter 12. Many of them have a few diagnostics among the utilities, including

- Norton Utilities — includes several diagnostic and test programs such as Disk Doctor, Disk Test, Format Recover, Directory Sort, System Information, and many others.
- Mace Utilities — does about everything that Norton does and a few other things. It

has recover, defragment, diagnose, remedy, and several other very useful programs primarily for the hard disk.

- PC Tools — from Central Point Software. It has several utilities much like the Norton and Mace Utilities. It has a utility that can recover data from a disk that has been erased or reformatted. It has several other data recovery and DOS utilities. It can be used for hard disk backup and has several utilities such as those found in SideKick.
- SpinRite and Disk Technician — from Gibson Research and Prime Solutions respectively. They are utilities that allow you to diagnose, analyze, and optimize your hard disk.
- CheckIt — from TouchStone Software. Checks and reports on your computer configuration by letting "you look inside your PC without taking off the cover." It reports on the type of processor, amount of memory, video adapter, hard and floppy drives, clock/calendar, ports, keyboard, and mouse, if present. It also tests the motherboard, hard and floppy disks, RAM, ports, keyboard, mouse, joystick. It can also run a few benchmark speed tests.

Touchstone also has CheckIt floppy drive testing system. If any of your floppy disk drives get out of alignment, you might not be able to read disks from other computers, and drives in other computers might not be able to read disks made from a defective drive. CheckIt measures how well the floppy drive is aligned and its rotation speed, checks its ability to read track O, and several other tests. The system includes precise test disks in both 3½-inch and 5¼-inch formats. It is inexpensive, but a valuable tool.

There are several other diagnostic software and hardware tools. Check the ads in the computer magazines.

Is it worth it to repair it?

If you find a problem on a board, a disk drive, or some other component, you might try to find out what a new one would cost before having it repaired. You can buy a floppy disk drive for about $50 or a network adapter board for about $100. A repair shop would charge $50 to $100 an hour to repair them. It is often less expensive to scrap a defective part and buy a new one.

Software problems

I have had far more trouble with software than I have had with hardware. Quite often it is my fault for not taking the time to completely read the manuals and instructions. For instance, I tried to install Charisma, a large program that works under Windows. I kept getting errors and it would not load. I finally read the manual and found that it requires at least 500K of memory to install. I have several drivers, TSRs, and other things in my config.sys file that eat up a lot of RAM. I had to boot up with a diskette that had a very simple config.sys file that left me over 500K of RAM. I had no trouble after that.

MS-DOS 5.0, DR DOS 6.0, DESQview, and several other programs can load drivers, TSRs, and other things into memory above 640K. They can leave as much as 630K of free RAM.

There are thousands and thousands of other software problems that you will use. Many vendors have support programs for their products. If something goes wrong, you can call them. A few of them offer toll-free numbers. With most of them, you have to pay for the call. Some companies charge for their support. Some have installed 900 numbers. You are charged a certain amount for the amount of time you are on the phone. It costs a lot of money to maintain a support staff.

If you have a software problem, write down everything that happens. Before you call, try to duplicate the problem (make it happen again). Carefully read the manual. When you call, it is best to be in front of your computer, with it turned on, and with the problem on the screen if possible.

Also before you call, have the serial number of your program handy. One of the first things they will ask for is your name and serial number. If you bought and registered the program, it will be in their computer.

There are still compatibility problems with updates and new releases of software. I had lots of problems trying to get the latest WordStar release to work with files I had created with an early version. It was mostly my fault because I didn't take the time to read the manual. Like so many other updates and revisions, they make them bigger and better, but out of necessity, they often change the way things are done.

Most software programs are reasonably bug-free. But there are millions of things that can go wrong if the exact instructions and procedures are not followed. In many cases, the exact instructions and procedures are not very explicit.

User groups

There is no way to list all of the possible software or hardware problems. Computers are dumb and very unforgiving. It is very easy to plug a cable in backward or forget to set a switch. Thousands of things can go wrong. Sometimes it can be a combination of both software and hardware. Often there is only one way to do something the right way, but 10,000 ways to do it wrong. Sometimes it is difficult to determine if it is a hardware problem caused by software or vice versa. There is no way that every problem can be addressed.

One of the best ways to find answers is to ask someone who has had the same problem. One of the best places to find these people is in a user group. If at all possible, join one and become friendly with all of the members. They can be one of your best sources of information when troubleshooting. Most of them have had similar problems and are glad to help.

Glossary

access time   The amount of time it takes the computer to find and read data from a disk or from memory. The average access time for a hard disk is based on the time it takes the head to seek and find the specified track, the time for the head to lock onto it, and the time for the disk to spin around until the desired sector is beneath the head.

active partition   The partition on a hard disk that contains the boot and operating system. A single hard disk can be partitioned into several logical disks such as drive C:, drive D:, and drive E:. Partitioning can be done at the initial formatting of the disk. Only one partition, usually drive C:, can contain the active partition.

adapter boards or cards   The plug-in boards needed to drive monitors. Monitor boards can be monochrome graphics adapters (MGAs), color graphics adapters (CGAs), enhanced graphics adapters (EGAs), or video graphics adapters (VGAs).

algorithm   A step-by-step procedure, scheme, formula, or method used to solve a problem or accomplish a task. It might be a subroutine in a software program.

alphanumeric   Data that has both numerals and letters.

ANSI   American National Standard Institute. A standard adopted by MS-DOS for cursor positioning used in the ANSI.SYS file for device drivers.

ASCII   American Standard Code for Information Interchange. Binary numbers from 0 to 127 that represent the upper- and lowercase letters of the alphabet, the numbers 0 – 9, and the several symbols found on a keyboard. A block of eight 0s and 1s are used to represent all of these characters. The first 32 characters, 0 – 31, are reserved for noncharacter functions of a keyboard, modem, printer, or other device. Number 32, or 0010 0000, represents the space, which is a character. The numeral 1 is represented by the binary number for 49, which is 0011 0001. Text written in ASCII is displayed on the computer screen as standard text. Text written in other systems, such as WordStar, has several other characters added and is very difficult to read. Another 128-character representation was added to the original 128 characters for graphics and programming purposes.

ASIC   Application-specific integrated circuit.

assembly language   A low-level machine language made up of 0s and 1s.

asynchronous   A serial type of communication where one bit at a time is transmitted. The bits are usually sent in blocks of eight 0s and 1s.

AT-type systems   The 286, 386SX, 386DX, and 486 are all based on the original IBM AT-type 16-bit bus.

autoexec.bat   If present, this file is run automatically by DOS after it boots up. It is a file that you can configure to suit your own needs. It can load and run certain programs or configure your system.

baby motherboards   The AT-type motherboards that have been shrunk to the size of the XT by combining and integrating several of the chips.

.bak files   Anytime you edit or change a file in some of the word processors and other software programs they save the original file as a backup and append the extension .bak to it.

BASIC   Beginners all-purpose symbolic instruction code. A high-level language that was once very popular. Many programs and games still use it. BASIC programs usually have a .bas extension.

batch   The batch command can be used to link commands and run them automatically. The batch commands can be made up easily by the user. They all have the extension .bat.

baud   A measurement of the speed or data transfer rate of a communications line between the computer and a printer, modem, or another computer.

benchmark   A standard program against which similar programs can be compared.

bidirectional   Both directions. Most printers print in both directions, thereby saving the time it takes to return to the other end of a line.

binary   Binary numbers are 0s and 1s.

BIOS   Basic input/output system. The BIOS is responsible for handling the input/output operations.

bitmapped   The representation of a video image stored in the computer memory. Fonts for alphanumeric characters are usually stored as bit maps. When the letter A is typed, the computer goes to its library, pulls out a preformed A, and sends it to the monitor. If a different size A or a different font is needed, it requires another bitmap set. Graphic images can also be bitmapped. They consume an enormous amount of memory. Newer techniques allow different sizes and types of fonts to be scaled rather than bitmapped. *See* typeface.

bits   Binary digits.

boot or bootstrap   When a computer is turned on, all the memory and other internal operators have to be set or configured. A small amount of the program that does this is stored in ROM. Using this, the computer pulls itself up by its bootstraps. A warm boot is sometimes necessary to get the computer out of an endless loop or if it is hung up for some reason. A warm boot can be done by pressing Ctrl-Alt-Del.

buffer   A buffer is usually some discrete amount of memory that is used to hold data. A computer can send data thousands of times faster than a printer or modem can utilize it. The data can be input to a buffer, which can then feed the data into the printer as needed. The computer is then free to do other tasks.

bug, debug   The early computers were made with high-voltage vacuum tubes. It took rooms full of hot tubes to do the job that a credit card calculator can do today. One of the large systems went down one day. After several hours of troubleshooting, the technicians found a large bug that had crawled into the high-voltage wiring. It had been electrocuted and had shorted out the whole system. Since that time, any type of trouble in a piece of software or hardware is called a bug. To debug, of course, is to try to find all of the errors or defects.

bulletin boards   Usually a computer with a hard disk that can be accessed with a modem. Software and programs can be uploaded or left on the bulletin board by a caller, or a caller can scan the software that has been left there by others and download any that he likes. Bulletin boards often have help and message services. They are a great source of help for a beginner.

burst mode   The bus is taken over and a packet of data is sent as a single unit. During this time the bus cannot be accessed by other requests until the burst operation is completed. This allows as much as 33Mb per second or more to be transmitted over the bus.

bus   Wires or circuits that connect a number of devices together. It can also be a system. The configuration of the circuits that connect the 62 pins of the 8 slots together on the motherboard is a bus.

byte   A byte is eight bits, or a block of eight 0s and 1s. These 8 bits can be arranged in 256 different ways. This is $2 \times 2 \times 2 \times 2 \times 2 \times 2 \times 2 \times 2 = 256$, or 2^8. Therefore, one byte can be made to represent any one of the 256 characters in the ASCII character set. It takes one byte to make a single character. Because there are 4 characters in the word byte, it requires 4 bytes, or 32 bits.

cache memory   May be a disk cache or a high-speed memory cache. A high-speed buffer set up in memory to hold data that is being read from the hard disk. Often a program will request the same data from the disk over and over again. This can be quite time-consuming, depending on the access speed of the disk drive and the location of the data on the disk. If the requested data is cached in memory, it can be accessed almost immediately. For some of the very fast 386 and 486 systems, the DRAM is too slow to keep up. A cache of very fast SRAM might be installed for these systems.

carriage width   The width of a typewriter or printer. The two standard widths are 80 columns and 132 columns.

cell   A place for a single unit of data in memory, or an address in a spreadsheet.

Centronics parallel port   A system of 8-bit parallel transmission first used by the Centronics Company. It has become a standard and is the default method of printer output on the IBM.

character   A letter, a number, or an 8-bit piece of data.

chip   An integrated circuit, usually made from a silicon wafer. It can be microscopically etched and have thousands of transistors and semiconductors in a very small area.

CISC   Complex instruction set computing. This is the standard type of computer design as opposed to the reduced instruction set computing (RISC) used in larger systems. It might require as many as six steps for a CISC system to carry out a command. The RISC system might need only two steps to perform a similar function.

clock   The operations of a computer are based on very crucial timing, so they use a quartz crystal oscillator to control their internal clocks. The standard frequency for the PC and XT is 4.77 million cycles per second (MHz). The 486 CPUs operate at 16 to 66 MHz.

cluster   Each track of a disk is divided into sectors. Two or more sectors is called a cluster. This term has been replaced by the term *allocation unit*. An allocation unit can be one or more sectors.

COM   Usually refers to serial ports COM1 and COM2. These ports are used for serial printers, modems, mice, plotters, and other serial devices.

.com   A .com or .exe extension on the end of a file name indicates that it is a program that can run commands to execute programs.

command.com   An essential command that must be present in order to boot and start the computer.

COMDEX   Computer Dealers Exposition. The nation's largest computer exposition and show, usually held in the spring in Atlanta or Chicago and in the fall in Las Vegas.

composite video   A less expensive monitor that combines all the colors in a single input line.

console In the early days, a monitor and keyboard was usually set up at a desk-like console. The term has stuck. A console is a computer. The command COPY CON allows you to use the keyboard as a typewriter. Type COPY CON PRN or COPY CON LPT1 and everything you type is sent to the printer. At the end of your file, or letter, type Ctrl-Z or press F6 to stop sending.

consultant Someone who is supposed to be an expert who can advise you and help you determine what your computer needs are (similar to an analyst). No standard requirements or qualifications must be met, so anyone can claim to be an analyst or consultant.

conventional memory Also called *real memory.* The first 640K of RAM, the memory that DOS handles. The memory actually consists of 1Mb, but the 384K above the 640K is reserved for system use.

coprocessor Usually an 8087, 80287, or 80387 that works in conjunction with the CPU and vastly speeds up some operations.

copy protection A system that prevents a diskette from being copied.

CPS Characters per second. When referring to a printer, it is the speed that it can print.

CPU Central processing unit, such as the Intel 8088, 80286, 80386, or 80486.

CSMA/CD Carrier sense multiple access with collision detection. A network system that controls the transmissions from several nodes. It detects if two stations try to send at the same time and notifies the senders to try again at random times.

CRT Cathode-ray tube. The large tube that is the screen of computer monitors and TVs.

current directory The directory of files that is in use at the time.

cursor The blinking spot on the screen that indicates where the next character will be input.

daisywheel A round printer or typewriter wheel with flexible fingers that have the alphabet and other formed characters. A solenoid driven hammer hits the assigned character and presses it against a ribbon onto the paper. Daisywheel printers can provide excellent letter-quality type, but are very slow.

database A collection of data, usually related in some way.

DATE command Date will be displayed anytime DATE is typed at the prompt sign.

daughterboard An additional board, such as for a modem or extra memory, that is plugged into a board that is plugged into a motherboard.

DES Data encryption standard. First developed by IBM. It can be used to encrypt data so that it is almost impossible to decode it unless you have the code.

DIP Dual in-line pins. Refers to the two rows of pins on the sides of most integrated circuits.

disk controller A plug-in board that is used to control the hard and/or floppy disk drives. All of the read and write signals go through the controller.

DMA Direct memory access. Some parts of the computer such as the disk drives can exchange data directly with the RAM without having to go through the CPU.

documentation Manuals, instructions, or specifications for a system, hardware, or software.

DOS Disk operating system. Software that allows programs to interact and run on a computer.

dot matrix A type of printer that uses a matrix of thin wires or pins to make up the print head. Electronic solenoids push the pins out to form letters out of dots. The dots are made when the pins are pushed against the ribbon and paper.

double density   At one time, most diskettes were single sided and had a capacity of 80K to 100K. The technology has advanced so that diskettes can be recorded on both sides with up to 400K per side. The 5¼-inch 360K and 3½-inch 720K disks are double-sided, double-density. The 1.2Mb and 1.44Mb disks are high-density.

DPMI   DOS protected mode interface. A proposed specification to govern the interaction of large applications with each other, DOS, and OS/2.

DRAM   Dynamic random access memory. This is the usual type of memory found in personal computers. It is the least expensive type of memory.

DTP   Desktop publishing. A rather loose term that can be applied to a small personal computer and a printer as well as to high-powered sophisticated systems.

dumb terminal   A terminal that is tied to a mainframe or a terminal that does not have its own microprocessor.

duplex   A characteristic of a communications channel that enables data to be transmitted in both directions. Full duplex allows information to be transmitted in both directions simultaneously. In half duplex, it can be transmitted in both directions, but not at the same time.

EATA   Enhanced AT attachment. A standard proposed by the Common Access Method (CAM) committee. Their proposal would define a standard interface for connecting controllers to PCs. It would define a standard software protocol and hardware interface for disk controllers, SCSI host adapters, and for other intelligent chip-embedded controllers.

echo   A command that can cause information to be displayed on the screen from a .bat or other file. Echo can be turned on or off.

EEPROM   Electrically erasable programmable read-only memory.

EGA   Enhanced graphics adapter. A board used for high-resolution monitors.

E-mail   Electronic mail. A system that allows messages to be sent through LANs or by modem over telephone lines.

EMS   Expanded memory specification. A specification for adding expanded memory put forth by Lotus, Intel, and Microsoft (LIM EMS).

EPROM   Erasable programmable read-only memory.

ergonomics   The study and science of how the human body can be most productive when working with machinery. Ergonomics includes the study of the effects of things like the type of monitor, the type of chair, lighting, and other environmental and physical factors.

errors   DOS displays several error messages if it receives bad commands or there are problems of some sort.

ESDI   Enhanced system device interface. A hard disk interface that allows data to be transferred to and from the disk at a rate of 10Mb per second. The older standard ST506 allowed only 5Mb per second.

.exe   A file with this extension indicates that it is an executable file that can run and execute the program. It is similar to the .com files.

expanded memory   Memory that can be added to a PC, XT, or AT. It can only be accessed through special software.

expansion boards   Boards that can be plugged into one of the eight slots on the motherboard to add memory or other functions.

extended memory   RAM that can be added to a 286, 386, or 486.

external commands   DOS commands that are not loaded into memory when the computer is booted.

FAT   File allocation table. This is a table that DOS uses to keep track of all of the parts of a file. A file might be placed in sector 3 of track 1, sectors 5 and 6 of track 10, and sector 4 of track 20. The FAT keeps track of where the parts of a file are located and directs the read/record head to those areas when requested to do so.

fax   A shortened form of the word facsimile and "X" for transmission. A fax machine scans an image or textual document and digitizes it in a graphical form. As it scans an image, a 0 or 1 is generated depending on the presence or absence of darkness (ink). The 0s and 1s are transmitted over the telephone line as voltages. *See* modem.

fonts   The different types of print characters such as Gothic, Courier, Times Roman, Helvetica, and others. Each is a collection of unique characters and symbols. A typeface becomes a font when associated with a specific size.

format   The process of preparing a disk so that it can be recorded. The formatting process lays down tracks and sectors so that data can be written anywhere on a disk and recovered easily.

fragmentation   If a disk has data that has been changed several times, bits of the files occur on several different tracks and sectors. This slows down writing and reading of the files because the head has to move back and forth to the various tracks. If these files are copied to a newly formatted disk, each file is written to clean tracks that are contiguous. This decreases the access time to the hard disk.

friction feed   A printer that uses a roller or platen to pull the paper through.

game port   An I/O port for joysticks, trackballs, paddles, and other devices.

gigabyte   One billion bytes.

glitch   An unexpected electrical spike or static disturbance that can cause loss of data.

global   A character or something that appears throughout an entire document or program.

googol   The figure 1 followed by 100 zeros (10^{100}).

GUI   Graphical user interface. It usually makes use of a mouse, icons, and windows such as those used by the Macintosh.

handshaking   A protocol or routine between systems — usually the printer and the computer — indicating a readiness to communicate with each other.

hardware   The physical parts that make up a computer system, such as the disk drives, keyboards, monitors, etc.

Hayes-compatible   Hayes was one of the first modem manufacturers. Like IBM, it created a set of standards that most others have adopted.

hexadecimal   A system that uses the base 16. The binary system is based on 2, the decimal system is based on 10. The hexadecimal system goes 0, 1, 2, 3, 4, 5, 6, 7, 8, 9, A, B, C, D, E, F. In the hexadecimal system 10 would be 16, and it starts over so that 20 would be 32. Most of the computer's memory locations are in hexadecimal notation.

hidden files   The files that do not show up in a normal directory display, such as the

DOS files that are necessary to boot a computer. They are hidden so that they will not be accidentally erased.

high-level language   A language such as BASIC, Pascal, or C. These program languages are fairly easy to read and understand.

ICs   Integrated circuits. The first integrated circuit was developed in the early 1960s by placing two transistors in a single can. Then ways were found to put several semiconductors in a package. This was called small-scale integration (SSI). Large-scale integration (LSI) and very large-scale integration (VLSI) soon followed. Today we have very high-scale integrated circuits (VHSICs).

IDE   Integrated disk electronics. Western Digital and other companies are manufacturing hard drives with most of the controller circuitry on the disk assembly, but they still need an interface of some sort to connect to the computer. They are somewhat similar to SCSIs.

interface   A piece of hardware or a set of rules that allows communications between two systems.

internal commands   Those commands that are loaded into memory when DOS boots up.

interpreter   A program that translates a high-level language into machine-readable code.

ISDN   Integrated services digital network. A standard for telephone transmission of voice, data, and images.

kilobyte   1,000 bytes (1K) or more exactly, it is 1024 bytes (2^{10}).

LAN   Local area network. Where several computers might be tied together or tied to a central server.

laser printer   A type of printer that uses the same type of "engine" used in copy machines. An electronically controlled laser beam sweeps across a drum. The beam leaves a static charge on the drum with an image of the letters or graphics that are to be printed. The charged areas of the drum pick up toner particles and deposit them on the page. The page is then routed through a heat process that fuses the toner particles to the page.

LIM EMS   Lotus-Intel-Microsoft expanded memory specification.

low-level format   Most hard disks must have a preliminary low-level format performed on them before they can be formatted for DOS. Low-level formatting is sometimes called *initializing*.

low-level language   A machine-level language. It is usually in binary digits that are very difficult for the ordinary person to understand.

LQ   Letter quality. The type from a daisywheel or formed-type printer.

macro   A series of keystrokes that can be recorded, somewhat like a batch file, and typed back when one or more keys are pressed. For instance, I can type my entire address with just two keystrokes.

mainframe   A large computer that can serve several users.

megabyte   1,000,000 bytes (1Mb) or, more precisely, 2^{20} or 1,048,576 bytes. It takes a minimum of 20 data lines to address 1Mb, a minimum of 24 lines (2^{24}) to address 16 Mb, and a minimum of 25 lines (2^{25}) to address 32 Mb.

menu   A list of choices or options. A menu-driven system makes it very easy for beginners to choose what they want to do.

MFM   Modified frequency modulation. The scheme for the standard method of recording on hard disks. *See* RLL.

MHz   Megahertz. A million cycles per second. Older technicians still call it cps. A few years ago, a committee decided to honor Heinrich Rudolf Hertz (1857 – 1894) for his early work in electromagnetism, so they changed cycles per second (cps) to hertz (Hz).

modem   Modulator-demodulator. A device that allows data to be sent over telephone lines. A modem creates digital voltages that are changed or modulated to analog voltages, transmitted over telephone lines, and demodulated by the receiving modem.

mouse   A small pointing device that can control the cursor and move it anywhere on the screen. It usually has two or three buttons that are assigned various functions.

MTBF   Mean time before failure. An average of the time between failures, usually used to describe a hard disk or other component.

multitasking   The ability of the computer to perform more than one task at a time. Many computers have this ability when used with the proper software.

multiuser   A computer that is capable of providing service to more than one user such as a server for a LAN.

NEAT chipset   New enhanced AT chipset from Chips and Technology. Chips and Technology combined the functions of several chips found on the original IBM motherboard into just a few very large-scale integrated (VLSI) circuits. These chips are used on the vast majority of clone boards.

NLQ   Near letter quality. The better-formed characters from a dot matrix printer.

null modem cable   A cable with certain pairs of wires crossed over. If the computer sends data from pin 2, the modem will receive it on pin 3. The modem sends data back to the computer from its pin 2 and it is received by the computer on pin 3. Several other wires can also be crossed.

OOP   Object-oriented programs. A type of programming that utilizes parts of existing programs to provide new applications.

OS/2 2.0   A 32-bit high-end operating system from IBM. It includes DOS 5.0 and Windows.

oscillator   Computers must have very accurate timing pulses. They use quartz crystals that vibrate at accurate frequencies when a voltage is applied to create precise clock timing signals.

parallel   A system that uses 8 lines to send 8 bits (1 byte) at a time.

parity checking   It is an error detection technique in the computer memory system that verifies the integrity of the RAM contents. This is the function of the ninth chip in a memory bank. Parity checking systems are also used in other areas such as verifying the integrity of data transmitted by a modem.

plotter   An X-Y writing device that be used for charts, graphics, and other functions that most printers can't do.

prompt   The > sign that shows that DOS is waiting for an entry. The prompt command can be programmed to display almost anything you want it to. If you place the command PROMPT PG in your autoexec.bat file it will cause the current drive letter and current directory to be displayed.

protocol   The rules and methods by which computers and modems communicate with each other.

QIC   Quarter-inch cartridge. A width of tape used in tape backup systems.

RAM   Random-access memory. This is computer memory that is used to temporarily hold files and data as they are being worked on, changed, or altered. It can be written to and read from. It is volatile memory. Any data stored in it is lost when the power is turned off.

RGB   Red, green, and blue. The three primary colors that are used in color monitors and TVs. Each color has its own electron gun that shoots streams of electrons to the back of the CRT, causing it to light up in the various colors.

RISC   Reduced instruction set computing. A design that allows a computer to operate with fewer instructions allows it to run much faster.

RLL   Run length limited. A scheme of hard disk recording that allows 50% more data to be recorded on a hard disk than with the standard MFM scheme. The MFM system divides each track into 17 sectors of 512 bytes each. The RLL system divides the tracks into 26 sectors with 512 bytes each.

ROM   Read-only memory. It does not change when the power is turned off. The primary use of ROM is in the system BIOS and on some plug-in boards.

scalable typeface   Unlike bit-mapped systems where each font has one size and characteristic, scalable systems allow typefaces to be shrunk or enlarged to different sizes to meet specific needs. This allows much more flexibility and uses less memory. There are also scalable graphic systems.

SCSI   Small computer system interface (pronounced scuzzy). A fast parallel hard disk interface system developed by Shugart Associates and adopted by the American National Standards Institute (ANSI). The SCSI system allows multiple drives to be connected. It supports a parallel transfer rate of 1.2Mb per second. The ESDI serial system can send 10Mb per second, one bit at a time. Because it takes 8 bits to make a byte, the ESDI and SCSI systems have about the same speed.

sector   A section of a track on a disk or diskette. A sector ordinarily holds 512 bytes. A 360K diskette has 40 tracks per side. Each track is divided into 9 sectors.

serial   The transmission of one bit at a time over a single line.

shadow RAM   A technology provided on some motherboards that allows the option to copy system ROM BIOS into unused portions of high memory. Because RAM is faster than ROM, this can speed up the system.

SIMM   Single in-line memory module.

SIP   Single in-line package. A memory module that has pins. Many small resistor packs and integrated circuits have a single line of pins.

source diskette   When using the DISKCOPY command, it is the original diskette to be copied from.

SPARC   Scalable processor architecture. A RISC system developed by Sun Microsystems for workstations.

spool   Simultaneous peripheral operations on-line. A spooler acts as a storage buffer for data that is fed to a printer or other device. In the meantime, the computer can be used for other tasks.

SRAM   Static RAM. A type of RAM that can be much faster than DRAM. SRAM is made up of actual transistors that are turned on or off and will maintain their state without constant refreshing such as is needed in DRAM. SRAM is considerably more expensive and requires more space than DRAM.

target diskette When using the DISKCOPY command, the diskette to be copied to.

time stamp The record of the time and date that is recorded in the directory when a file is created or changed.

tractor A printer device with sprockets or spikes that pull computer paper with holes in the margins through the printer at a very precise feed rate. A friction-feed platen might allow the paper to slip, move to one side or the other, and not be precise in the spacing between the lines.

Trojan horse A harmful piece of code or software that is hidden in a software package. It is unlike a virus in that it does not grow and spread.

TSOP Thin small outline packages. A new standard proposed for memory cards such as those used in laptops. It is about the size of a credit card.

TSR Terminate-and-stay-resident. When a program such as Sidekick is loaded in memory, it will normally stay there until the computer is booted up again. If several TSR programs are loaded in memory, there might not be enough memory left to run programs.

turbo Usually means a computer with a faster-than-normal speed.

UMB Upper memory block. Refers to the memory above 640K. With the DOS versions greater than 5.0 and other memory managers such as DESQview, this area can be used for such things as TSRs and device drivers. This frees up more space in the lower 640K.

user-friendly Easy to learn, use, and understand. It should make using the computer easier.

user group Usually a club or a group of people who use computers. Often the club will be devoted to users of a certain type of computer, but in most clubs anyone is welcome to join.

vaporware Products that are announced, usually with great fanfare, but are not yet ready for market.

virtual Something that is essentially present, but is not in actual fact. If you have a single disk drive, it is drive A:, but you also have a virtual drive B:. If you want to copy a file from one floppy disk to another on your single drive, you can use the command COPY A:filename B:filename (replace filename with the actual name of the file you want to copy).

virus Destructive code that is placed or embedded in a computer program. A virus is usually self-replicating and will often copy itself onto other programs. It might lie dormant for some time, then completely erase your hard disk or destroy data.

volatile Refers to memory units such as RAM that lose stored information when power is removed. Nonvolatile memory is similar to that of ROM or a hard disk.

VRAM Video RAM. A type of special RAM used on video or monitor adapters. The better adapters have more memory so that they can retain full-screen high-resolution images.

windows Many new software packages are now loaded into memory. They stay in the background until they are called for, then they pop up on the screen in a window.

Windows 3.0 An excellent graphical user interface program from the Microsoft Company. It provides an operating environment for programs that can make them easier to use.

Index